DAVID POMEROY

LEADERSHIP

IN THE

TRENCHES

A ROAD TRIP IN REALITY TO

SUCCESS

DAVID POMEROY

with
Jonathan Richards, M.B.A.

Produced by Scottsdale Multimedia, Inc.

DEDICATION

This book is dedicated to all of the brave men and women in uniform who work incessantly and even risk their lives to protect us all from those who are enemies of freedom.

All net proceeds from the sales of this book are being donated to the Wounded Warrior Project.

CONTENTS

Meet the secret to success: the Fourth Gear. Learning how to ignite your Fourth Gear will enable you to achieve success in ways you never dreamed. This book will teach you the principles you need to know.

Form over Substance is the new-age nobility of the corporate world—and it's a common, serious problem. The Ego can be a great tool to build relationships, or a devastating weapon to destroy them, depending on how it's used. Hard Work isn't the who, where, when, or why; it's the what and how of getting things done.

Success requires an understanding of people and their motivations—including your own. Personality, Character, Self-Efficacy, Self-Image, and Self-Awareness all play in to discovering and understanding your own strengths and then identifying the strengths of others. These concepts form the foundation of Emotional Intelligence, the new IQ.

Some people resist because they are obstinate; others resist out of genuine concern. Ignorance requires training; defiance requires termination. Can you tell the difference? The Fundamental Attribution error makes that question harder than you might think.

Cognitive Dissonance is trying to hold two mutually exclusive ideas in your head at the same time. It's an uncomfortable feeling that people experience frequently when they learn. Confront Cognitive Dissonance and use it to motivate ingenuity and growth rather than Rationalizing it away.

Expectations are a powerful way to build or erode trust. Be explicit in what others can expect in you; also be clear on what others expect from you. Success comes from setting clear expectations for the future and doing whatever it takes to reach those expectations, and then you must enforce accountability for yourself and others.

Understanding Financial Reporting and identifying trends is critical to determining the health of a company, division, or organization. Financial reports provide the information you need to lead your organization safely to success. The most critical reports are the budget, and budget to actual.

ACKNOWLEDGMENTS

I would like to thank all of those who have assisted me in researching, writing, editing and producing this book.
Jonathan Richards, M.B.A., lead business writer for Scottsdale Multimedia, Inc., for helping in all aspects of writing and editing the work

.

INTRODUCTION: UNFOLDING THE MAP

The world is full of advice about how to succeed in business. With so much research and material out there, why is it that people still fail? When people think they know what it takes to succeed, why do so many _not_ succeed? They don't understand what it means to lead.

Most of us have heard the startling idea that 9 out of every 10 business ventures fail in the first five years. In light of that, you have to ask yourself _why_ so many businesses fail. If you think about it, ask around, and do a little research, you'll come to another startling conclusion: there is a shortage of quality leadership in the world.

The quality of managers has increased as the quality of education has increased; however, while "managers do things right, leaders do the right things" (Pascale 1990). Too many managers, team captains, and business entrepreneurs are missing the critical qualities that could lead them to success. The world lacks a pool of real leaders who can lead at any level.

Everyone wants to grow; they love competition and the taste of victory. Everyone wants to move to a new level of performance. The spirit inside them drives them to be better today than they were the day before. Whether that's in the sense of moving from salesman to sales manager, from chef to owner, or from trainee to top performer, everyone wants to progress and have success as they see it. The reason that so many fail is because they don't have a map, and they haven't awakened their inner leader to show them the way.

With all due respect to Anthony Robbins[1] and Dr. Stephen Covey[2], their principles were great but just a lot of motivational words. The real key

---

[1] Author of _Unlimited Power: The New Science of Personal Achievement_

[2] Author of _The Seven Habits of Highly Effective People_

to success lies not in hard work or even smart work. The real key lies in self-awareness and understanding human nature. To have true success, you have to become a student of human nature. Once upon a time, people could get by and make great contributions by being technically brilliant and by understanding the 'mechanics of management.' Those days are gone.

Unfortunately, most of the available literature and training material continue to support the idea that careful management tactics are the key to success; they aren't. Despite the number of training manuals with which managers load their bookcases, the main reason people leave an organization today is because of bad management. Is that because people are selfish and lazy and just want to badmouth their managers in an effort to get away with doing less on the job? I don't believe so.

I fully believe that, on an individual level, people are intelligent and driven, and that they crave success. When people leave a company, it's because they don't see enough opportunity in their current circumstance anymore. I believe that people want to find that next level inside themselves, but they don't always know how to do it on their own. They try something new—but wrong—and it works once. Over time, that technique turns into a bad habit, and then they can't figure out how to escape it on their own. They want to grow—and they have the ability—but, without the right kind of leadership, they can't always find the right path.

My belief is that everyone has a set of gears inside them. The first gear is the 'slow' gear. People don't generally want to stay in that gear, but they pass through it while they're learning the job--during training and similar experiences. The second gear is the 'average' gear. This is where people slump back to if they've tried something new and been put down by a bad manager. This is also where people shift when they've been told that the status quo is the best way.

The third gear is the 'fast' gear. This is where management thinks it wants people. This is where you know the job, and you can just perform all day. You're doing good work, and everyone's happy. At least, mostly happy.

What people don't realize is that, buried down deep inside, is another gear. This one's a little rusty for many people. Most people don't even know it's there. I call this Fourth Gear the Gear of 'Desperation.' This is the gear that people engage when failure is not an option. When they'll do anything and everything to find their way to success—tooth and nail, if necessary. This is the Gear that controls the 'next level' that everyone says they want to reach.

This Gear is so fast and so powerful that it will make other people stop and blink in surprise. This is the Gear that engages when you've got a deadline to meet, and you won't accept anything less than your best. This is the Gear that drives the humble and propels them to work longer, harder, smarter, or whatever else it takes in order to rise above their current situation. This is the Gear that runs soldiers when, tired, defeated, and behind enemy lines, they fight on so they can bring their brothers and sisters home. People say necessity if the mother of invention. I say that invention is the Fourth Gear.

Everyone has that Fourth Gear; it's not something special that only the chosen few are born with. The key is dusting it off and igniting it. In order to power up this Gear, you first have to develop the willpower to keep it engaged. Make no mistake, when you light up this Fourth Gear, you will be able to do things that surprise even you. Those things may not be easy, and they probably won't be quick, but they will definitely be worth it. You'll be churning for real success.

This book is designed as a roadmap to that Fourth Gear. The willpower you need has to be learned, and this book is designed to help you learn it. Self-awareness and the understanding of human nature are the keys. Most management training is centered on efficiency and effectiveness of current processes. It focuses on looking at situations or 'rules' or 'quick, simple tricks' to get people to do what you want them to.

I believe that's backwards. I believe we should be focusing on *why*— not *how*—certain things need to get done, helping people catch that vision and understanding, and then letting them create new and innovative methods to achieve the goals.

Success is more like a marathon, not a sprint. It's not about winning, it's about finishing. Leadership in the trenches is the same. It's not about being 'better' than someone else—unless that someone else is yourself. Leadership is about awareness, ingenuity, trust, and respect. It's about picking up the flag and leading the charge. This is the kind of leadership that can be done regardless of a person's title—or lack thereof. This is Leadership at any Level. This is the kind of leadership that's missing in business today, and it's driven by the Fourth Gear.

What I offer here is something deeper than a fifteen step program or a list of fifty-two rules. Something more meaningful. In this book, I will try to convey the principles and truths I, an uneducated man, have fought and bled to learn through 40 years of business in the trenches.

These are keys of leadership with regard to the self and others. This is about learning why people do—or don't do—what they do. I pass on my these principles in hopes that others—like you—can use them to unlock that Fourth Gear and, in turn, work to make your life better than it was yesterday.

While these keys are designed and presented with business in mind, be assured that they apply to life outside the office as well. Many community organizations struggle from the lack of leadership too. And, even on a smaller but no less-important scale, families also need leadership.

As Robert M. Hutchins[3] once said, "The most distressing aspect of the world into which you are going is its indifference to the basic issues, which now, as always, are moral issues." The only way to shore up those foundations and prepare the next generation to face those moral issues is to develop leadership in the home.

Leadership of this kind is more than simply telling people to be motivated. All that does is stir resentment inside them. They already know they need to be motivated. Until you got on their cases, they probably _were_ motivated. Leadership at any Level isn't about telling people what to do, it's about taking the lead, engaging the Fourth Gear to do what needs to be done, and then trusting people to be motivated enough to follow you.

So, as we go through this journey together, look for the specific keys that will help you unlock your own, personal brand of success—your Fourth Gear. Feel free to take notes in the margins to record your thoughts and impressions.

Think of this as a guidebook—your personal mentor. You'll probably want to read through it once from cover to cover, just to get a lay of the land. Then, as you recognize situations in your life where these principles apply, come back to this roadmap and review the applicable sections for help, guidance and ideas.

If you can get one helpful lesson from the time and effort this book represents, I will consider it a success. If there is just one principle in here you can embrace—one solution—then this will be worth everything that went into it, 1000-fold.

---

[3] Former Dean of Yale's Law School and, subsequently, the President of the University of Chicago

LEADERSHIP IN THE TRENCHES – THE START

Go into a room with a hundred employees from all levels of a company and ask them to raise their hands if they think they need to be managed. How many hands do you think will go up? If your experience matches mine, none.

How about you? Do you feel like you need to be managed?

We have a problem in business today that runs deeper than market trends and is more destructive than price competition. That problem is the shifting meaning of the word 'management.' Too many managers nowadays seem to be straying further and further into the mistaken belief that they are the ones with the answers.

Too many have lost the vision of the manager as a coach and have come to believe that they know everything, and know it best. Too many seem to believe that their coworkers wouldn't be able to get anything done without close supervision and correction. Too many somehow think that, like the *Wizard of Oz* (Baum 1900), they can sit behind a curtain and project some larger-than-life image of themselves to make everyone else 'fall in line.'

I'm here to debunk that myth. To start our road trip together, we're going to throw back the Wizard's curtain and reveal the little man of 'management' for the misguided title that it has too often become. Ask those hundred employees in the room what they want from their 'manager,' and you'll hear things like 'support,' 'training,' 'more business,' or 'strategic vision.'

People don't want someone telling them what to do or when to do it. People want to feel like they're part of something great and grand and worthwhile. They want to know what's expected of them and then have everyone get out of their way, so they can really show just how good they are.

People are more intelligent than the current concept of 'management' gives credit. When people run into a situation they don't understand, they may want some help figuring it out, but, once they've got it under control again, they want everyone to step aside and let them shine. You see, as social creatures, people want to find success.

So, if management in its current form is becoming almost more of a hindrance than help, why does it even exist? In its original form, management served a vital purpose: without some kind of supervision, every part of a business would head a different direction and the organization would collapse on itself.

The answer is less focus on how to 'manage' and more focus on how to 'lead.' What the business world needs—along with the world in general—is more leaders. In fact, the world would do well if everyone would step up and be a leader in their own way, in their own sphere.

Of course, there are entire libraries of books written about leadership. This book isn't designed to summarize that wealth of information. This isn't about checklists, cheerleading, and pithy phrases.

Instead, this book is about getting to the substance beneath the form. This book is about self-awareness and understanding why people do what they do. This book is about what you can do to navigate your way to success an environment so littered with obstacles. This book is about doing less managing and more leading. Still, getting people to do what needs to be done is leadership in its most basic sense, so let's spend a few minutes on how we'll be using the term in this book.

President Dwight D. Eisenhower[4] once said, "You do not lead by hitting people over the head. That's assault, not leadership." In other words, you can't beat on people and expect them to follow you. Unless you are coordinating air strikes from the Pentagon, you need to be leading your troops in the literal sense—by going in front of them.

An extension of this concept is that you should never ask someone else to do something you are unwilling to do yourself. To clarify this concept, let's dispel a myth and cite the dictionary at the same time. To lead means "to go before or with to show the way; conduct or escort" (Random House Webster's Unabridged Dictionary 2001).

In other words, the concept of leading from the executive suite—sitting behind a desk and barking out orders to the 'lower' ranks—is wrong; it's flawed at its very core: it's not leading. To lead is to set the example, to show how things should be done.

For evidence of this we need not look further than the New Testament of the Bible. The metaphysics of Jesus' life aside, he is widely praised across religions and creeds as one of the most effective leaders and

---

[4] The 34th President of the United States of America

teachers this world has ever known. It's no accident that those two concepts are tied together: leader and teacher.

A leader has to show the way and then teach those that follow. That's their role. If the way is already clearly laid out, anyone with half a brain can follow it without the 'help' of a leader. If the policies and methods are clear enough, people don't need someone there to 'lead' them to follow the manual. People are intelligent enough to do that on their own, and trying to tell them they need a 'manager' is something of an insult.

No, people need a leader when they forge into the unknown—when they explore new, untapped opportunities—when the way isn't clear ahead. To be that kind of leader doesn't require a special appointment or designation. In this way, you can be a Leader at any Level. At every level.

There is a famous poem by Will Allen Dromgoole[5] called the "Bridge Builder." It's a little long and the language is a little out of date so I'll just summarize it here (see Appendix A for the full text). In the poem, an old man is building a bridge over a dark and dangerous river. A passerby remarks that the man has already crossed the river; why build the bridge now? The old man's reply is that a young, innocent child is following after him and will need to cross as well. The bridge is being built to protect that child from the likely death of the treacherous river.

The old man was a leader in the truest sense. Perhaps he wasn't taking the young boy by the hand and personally guiding him across the river— and he certainly wasn't giving him step-by-step instructions on how to get the job done—but that doesn't change the facts. The old man was preparing the way so that anyone could follow in his footsteps. The man had taken the lead—the initiative. He had explored the path, found the best way and then, using his experience, leveraged it to prepare an even better way for the next travelers. He was following the instruction of Ralph Waldo Emerson[6]: "Do not go where the path may lead, go instead where there is no path and leave a trail."

As a leader, you can and should do the same thing. You should be striving to be the best at what you do and then leading in whatever position you hold. You can lead at some level regardless of what level you think you hold. CEOs aren't the only ones who can lead. You need to be ready and willing and able to do whatever needs to be done—within the bounds of the law and ethics, of course—to get results. That's what it means to ignite your Fourth Gear and Lead at any Level.

Leading by going first means you can't be asking someone else to do something you're unwilling to do. If you ever feel the need to check your leadership ability, go clean the restroom. If you can't bring yourself to do it,

---

[5] A best-selling, female novelist and poet in the 1890s
[6] An American poet and transcendentalist philosopher

you might have a problem. Cleaning the toilets is a humble, thankless task; it's unlikely to earn you glory or prestige. Still, the restroom says a lot about a company, and somebody has to clean them. As a leader, why not you?

You have to be personally willing to do anything in the business that needs to be done. Even if that means cleaning the bathrooms. As a Leader at any Level, you need to be willing to step in and get the job done where no one else is willing to go, and the people you work with need to know it.

I requested that one of our Senior VPs come in wearing jeans and work in our distribution center on an occasion after he brought a complaint to me and it became apparent the man felt he was above the people he worked with. He wouldn't do it because he thought it was a stupid assignment and too far 'beneath' him.

To me, that was a final signal that he didn't want to lead; he wanted the easy way out. Thankfully, I'd already found his replacement. I needed someone who was willing to ignite their Fourth Gear—to do whatever it took to get the job done and find success—someone who was willing to lead others in the same path.

Truly exceptional leaders don't spend their time admiring their 'empire' from the umpteenth floor of the corporate headquarters. Truly exceptional leaders get out into the trenches with the people who control the success of the company. They go 'out onto the front lines' with the people in their organization. They get 'up close and personal' with their customers. They rub shoulders with the people who make the top line—and the ones who keep controls in place to preserve the bottom line.

If you want to be a truly extraordinary leader, do the things people would never expect: the things that traditionalists would consider to be 'beneath' your position. If you just do what everyone else is doing, you'll just be ordinary. Do you want to be ordinary or do you want to be extraordinary? 'Average' just means best of the worst and worst of the best. What's your choice?

And, while you're at it, remember that a leader is there to serve. In other words, nobody is beneath you. If anything, you're beneath them. Think about that. Where does your paycheck come from if they all stop doing their jobs?

So instead of asking one of the salespeople how many calls he made that day, sit down with him in the morning and make calls together. Show him how important that responsibility is. Take the first call. People often fear rejection. Show them that a 'no' answer is really nothing to fear because it means you don't have to spend any more effort there. Your coworkers will be stunned to see 'the boss' getting his fingernails dirty—doing the job—and your customers will feel honored to receive the attention. Show your colleagues how critical their job really is and help them ignite that Fourth Gear.

Ask anyone who's ever been in the military, and they'll tell you: leadership isn't about pointing at a hill and commanding the troops to go secure it. Leadership is about taking point with your trusted soldiers at your back and, together, you take the hill and leave no one behind. According to Albert Schweitzer[7], "Example is not the main thing in influencing others, it is the only thing."

Leadership is about understanding the pulse and culture of the company. It's about understanding what the people around you like and dislike. It's about getting honest feedback and acting on it. It's about defending the company and the people in it—instead of badmouthing the company or agreeing with another's criticisms. Again, it's about leading by example.

True leaders earn respect by modeling the behaviors that bring success. They earn it by delving into human nature, so they can work with people more effectively. They earn respect by being able to set the proper attitudes and expectations—and by igniting their Fourth Gear to work through resistance. They learn how and when to trust, and how the double-edged sword of loyalty really works. They earn that respect through careful communication.

By working to have all these tools at their disposal, leaders can COmmand respect, instead of ineffectually DEmanding it. They don't have to rely on a title or executive order or some other fictitious source of power to create results and success because they will have that self-control and power already within themselves.

Form Over Substance

It's interesting that, in setting the stage for the foundation of America, the Founding Fathers threw off the concept of the English nobility. Instead of an aristocratic class system where people succeeded or failed based on who their parents were, the Founding Fathers wanted to establish a country where all were free to succeed based on effort and merit. Countless men and women have given their lives to protect that ideal, so it's lamentable that, after less than 250 years, we've essentially regressed back to a class system—and are suffering many of the same problems.

Instead of a royal nobility, we now have a corporate nobility. We have directors instead of knights and CXOs instead of Lords and Ladies. In startups across the nation, men and women take the title of CEO or Chief Whatever Officer the moment they sign the filing forms to register with the state. Most view it as a prerequisite to being a leader, but what are they executives of? What are they leaders of? Dreams, mostly. At least at first.

Because of this new-age nobility, when you ask someone what they do,

---

[7] A medical ethics pioneer and recipient of a Nobel Peace Prize

you nearly always get a title in response. Instead of hearing that a person teaches ancient near-east studies, you find out he's a professor. Instead of learning about how he operates an international team securing parts for an automotive assembly line, you find out he's a vice president. Instead of finding out that he manages the overall budget for a 3 billion dollar company and a staff of several hundred accountants, controllers, and support staff, you find out he's a CFO. Or, my favorite, instead of learning about the intricacies of making furniture in a garage and selling it in the front yard, you find out the man is a CEO.

But what, exactly, does a CEO do? Or a vice president? How is learning a person's title in any way interesting? How does it build a conversation, let alone a relationship? And, since there are both 'good' and 'bad' CEOs today, what does the title even say about a person's leadership ability? A title says nothing about your character or personality; your integrity defines those attributes.

A CEO, or Chief Executive Officer, is a reporting position for a public company (Chief Executive Officer n.d.). Privately held companies don't even—technically—have CEOs. Private companies have presidents and vice presidents—like the American government—or, in the case of LLCs, they have managing members.

The CEO is responsible for maintaining the strategic vision of the company. He is responsible for selecting a management team capable of executing on that vision and then providing support for the management team as they move forward. Really, a CEO is an inspirational figure. CEOs lead and motivate at a high level, not in the day-to-day.

It's almost unfair to them that they take so much guff from the press and the public when, at the heart of things, they have very limited control over what actually happens 'at the front line'—all the while being pinned with all the liability if anything wrong happens (that's what it means to be a company officer of any kind: you're responsible for the liability).

The rest of the executive team, the VPs, and the middle management have more power. In reality, the closer to the customer you get, the more power you have—real power that is—to grow or cripple the company.

The point is that the titles are meaningless—especially in light of the current, transmuted management hierarchy. There is a concept of 'form over substance' in the way we use titles today. Everyone wants the bigger title and the corner office even though those aren't the things that make a business successful. Those also aren't the things that make a person successful—they don't define you.

There was a time when I owned seven companies—different franchises of Computerland. I didn't have an office at that point. When people asked why I didn't have an office, I explained that I didn't need one. Rather than go and sit in an office all day, I was traveling between my seven locations—staying out in the field.

Invariably, I would visit a store to find that a sales rep was out making calls for the day, leaving a desk open. I used the open desks. The only things I needed were a phone, a desk, and my briefcase. That briefcase was my office. I didn't need French doors or mahogany furniture. I wanted to be out with my coworkers, making joint sales calls and actively helping the business—it didn't hurt that I was avoiding overhead and saving money too.

Form over substance, at its heart, is the idea that the appearance of success is more important than real success. Being CEO of a company of 10 is form over substance. Taking on unnecessary titles just to pad a résumé is form over substance, and people see right through it. The important things in business are hard work, integrity, and getting results. You can do that regardless of any contrived title—or the lack thereof—and, as my wife would say, you can still take out the trash no matter your net worth.

I remember one particular swim meet when my daughter Traci was nine. Traci was a good swimmer; she won two events and came in near the top on a third. At the end of the day, she was tied with another girl. The two of them had 'high points'—tied for 'first place.' At this meet, there happened to be a fairly large trophy for the winner—but only one trophy because there was only supposed to be one winner.

Because Traci and the other girl had tied, they had to flip a coin to see which of them would get the trophy. All the adults had to know that the coaches would go out and get a second trophy on the following Monday, but it was unlikely that these two girls knew that—they were still young.

As it turned out, Traci won the coin toss. She got the trophy. What did the other little girl do? She ran off crying. What did Traci do? She went after the girl to give her the trophy. What means more? Having a gaudy trophy or winning high points?

Trophies are a perfect example of form over substance. A trophy doesn't mean anything intrinsically—just like a title doesn't mean anything intrinsically. You can carve something into the plaque at the bottom of the trophy, but it still doesn't mean anything.

Have you ever been to an upscale restaurant and been disappointed by the quality of the food? That's form over substance. In marketing, they talk about having "all sizzle and no steak." The sizzle is the look—the atmosphere and appearance. It's all the temptation that draws you in. The steak is the actual substance. It's what brings you back time and again. There's nothing wrong with sizzle—with form—but it's the steak that you came for, and the steak will bring you back—or not.

Can you imagine walking into a restaurant and smelling the most delicious food, but getting served an empty plate? Would you go back? If the Senior VP of Sales is losing your customers, are you going to keep him because he has the fancy title and looks great in his Armani suit? Of course not.

People see through the façade in a heartbeat; they're too smart to be fooled by elaborate titles and fancy clothes. Contrast those title-mongers with the dedicated employee (or two) who, day after day, does an amazing job no matter what job he's doing. He's the innovator, the hard worker, the one who refuses to quit until he's exhausted all the options. He's ignited his Fourth Gear. It doesn't matter to him whether his title is 'Intern,' 'Associate,' 'Cook,' or 'CEO;' he's going to get the job done because he's failure averse. He's going to get the job done because he's a real leader: a Leader at any Level.

One of my heroes in this regard was the owner of the first car dealership I worked at. He was an incredibly savvy businessman with a number of successful investments in various businesses. The thing is, you wouldn't know it from the look of him. His only title was 'owner.' He never claimed to be CEO or anything else of any of his number of businesses.

He drove a modest, 4-door sedan—an Impala—even though he owned a dealership and could have had whatever he wanted—like a Corvette. His house was nothing extravagant. It was nice, to be sure, but modest. He wasn't one of those guys to go off and build a mansion at the first hint of success—or at the first influx of investor capital, as seems to have become the trend. Even his boat—which, admittedly, he had—was modest.

Part of that was his shrewd business sense—when the dealership needed to be repainted, he told us to just get a bucket and touch up the trouble spots rather than paying for the whole building to get a new coat. Part of it, though, was his self-image. He was confident in who he was and what he had. He didn't need to flaunt his success to everyone around him.

He wasn't the type to walk in and beat you on the head with how many successful businesses or investments he had. He had the substance, so he didn't need the form. Truly successful people often have that kind of confidence. They recognize that money and 'stuff' come as a residual to real success, and they focus on igniting the Fourth Gear and earning success.

These kinds of people don't need the crutch of a fancy title because they know what they've accomplished. They don't need to be fawned over because they're already secure in their own minds. They have real confidence; the confidence you can only get from actually doing things—instead of sitting around and talking about doing things.

The people who put out their titles first often do so because they're insecure. They put out their title like a shield, hoping it will protect them from further scrutiny—because they know in their hearts that scrutiny will uncover that they are faking it. "Oh, he's a Senior VP; he must know his stuff." This is the social shield they rely on to cover their lack of ability.

Look around when you go to parties. You'll see it easily enough.

When my business partner and I started selling computers, we did it out of a 500 square-foot room in someone else's office building—it was practically a closet. There was just enough space for a desk, a phone, and a couple boxes of inventory. It wasn't really big enough to be called an office. But we were really only interested in the substance; we didn't have to wait for the form of the fancy new building; we didn't need flashy uniforms or pens with logos on them. We knew how to sell, and that's what we were going to do.

When it comes right down to it, in order to 'do' something, that something must be a verb. I can 'sell' computers. I can't 'CEO' something. And what, exactly, does 'managing' look like? I dare you to show me what it looks like to 'manage' someone and have that someone enjoy the process.

Keep all this in mind the next time someone asks you what you do. Hiding behind a title is an exercise in ego. The wrong kind of ego.

Manage Your Ego

Which brings us to a very interesting leadership topic: egos come in all shapes and sizes. Some are big, some are small. Some are strong, some are weak. Basically, the ego is what you want other people to think about you. The problem is, the outward display is not always in line with what you consciously, actually want to be known for.

Ego is generally associated with pride—and generally in a negative way. That's deserved, to an extent. For our purposes, we're going to make a distinction between two general types of ego. To keep it simple, we'll just call them good ego and bad ego. There are subsets and different flavors of these two main types, but we'll leave that for the psychology textbooks and keep things understandable here.

People with "good" egos know when it's appropriate to have an ego and when it's not. They know how to check ego at the door when they go to meet with someone else. If they talk trash on the links, it's good natured and it stays out there on the green, because they understand that your skill at golf doesn't define how good or bad you are as a person.

Because people in control of their egos are confident in themselves and have a healthy self-image, they don't need to beat on other people to feel validated—and they certainly don't need to rub any victories in other people's faces. In conjunction with this, they don't care as much about who gets credit for a job well-done. They just want to know the job gets done well.

In order to control your ego, you have to know yourself—be able to identify your own strengths and weaknesses—and ask for help when appropriate (we'll talk about this more in the next chapter). People with good egos don't have to worry about looking bad because they know they'll shine when the time comes for them to do what they're good at.

These kinds of people are also much more pleasant to communicate with because they don't feel a need to dominate the conversation—and make everything be about their own exploits and victories. And, when a person with a good ego is in the presence of someone successful, he'll sit and listen and learn, rather than ruining an opportunity for mentorship by trying to show how smart he is.

A good, controlled ego also lends itself to recognizing the contributions of others. Because the person is already confident, he doesn't need to draw all the glory and attention to himself. As a result, he is much more likely to acknowledge the contributions of the team—and much less likely to use the word "I."

This type of leader hesitates in taking a disproportionate amount of credit for himself because he is humble enough to know he couldn't have done it on his own. And his humility is honest—not false modesty. That said, this type of person isn't out to give away all the credit either; he just doesn't feel the need for more than his fair share. Also, if someone with a controlled ego gets less credit than due, he doesn't let it bother him. He has the confidence to know that his work speaks for itself, and that he will come out where he wants to be in the marathon for success.

That confident, accurate assessment of his own ability also allows him to set good "stretch goals." These leaders have no illusions of grandeur or inferiority regarding their abilities, so they can set high but realistic expectations, then ignite the Fourth Gear and work to meet those expectations. They are able to accept setbacks and blame without getting pushed off track. That's the kind of attitude that earns respect.

On the other hand, someone with an unhealthy, "bad" ego is more likely to shoot for the stars with unrealistic goals and expectations. Then, when the goals aren't met, a bad ego will look for excuses and try to place blame on anyone but himself. Rather than striving for collaborative success, a bad ego will go with the flow until he gets a chance claim the credit—even if that means lying, cheating, or stealing. When credit is passed down, the bad ego wants an unfair share of it; usually, as much as possible—preferably, all of it.

This kind of glory-hogging problem is generally caused by one of two conditions: a lack of self-confidence or a desire for undeserved security.

First, people with uncontrolled, bad egos have no real understanding of themselves and no confidence in their abilities. As a result, they are always trying to draw external validation from others. They want the people around them to be awed at their abilities.

This causes people with bad egos to surround themselves with 'yes' men. People who are too weak to protest—or too self-interested to care. This gives the bad ego an illusion of grandeur and power. Unfortunately, an inability to accept failure stunts their ability to learn from their mistakes which means they are unable to show any real progress or growth.

In turn, the inability to learn and grow guarantees that someone with a bad ego will only be as successful as their highest level of incompetency. In other words, since they can't develop, they can only reach their current limit before a string of failures will bring them down. If they were humble enough to accept their mistakes and learn from them, these people could continually push out those limits and reach ever-greater levels of success.

The other reason for taking as much glory as possible is that people with uncontrolled egos want to create an aura of power and effectiveness around themselves. This is a form of protection for the inevitable point when their self-destructive tendencies drive them to cut a corner, and it backfires.

People with bad egos want to seem amazing in an effort to make themselves seem indispensable. They are trying to secure themselves and their jobs at any expense—usually their employer's—because they know, deep down, that it can't last.

People with ego problems tend to grasp at titles for the same reasons that they hog credit. They don't necessarily want the responsibility nor have the skill set necessary to support having a title, but they want it anyway so they can have the shield. They don't concern themselves with the substance—the character—because all they're really interested in is the form—the appearance. They want the corner office for its perceived value because they want to appear too important to lose.

These are the same people who take business for granted. Instead of valuing the customer, people with bad egos believe customers should be honored to be customers. These kinds of people feel like they are the greatest thing to enter the business world; even though, more often than not, they haven't done anything to earn greatness.

In their heads, people with uncontrolled egos don't see a need to prove their greatness. They have false bravado in spades and somehow believe that's enough proof of their value. Of course, this leaves their egos paper thin because the moment their claims are challenged, they evaporate into the hot air they're made of.

This is the same reason why uncontrolled egos tend to increase their lifestyle rapidly once they have a little success. Rather than living cautiously within their means—being humble and patient—bad egos want all the rewards yesterday, for all their 'hard work' tomorrow. They want everything now because they know their success just a farce. They know they don't really deserve the reward, so they want to squander everything before anyone else catches on and takes it all away.

That's why you'll find people with this kind of ego taking money out of the business before it's even making money, drawing large salaries from investor money. The core of this kind of person is devoid of true character—the kind earned by overcoming adversity—so they change their lifestyle quickly to embrace and flaunt even the smallest bits of success.

At one point, I knew of a Board of Directors that was justifying the expenditure of 10 million dollars on a new enterprise system when their company was already losing money. They told themselves that, because there was cash on the balance sheet and available credit with the bank, the infrastructure investment would return the company to profitability. They thought they had all the right answers because they were the Board, but you can't spend your way into profits. It's unsustainable. However, a person with an uncontrolled ego won't recognize the problem because he is too busy trying to keep up appearances; he is too concerned about the form to spend time worrying about the substance.

Having a bad ego also tends to result in a lot of resentment, both from within and from without the individual. Bad egos tend to resent authority for establishing rules and administering justice. Bad egos want to cut corners and take shortcuts to glory, and they don't want someone checking on their progress or watching over their shoulder. They always think they know best, so, because they tend to avoid help, they often make mistakes.

Then, to hide from an uncomfortable situation (people who are always right don't make mistakes), people with bad egos will generally try to hide those mistakes (or at least their part in it), shift the blame to others (even innocent bystanders), and hope everything just goes away. Sometimes, they do this whole dance without even being aware of it, which is really a reflection of weak character.

In keeping with that weakness, bad egos also tend to resent people of strong character. This stems from jealousy. While they won't admit it to themselves, bad egos know that they personally have no ground to stand on. They know they don't have a solid inner foundation, and they know they won't stick out the hard battles long enough to earn anything. That's why they just want credit where credit isn't due. They would never get anything otherwise.

The really dangerous thing about ego is that it's like a pet dog. A big, toothy one. Think Rottweiler or Bull Mastiff. People can usually tell pretty quickly whether it's well trained or not. If you have a bad ego, it's like a disobedient big dog. It gets in people's faces and makes them less likely to want to interact with you in the future. Worse yet, it's not like it's something you can hide. A bad ego dominates you in the same way a big, disobedient dog would. You can pretend you're in control but it doesn't take a dog whisperer to know what's really going on.

On the other hand, a good ego is like a well-behaved dog. Regardless of whether a person likes dogs or not, seeing a very obedient, respectful one says a lot about the owner. It says he is calm and controlled. It says he is patient. We are more likely to respect a person if he knows how and when to control his ego in the same way we respect a person more when he knows how and when to control his dog—even if we disagree with the person about the actual topic of discussion.

As we know, not all egos are created equally. If there really were only two types, it would be easy to weed out the good from the bad, and then hire—or associate with—only the good. Unfortunately, there is a spectrum when it comes to egos. As an example, allow me to describe three different people. One of them will be clearly good, one clearly bad, and one somewhere in the middle.

The first example of ego is Spencer. Spencer is the COO of a big technology firm. He's a likeable guy and generally has a good word for his coworkers. He loves to be successful and tends to get a new gadget to show off every time he gets a promotion or lands a new deal—just his little way of celebrating and enjoying success. He loves to be in the know and works hard to maintain his network, so he can stay on top of all the latest news. He loves to go in to work, but he prefers to work alone. He's got an attitude of persistence, but sometimes the market conspires against him and makes it impossible to hit his goals. He can't understand why people always want to focus on the little things though instead of the success he did have. He's a good, hard worker, but he doesn't mind stepping on a few people in his climb up the ladder—but only if they get in his way, of course.

We'll call our next hypothetical example Wes. He's an ex-professional athlete of no small talent. He loves to be surrounded by his adoring fans, but he couldn't tell you the name of a single one. He has a lot of sports experience—though he can't stand the business side of things—and thinks he knows how to play his position correctly. In fact, he gets frustrated when people try to tell him what to do or recommend a different way. He can't understand why he spends so much time on the bench, since he's clearly the best player on the team. It's really depressing to him that the owners keep recruiting other players that can't make plays—which then makes him look bad. He can't believe how often people try to abandon him or try to blame him when things go wrong. It's like everyone is out to get him. He has fans but no true friends because nobody seems to give him the respect he thinks he deserves. He's happy to be good enough at what he does that things just go his way most of the time, and he can't understand the people who stick around when things get ugly—there are plenty of other, easier opportunities when things get rough.

Last is James. He's a small business owner who believes fervently that his customers are his life. He is tough on his coworkers but toughest on himself. He's very careful to listen to all sides of the story and tries to be as fair as possible. Still, this puts him in a position that, sometimes, people don't like him. While that hurts, James is willing to accept the resentment if it's for the right reasons. When things go wrong, he's willing and able to handle the blame and get things moving in the right direction again. He's also mindful of the weaker members of his team and tries to give them personalized time for training and mentoring. He wants to see them get stronger, so they can rise to the top. He has a 'never give up,' persistent attitude, and he's willing to throw things at the wall to see if they stick. He spends much of his time motivating and coaching his colleagues but never lets discipline slip.

It should be fairly obvious that Wes has the bad, uncontrolled ego. Hopefully, it's equally obvious that James is the example of the good ego with Fourth Gear engaged. By default, that means Spencer is the example with the gray-area ego. A closer look, however, reveals just how tricky his ego problems really are.

First of all, he's a 'likeable guy,' but doesn't mind stepping on people if it advances his position. That seems a little conflicting and should raise a flag. What's more, he always wants to be in the know. He's the type of person that wants to know all the secrets but wouldn't hesitate to rat someone out if he felt it would get him ahead. He most likely prefers to work alone because it allows him to take all the credit for any success but also because he sees his coworkers as competition, and he wants to be the one making the big bucks and receiving all of the accolades.

This craving for success and, more importantly, money is likely to lead him to do some things outside the normal order of business—but not good things. Spencer is likely to cut corners and cheat a little. He's probably cautious about it out of fear of getting caught, but no matter how careful he is, it will eventually catch up to him.

His tendency to 'shoot for the stars' is also worrisome. Psychologists have found that a difficult but achievable goal has the effect of motivating a person. On the other hand, if the goal is set too high, it actually has the opposite effect (Ordóñez, et al. 2009). Goals that are considered unrealistic have a demotivational effect on people.

Spencer has a tendency to set just those kinds of goals, goals that his colleagues can't meet. Then, when they don't meet the goals, he blames the failure on them. Basically, he's punishing them twice—once in the goal setting process and again during the performance review.

Last is his interest in form over substance. He's clearly the kind of person who's focused on the next title and the next pay raise. He's probably making great money but still overdraws his bank because, no matter how successful he is, he still wants more. His lifestyle changes quickly with his success, demonstrated by the gadgets he buys as 'trophies.' This impulsiveness implies a lack of strong character—an inability to stay true to an inner core. It will also make him desperate for ever-increasing success, which will drive him to riskier and riskier deals as he struggles to find his next big payoff. Sooner or later, he'll take a gamble on the wrong deal and sink himself—and possibly his company.

In conclusion, while Spencer might not seem so bad on the surface, without careful attention and mentoring, he is something of a time bomb for the organization. Symptoms of his presence are likely to include bitterness and jealousy among employees, shady deals with disgruntled customers, and rising expenses for level or even falling sales. In other words, Spencer's ego will drive out the good people and slowly rot the business from the inside.

Ego is a powerful force in leadership. People will instinctively be drawn to a good ego because the owner of the ego is trustworthy and good to work with. The good egos are supportive and humble. If a manager has a bad ego, however, people will see right through the façade and start to leave.

What is Hard Work?

People go on and on about how hard work is critical for success, but how many people understand what hard work really is? So many think that 'hard work' is coming in early and leaving late. That's not hard work; that's long work. Hard work is what you do when you're in (or out of) the office, not how long you fill up a chair. Hard work is all about igniting the Fourth Gear: never saying never and inventing ways to get things done.

We used to tell our top salesperson that he never had to come into the office again. It's true. We didn't care whether he attended a sales meeting or anything else. As far as we were concerned, he could spend all day every day out at the golf course. As long as he continued to produce top results and violated none of the laws of man, we were okay. As long as he didn't do anything to ruin the name of the company, the sky was the limit.

The way we saw it at Pomeroy IT, to have top success, he must have already been doing the hard work—the real work—so what did we care about the hours he put in? Or when he put them in? To have top success—and sustain it—that person was already igniting their Fourth Gear and creating new ways to gain success. They were desperate, and we didn't want to get in the way.

Hard work—the Fourth Gear—is about studying, using intelligence, gaining an understanding of people, making the hard calls, taking responsibility when something goes wrong, fixing problems, being an example, and getting "it" done—whatever "it" is.

Hard work is having a machine that only builds 90 widgets a day when you really need 100 widgets a day—and then making it happen. Hard work is being the cancer researcher that goes through a thousand failures before finding the tiniest win. It takes patience, dedication, ambition, tenacity, and courage. It's igniting the Fourth Gear.

In short, hard work is being a Leader at any Level. You don't have to know everything, but you have to be willing to learn anything—no matter the personal cost in time and effort. One of the things I have always loved about college graduates is that they understand homework. They understand that, after a long day of classes (work), they can't just go home and party. Not the serious ones, anyway. They understand that they need to take their work home and learn more about it.

In the computer industry, back when it was getting off the ground, the amount of experience and education a person could get that would be relevant to the actual job wasn't very high or, to be fair, particularly important. We were in the heart of the computer revolution and things were changing so fast that a solid understanding now would be obsolete in less than a year. I liked college graduates because they knew how to study to stay on top of the changes. They knew how to do that hard work and maintain their knowledge and expertise.

So, to summarize, leadership is the ability to stand for something important and then do whatever it takes—hard work—to make that vision reality. True leadership is that rare ability to choose a course and stick to it, marking the path for others to follow. It's the ability to catch the vision and be an example of it.

Leadership is standing up to your colleagues at lunch when they all want to bad-mouth the company or boss, and then showing those coworkers what it means to believe in something greater than bricks and mortar and give someone the benefit of the doubt. It's taking the reins of a billion-dollar enterprise and turning it around from failure to growth by showing what it means to be motivated and ingenious.

Leadership is talking to your parents, family, or friends and showing them how to celebrate success by exercising restraint and living well within their means instead of blowing every penny of a raise on a new toy that screams to the world how "successful" they are. It's about doing what's best for the family, community, or business, instead of pushing your own agenda.

Leadership is not a title. It's you. You are a leader in everything you do—so long as you do it right and do it well. You are a leader if you want to be. Sometimes you're a leader even when you don't want to be. Leadership isn't just for executives. It can be for anybody. It should be for anybody. It should be for everybody. So square your shoulders, set your vision, ignite your Fourth Gear, and lead wherever you are in whatever you do. Be a Leader at any Level—at every level.

Chapter Summary
- Leadership is displayed by example; it means to go before and pave the way
- Focus on the substance—getting the job done—and the form will come on its own
- Control your ego or it will control you; everyone can see through your ego anyway
- Hard work is figuring out problems; it's study, research, and ingenuity

---

IQ OR EI – READ THE SIGNS

In order to be a leader, one must master his own ego, engage the Fourth Gear, and then understand people. We talked about ego in the last chapter. In this chapter, we'll build the foundation for what it takes to understand people—including yourself—a skill set that allows true leaders to be self-aware and emotionally fluent.

For a number of years, the magic predictor for workplace success was believed to be IQ, Intelligence Quotient. Over the past couple decades, however, psychologists have tended to debunk this theory. It's common sense now to say that just because a person is smart doesn't mean he'll be successful.

For example, Ted Kaczynski is reported to have had an IQ north of 160. The average of American IQs is around 100. Approximately 97.5% of the population is supposed to be below 130. That makes Ted a real genius. Ted also happens to be the Unabomber. Clearly, IQ should not be the only factor we use to predict success.

In more recent times, experts have been focusing on a concept called EQ, Emotional Quotient, more properly known as Emotional Intelligence, or EI. By definition, EI measures the ability of a person to read and understand the emotions within himself and within others. The power in this lies in the fact that, once you understand the emotions in play, you can begin to make them work for you—or at least minimize how they work against you.

As a leader, this ability allows you to better guide people to harnessing their Fourth Gears; you'll be better equipped to understand and resolve their concerns, and you'll be more in tune to support them when they need it. Perhaps most importantly, you'll be more careful and offend people less often.

In order to better understand Emotional Intelligence, both as a general principle and as it applies to you in your leadership and success efforts, we'll need to first go through a few fundamental ideas. These are the major components of EI and what makes it so powerful. By learning these concepts and how they work together, you'll be learning how to control your emotions—instead of letting your emotions control you.

Personality

First is the concept of Personality. Quite simply, personality is the response pattern your behavior follows when you're confronted with a given situation. For instance, a coward might run when faced with an angry dog. Then again, so might a wise person. A teenage boy might face the dog to 'prove' how macho he is. A strong man may simply ignore it. There are any number of possible responses to the stimulus of an angry dog. A person's personality is comprised of the most likely response he would employ.

Often, personality is broken down into the emotional responses one is most likely to display. Therefore, "he's angry all the time" becomes a description of what someone's personality is perceived to be.

However, this is deceptive. Personality is influenced by many factors: social setting, previous experience (both recent and more distant past), company (both in the sense of the people around them and the culture of the organization(s) to which a person belongs), desires / goals, stressors, material goods, religion, etc.

Simply moving from one room of your house to another can change your response set, and therefore, your personality. In fact, a change of scenery—like stepping out of your office into the hall—can drastically change the way you deal with situations. There is something to be said about being on your 'home turf.'

It's interesting to note that people can display different personalities depending on the setting and who they're with. Thus, I can be loving, gentle and thoughtful at home with my family but be something of an autocratic jerk when I'm at work. Just because a man ignores and neglects his dog doesn't mean he will do the same with his children—though it is a dangerous indicator.

Because of these variations, it can be difficult to accurately 'type' someone's personality—that's why you shouldn't judge someone until you really know them. If you develop the reputation of being a person who doesn't judge others too quickly, people will respect you for it.

This is important to learn and understand because of a principle called cognitive dissonance (which we'll delve into in Chapter 4). For now, the point to understand is that a person can be a complete jerk to everyone at work, yet still think of himself as a nice person because, outside of work, he is. What we think of our own personality and what other people observe of our personality are rarely ever perfectly aligned. Generally, people only have the chance to see one or two sides of us. Few people see the full range of who we can be.

Still, psychologists believe there are generally common traits within a person that manifest on some level regardless of the environmental and social influences of any given moment (i.e., you may act differently in different places, but deep inside, you're still you). Certain psychological tests, when administered to children, give significantly similar results when re-administered to those same people as adults; some people are just always introverted. They may learn to be gregarious in social settings in order to better fit in, but, at heart, they still prefer to withdraw. In order to best understand yourself, you have to know where your strengths and weaknesses lie and get a clear picture of the way your personality reacts in a given situation. Recognizing your weaknesses and being honest about them will earn you respect.

Character

Next comes Character and what it means in the context of our discussion. Character, in the simplest terms, is the result of a long series of decisions. In many ways, character is very similar to personality. The main difference is that personality is a list of your predispositions; character is more like an accounting for what you've actually done. In most people, these two things will be essentially the same. In a few individuals, however, their recognition of their personality has given them power over shaping their character.

A person may be predisposed to run from an angry dog but make the decision not to. Whether because he is facing his fears or because he is making a higher judgment of the situation or for whatever other reason, he has the power to shape his character. In time, an individual's personality will tend to become more like his character and vice versa. That's why it's so important to understand what character and personality are, so that you can better control them and, in so doing, control yourself.

Good character is earned, not given. It's the result of facing difficulty, engaging the Fourth Gear, and claiming victory. Weak character results from running from challenges—from indulging in handouts, rather than leveraging them.

When we look at historical figures like Washington, Lincoln, or Churchill, what we tend to admire is their character: their drive to go and do the right things no matter the obstacles. People with strong character have a habit and history of knowingly and willfully making the right decisions—regardless of any contrary predisposition or external opposition—and then pushing through to see the end goal. These are the people who tell the truth no matter how much it might hurt.

Strong character has another benefit too: people learn that they can count on you. That makes it easier for them to understand how they should interact with you. It's easier to read a strong character 'like an open book' because you can be sure of how they'll act.

Someone with weak character is much more likely to vacillate from one view to another and back again. Think politicians. Any inner character aside, the outer character of trying to always people-please gives the appearance of having no character and no conviction. How can you count on someone like that? You can't ever be sure if he believes in what he's doing, or if he's about to drop everything and walk away to try something else.

Additionally, having well-developed character allows you to build a strong foundation from which to direct your life—both business and personal. It helps you to find patterns and consistency to give you emotional stability. Examples of this are the people who can hold their peace during a meeting. Rather than needing to speak out about everything, these people sit quietly and listen. They don't need to voice their opinion until someone asks them to. They are confident enough to respect the speaker—and they earn the same respect in return.

In a way, character can take a lot of the stress out of a number of situations because you don't have to weigh the morality of them each time. Instead, you've already drawn your line in the sand, and you already know what to do. You don't have to stop and puzzle it out each time a new iteration of an old problem arises.

Interestingly, Helen Keller[8] once said, "We could never learn to be brave and patient if there was only joy in the world." While her statement is a little surprising on the surface, when you look deeper, it makes sense. How would you ever know what good was like if you never experienced hardship? My parents were good examples of that. My dad spent time in a Nazi concentration camp during World War II. It nearly killed him, but I fully believe that he was stronger for it. It gave him perspective on life that people just don't gain by accident.

The famous Nietzsche[9] quote, "That which does not kill us makes us stronger," holds true for people wanting to build deep, strong character. By extension, we can include the old bodybuilder's axiom: no pain, no gain. It is a physiological truth that, in order to strengthen muscle, you have to overload it to the point of doing physical damage. This causes real, physical pain called DOMS (Delayed Onset Muscle Soreness). Then, as the body works to rebuild the injured tissue, it will build it back stronger than before

[8] A deaf and blind author and public speaker, recipient of the Presidential Medal of Honor, and National Women's Hall of Famer

[9] A German philosopher

in order to prevent such damage in the future. This is why the military does such an effective job of breaking down new recruits—physically and mentally—so they can be rebuilt in a stronger, more dedicated form.

The same principle holds with character. It's the adversity and difficulty that tear us down which allow us to ignite the Fourth Gear and come back stronger. If life was always easy, we'd never appreciate it. If everything was beautiful, we wouldn't be able to distinguish between the mundane and the magnificent.

So, instead of complaining about the hardships, think about them. Learn from them. Ask yourself why you're facing a challenge and what you can learn from it. If there's something in your life you can change to avoid future repetition of the difficulty, consider changing. However, no matter what the outcome, don't regret facing hardship. Instead, remember that you'll come out stronger after facing the trial; remember the words of Emerson: "Unless you try to do something beyond what you have already mastered, you will never grow."

It's never too late to start building character. Now, certainly, the longer you've avoided building character, the harder it may be to start, but you can still do it. If you've always rolled with the punches and caved on difficult choices in the past, start small. You'll need to build your willpower and build your character before you take on the bigger challenges—but the fact of the matter remains: you can do it. You can improve your character. And what if you feel like you've done something really wrong? Well, start by never doing it again. Period. Ever. Reinvent yourself and move on, starting today.

If you feel you already have strong character, now that you're more aware of certain weaknesses and flaws, you can actively focus on strengthening yourself in those weaker areas. This doesn't mean you need to go out of your way to seek hardship, but it does mean you probably should stop going out of your way to avoid it. The sad fact is that it often takes less effort to just face down a challenge than it does to invent some elaborate, time-consuming work-around to avoid the challenge.

The beautiful thing about the human mind, though, is that if you really want something, you can find a way to make it happen. The Fourth Gear makes that possible. If you're really ready to strengthen your character, you'll find ways to establish and reinforce yourself.

Self-Efficacy

Another critical concept is that of Self-Efficacy. Self-efficacy is, in its simplest terms, how well a person thinks he can perform a task. It's important to note here that self-efficacy has no relationship to a person's actual level of skill; it's only a reflection of one's confidence—one's self-assessment of whether or not he can perform a task and how good of a job he thinks he can do. Self-efficacy is based in perception and, therefore, has only a limited connection to reality. The power of self-efficacy is that it affects our individual perceptions of reality.

Self-efficacy tends to be kept internally but reinforced externally. We have our own opinions about what we can and can't do, and no one can 'change' those, per se. However, our perceptions tend to mirror the average of the external feedback we receive.

For instance, when I was at Beneficial Financial at the beginning of my career, I quickly became one of the best collectors they had. It wasn't that I was necessarily any better at working with people or anything like that. Largely, it was due to my drive and fearlessness-my Fourth Gear. I was willing to work the cases no one else would touch.

Having success in collecting and being recognized for that success contributed heavily to the growth of my self-efficacy. To an extent, this got me into a few situations where my confidence in my ability exceeded my actual ability to collect. Or, perhaps more accurately, my confidence was exceeded by another individual's confidence that they did not have to repay. In either case, while my opinion of my ability was kept inside me, the outside factors moved the needle up or down. Closing a difficult case gave me a boost to my confidence. Having a man pull a gun on me shook that confidence. Then finding out he came in to pay up his debt helped me up again.

An important distinction is that self-efficacy and pride are not analogous terms. Self-efficacy is how I feel about my ability regardless of how I perform in relation to others. I can be the worst Olympic shot-put thrower and still feel pretty confident in my shot-put ability. I can be the worst performing salesman in my organization but, given the strength and skill of my colleagues, still feel very confident in my ability and still close a lot of deals.

Pride, on the other hand, is when I try to compare my perception of my self-efficacy with my perception of someone else's efficacy. If I feel I'm better at a task than someone else, that's pride. Thinking I'm the 'best collector' at Beneficial is pride. Thinking I'm a good—or even a great—collector is not, because it isn't comparative. I'm not claiming to be better than anyone else.

Where this comes into play is with ego. If I have good control of my ego, I can have a very high self-efficacy in a task without feeling the need to flaunt it to my coworkers. Your coworkers are important too, and you're going to need them some day. You can be the number one sales rep and be humble about it. On the other hand, having bad ego control and high self-efficacy is a dangerous recipe. That's when a person begins to gloat to their colleagues, and, over time, this behavior will erode relationships and poison the cultural well of a company.

Still, there are some advantages to high self-efficacy. For instance, high self-efficacy allows us to have confidence in taking risks. If I believe I'm a good collector, I'm willing to take a shot at the cases no one else will touch. I may also be more willing to try similar tasks in a new field. For example, my confidence in my ability to sell and my confidence in my knowledge regarding credit gave me the confidence to partner with my friend to buy a number of Computerland franchises. I had never sold a computer before.

In fact, as difficult as it might be to believe now, computers hardly existed at that time. Cellphones today have far more power than the computers did back then. So how could I have any idea whether I would be good at selling computers or not? I didn't. But I knew I could sell from my time in car sales, and I knew I could learn what I needed to because of my time teaching myself at Beneficial. Put the two together, and I was confident I could learn to sell computers. I was willing to take the risk.

The take home here is to have an understanding of a person's confidence level for different tasks. If they know nothing about accounting, don't ask them to prepare a P&L (profit and loss) statement unless you're willing to walk them through it. On the other hand, you shouldn't need to worry too much about your salespeople being able to sell that new product you're introducing—as long as it's complementary to your existing line.

Paper salesmen might have difficulty selling luxury yachts; private jet salesmen might not have that same challenge. So be aware of self-efficacy when you're making assignments, and you'll be less likely to leave people feeling overwhelmed by their new tasks.

Self-Image

Closely related to self-efficacy is the idea of Self-Image. This is, in essence, how a person sees himself. Self-image is made up, in large part, by the previous concepts. To be clear, however, this is not self-esteem. Self-esteem is how a person feels about what he sees when he looks at himself. In other words, self-esteem is how a person feels about his self-image.

Self-image, however, is at once simpler and more complicated than self-esteem. Self-image is what a person sees in the mirror. Are you tall, short, fat, skinny, bald, hairy, ugly, beautiful, etc.? But it also goes deeper than just surface characteristics.

For instance, I see a computer salesman when I look in the mirror. I see a person who can sell anything honest, given the right opportunity to learn about the product. I see someone who can weather a storm or three without losing sight of the vision. I see someone who cares deeply about his family—past, present, and future. I see someone who values freedom and honesty and responsibility. I see someone who values success and helping others achieve it.

At its core, self-image is the amalgamation of personality and character with skills, talents, dreams, and desires. It includes an assessment of a person's self-efficacy. It's a picture of everything a person feels that he is or isn't. Unfortunately, because it's monitored and controlled by the 'self,' it's not always entirely accurate to reality. All too often, people fail at things because they don't see themselves as being successful—even though they actually had the skills necessary to succeed. Because of that distorted view, they don't give themselves permission to be successful and end up sabotaging their own efforts. As Henry Ford[10] said, "Whether you think you can or you can't, either way, you are right."

That's why it's so important to understand these principles. If you can't understand how people see themselves, you won't be able to gauge their reactions and efforts accurately. As a Leader at any Level, you need to know the people around you well enough that you can work with them in the most efficient manner. Whether that means a little more hand-holding for one and a little more correcting for another, understanding these concepts—understanding Emotional Intelligence—will help you know how to be the best leader you can be.

In order to lead, you first have to be able to manage your ego and maintain your own self-image accurately. If you don't have those things firmly under control, how can you expect to have the confidence to take risks on new ventures and ideas? Without solid character, how can you expect to weather the trials and adversity of paving a newer, better way?

Self-Awareness

There came a time at Beneficial when a management position opened up at a branch in northern Kentucky. My boss at the time put in a good word for me, and I got the job. I would be on my own to lead a good branch. At first, I was thrilled. I had started out young and worked hard. I had earned this promotion, and I was excited about it. At the same time, however, I realized that I might be getting in over my head. I was only 22, which meant the entire staff would be older than me. I would be the boss, but they would have more experience.

I didn't really know how to get started, so I called my supervisor. I asked him what I should do to manage the people in this new office, and he told me not to 'manage' them. He pointed out to me that most of the men and women who would be working 'for' me had 20 or 30 years of experience. He reminded me that they knew what they were doing; they didn't need to be managed. They knew their jobs, and they were smart people.

He said to do nothing with them and wait to let them come to me. He

---

[10] An industrialist from the early 1900s widely considered to be the father of the assembly line

suggested that I listen to them and learn from them, and that I should just go in there and start making loans and doing collections like I always had—that the people would respect me more for that than for trying to order them around. It was the best advice I could have received at that time—I could feel the respect right away, and the employees came just as he'd predicted—it was also advice I never would have taken if I hadn't checked my ego and been self-aware.

Self-awareness is the ability to take off your glasses and look at them. Everyone has a set of figurative 'glasses' through which they see themselves and the world; some people call it a 'paradigm' or a filter, but the meaning is the same. That set of glasses is comprised of all the aspects of the self-image and tempered with the different experiences life has offered. No two people have the same set of lenses. In effect, we all have different prescriptions.

Unfortunately, we also don't have 'paradigm doctors' around to calibrate our lenses and make sure we're seeing through them properly. Until we do, it's up to each of us to monitor our viewpoints and watch for the inevitable bias that creeps in. Don't judge too quickly.

Let's try an experiment. You're running late for an important meeting. Maybe it's a date with the person you think you want to marry. Maybe it's an important client. Maybe it's just your parents, but they only have an hour on their layover before they head out to Hawaii. Think of a reason. A real reason. Make it something important to you. Got it?

So you're flying down the freeway, running late. Up ahead, you can see a little traffic forming—one of these little dozen-car packs that just amble up the highway and slow everyone down—but you can clearly see a gap in the cars that will let you through so you can be on your way. Then, out of nowhere, a little Honda Civic comes flying up beside you, swerves dangerously in front of you, and nearly takes off your bumper.

You lay on the horn and the little car slams its brakes, nearly becoming your new hood ornament, before taking off again, cutting through your gap in the traffic just before it closes. Now you've missed your chance and have to fall in with the little pack, hoping that another opening will appear.

How do you feel? Frustrated? Angry? Do you pray the punk gets a flat tire—or something worse? Think about that. Keep it in mind as we continue.

Let's say you end up arriving twenty minutes late to your important meeting. The significant person there tries to wave it off, but how are you feeling? Do you think your mood will affect how the meeting goes?

Now, let's be fair here. You've had a string of bad luck. No one's going to argue with you about your right to be disappointed in what's happened. However, how does that help? What does getting mad fix? You can't turn back time and have another go. Even if you could, how are you sure you didn't already have the best outcome. Maybe every other option would have led to a wreck and you'd have missed the appointment entirely.

The concept of self-awareness isn't just about anger management, however. It's about how your emotional state from one event can spill over and taint another event. If you get cut off on the way to an important meeting, and it ends up making you late, you have two choices; you can be mad or you can forget about it. If you decide to be mad, you're likely to go into your meeting mad. Now let's turn that around.

Have you ever had someone come to meet with you (a friend, colleague, vender, family member), and they came in all hot under the collar? How did that affect you? Did you get defensive? Offensive? They brought a mood in with them, and it potentially changed the nature of the game. What might have been a relaxing, productive meeting could suddenly turn into a battlefield. If they had just taken a moment to calm down and get their head on right, things might have gone more smoothly.

When I was working at Superior Chevrolet, we were painfully aware of this phenomenon. The receptionists were critical to us. They were the face of our business. If they were having a bad day, every customer who came in would see a grump first. Do you think that doesn't affect business? Think again. We used to ask the receptionists to stay home if they were having a bad day—or at least fake a smile until they could get past whatever was getting them down. We didn't need our customers to go through that. Setting an expectation of pleasantness for the face of the company is critical.

So how many times have you carried the loaded weapon of emotion into a meeting? Keep in mind that it works in both ways. If you're having a great day, you can bring that to others. Like when that random person smiles at you on the street and you can't help but smile back. However, if you're miserable, you can bring that around with you instead. The point is that, whatever emotional baggage you're carrying, you will off-load some of it onto the people around you if you're not both careful and self-aware. There is a saying that "Everybody brings joy to a room: some when they enter, others when they leave." Which type of person would you rather be?

Here's the key: how often do you stop and take stock of your emotional state? How often do you sit back and think about the baggage you're carrying? Most people don't think about it very often at all. Most people just take their emotional state for granted. Instead of mastering their emotions, they tend to be mastered by them. If they have a blow-out with their spouse just before heading off to work, they arrive at work grumpy, and it affects their productivity and office relationships.

On the other hand, if they get their favorite parking spot or their favorite song comes on the radio just before they come into the office, they may come in with a smile. That smile can improve their whole day. People tend to be their very best when they're smiling—and smile when they're at their very best.

The beauty of being self-aware—of having high Emotional Intelligence—is that you can then have more self-control. When you pause to take stock of your emotions periodically, you can regulate them. Being cut off on the freeway may not be any less frustrating in the moment, but it doesn't have to cloud your mood for the remainder of the day. Instead, you can stop, take a deep breath and regain control.

Emotions are one of the major components of how we see the world. They provide a very strong bias in what we see because they have a tendency to be self-reinforcing. In other words, if you're angry, you'll tend to see things that make you angry. If you're happy, you'll tend to see things that make you happy. In psychology this is called confirmation bias. In other words, we see what supports how we already feel. No one has enough attention to see everything all the time, so the lens you use is extremely important: it determines what filters through to you.

Know Your Strengths—and Weaknesses

In addition to being able to regulate your mood, thereby maintaining better control, there's another aspect of self-awareness: knowing your strengths and weaknesses. This ties back to having an accurate self-image. First of all, everybody has weaknesses. It's part of life. No one is good at everything. And that's a good thing. If you honestly could do everything yourself, why would you ever need another person? Especially if you were better at any given task than anybody else. Think of all the relationships and growth and opportunities you would forgo because you could just do everything on your own. How boring would that be?

Instead, we all have strengths and weaknesses. Don't be ashamed of your weaknesses—everyone has some; just be sure to recognize them. I haven't always been the most skillful at treating others nicely in business. I expect a lot out of people, including myself, and it's hard for me to accept when they fall short on their promises.

However, I recognize that aspect of myself, and, in recognizing it, I'm able to keep my demanding nature in mind. I haven't turned it into a strength, but, certainly, I'm less weak when I'm thinking straight; i.e., knowing where my weaknesses are allows me to try to work things around them. It allows me to avoid situations where I'll be weak by sending in someone stronger instead.

Having an accurate picture of your strengths and weaknesses will not only help you avoid potential pitfalls in business and life, it will also give you a better view of the lens through which you are viewing the world. In essence, this is getting a clear view of where you should have self-efficacy—and where you should be more cautious about charging in head first.

Knowing your strengths and weaknesses allows you to track down and hire the kind of people that have strengths where you have weaknesses. Shortly after my partner and I began operating our Computerland franchises, we realized that we were growing fast enough to need a real accounting system. But we were salesmen. We were learning logistics and new products and training new personnel; we didn't have the accounting know how, and we didn't have the time to develop it on our own because we were too busy trying to drive more business. We recognized a weakness.

Rather than be willfully blind, we looked at it as an opportunity to shore up our operations. Thankfully, my partner had a friend who happened to specialize in accounting. It was one of the best hires we ever made. Ed was brilliant when it came to accounting. He had a strength where we had a weakness. Immediately, we were able to put the back-office operations in his capable hands and focus on our own strengths.

So how do you figure out where your strengths and weaknesses are? Well, the easiest answer to that question is to ask someone. In particular, ask people you trust—ones who also know you well. You may trust your banker, but, unless you've spent considerable time together, he's unlikely to have an accurate picture of you. Instead, ask mentors, friends and family; people you know will give their honest opinions—and have enough experience with you to base an accurate opinion on. Before doing this, though, you need to recognize a couple of things.

First, if they give you their opinion, you'd better be prepared to act on it. It's awfully easy to lose a lot of respect when you ask someone for their candid opinion and then ignore it. When was the last time that you had to say "I told you so" to someone? Sometimes, it's fun to be able to say that. Like when it means you won an insignificant argument.

Then again, if a colleague, child, or friend asked for some advice and then did something else entirely, how would you feel about them? On the one hand you want to give them the benefit of the doubt, but, on the other hand, you question why they wasted your time asking you—especially if they never seemed to give your suggestion any consideration.

Second, you need to realize that you might not like everything they have to say. Sometimes it hurts to hear what other people think our strengths and weaknesses are—especially when we value the opinion of the person. You might, for instance, think you're a great public speaker. Chances are, you're not half bad. However, your friend and colleague might hear you say 'um' too many times as you gather your thoughts. Maybe you think you're a great driver. You've got zero tickets in the past decade and no accidents. Your record may be spotless, yet your kids or friends are terrified to get into the car with you at the wheel. Things like that can feel like a bit of a curve-ball.

Of course their feedback about your strengths can be equally surprising. They may tell you that you give the best presentations but you feel you're always fumbling for words. Your kids may think you make the best cookies but you always feel like they turn out a little burned. The point is, our perceptions of ourselves are rarely identical to others' perceptions of us. Recognize that going in, so the surprises will be less alarming.

Third, keep in mind that each of the people you go to will have a different perspective on your strengths and weaknesses. It's generally a good idea to reflect on the areas that multiple people bring to your attention and spend less time on the outliers. If only one person mentions something, it's probably not a big deal. If everyone mentions the same characteristic, you should probably pay attention to it—even if the combined opinion is the opposite of your own.

Finally, once you've polled your friends and developed a list of strengths and weaknesses, get to work. Now that you're aware of those aspects, do something with the knowledge. Work on improving yourself. The true power of self-awareness doesn't manifest until you begin to act based on the knowledge. If you know you're a strong presenter, seek more opportunities to present. If you're weak at sales, get the great salespeople to help you improve, or get yourself out of that sales position.

The key here isn't to try to improve the areas you're weak in. Chances are, you're far enough behind the curve that trying to become an expert in something you are currently bad at is a waste of time. This is especially true when you can just partner with someone who's already strong in that area. More importantly, current research indicates that the greatest improvement gains happen when people focus on improving their strengths (Aguinis, Gottfredson and Joo 2012). So just focus on what you do well and leverage the strengths of others for the things you aren't good at.

It's interesting, in that regard, that we try to compartmentalize nearly everything in life—except ourselves. We have different tools for different situations. The people in customer service don't generally need access to the same programs as the people in research and development. The accountants don't measure things the same way as the HR folks. There isn't one magical pot or pan that can effectively cook every meal. We all recognize that, as often as not, one size really doesn't fit all, and yet we insist on being one size ourselves. We insist on being the right fit to create every solution. The truth is, we'd be better if we focused on our strengths and allowed others to do the same. No matter how brilliant the brain surgeon may be, he still has an anesthesiologist put you to sleep.

Self-awareness allows you to see the world more clearly and recognize the twists and blemishes in your lens that might be distorting your perception. It involves having an accurate account of your strengths, weaknesses, and personality. It gives you more control over the character you are creating, and it helps you to better focus your efforts on those areas that will bring you the most success. It's the difference of steering your life instead of just riding shotgun.

Emotional Intelligence (EI)

Self-awareness, in turn, prepares you to better understand and accept the tumultuous emotional states of the people around you; it forms the foundation for true Emotional Intelligence. If you lose control of your emotions, you've lost control of the situation. To demonstrate this, let me tell you two stories. The first was a mistake I made early in my career; the second is a victory I experienced after learning from my mistake in the first story.

When we were still fairly young at Computerland, we had a representative come in from a major grocery store chain. In those days, computers didn't have fancy, pre-loaded software. When you bought a computer, you bought a box of potential—potential you had to program yourself. Everything came separately. So this rep comes in demanding a software program that's supposed to hit the market soon, but in reality, isn't quite out yet.

We went back and forth for a bit as I tried to explain that it wasn't out, but this guy wouldn't take no for an answer. He needed the software, and he needed it yesterday. Finally, I had an idea. I'd received a demo copy of the software, so that I could 'sell' customers on the features of the upcoming program. The idea was to show them how great the software was, so they would line up for it once it finally hit the shelves. I offered to let the rep take our copy of the software to use until we could get the real thing in stock for him.

Now, as it turns out, the demo copy had a bunch of locks built into the software to prevent resellers from receiving a 'free' copy and turning around and making pure profit on it. I didn't realize that because I hadn't had time to check it out yet.

Well, the rep comes back within a week, and he's just steaming out the ears. He's absolutely livid. He starts going off in some very colorful language about how worthless the software was and how unprofessional it was to give him such crap. Well, I was kind of blindsided by this. Here I was thinking I'd done him a huge favor, and he comes back in to accuse me off all sorts of unprofessional behavior. I kind of lost it.

We had a little shouting match to see who could use the worst language. He swore the grocery chain would never come to us for anything ever again, and I swore I'd forbid our employees from ever shopping in his stores again.

I know. In retrospect it's easy to see how childish it all was. Still, in the moment, it was real, and it was intense. Afterward, my partner came up to me and chastised me for losing my cool. He reminded me that we couldn't afford to be chasing off business—especially not big business like that. New customers cost far too much to recruit.

According to the White House Office of Consumer Affairs, a customer with a negative experience will tell eleven other people about that bad experience. Customers with a good experience will tell only three. That means you need four good customers for every one bad customer just to break even.

It hurt to have my partner chew me out, but I couldn't argue because I knew he was right. And the rep hadn't lied either. That grocery store chain didn't do business with us for more than a decade. By losing control of myself, I lost control of everything else, and, as a result, lost a very lucrative prospect. But, the good news is that I learned from my mistake.

Later in life, after the company had grown significantly, we were in a position where a very large manufacturer owed us a significant amount of money from a rebate program it had been running. We were owed a little over $20 million, to put things in context. It was money Pomeroy IT couldn't afford to just write off. Over the course of years we met with senior executives from that company and made numerous efforts through correspondence as well. Then, toward the end of the ordeal, I had a meeting I'll never forget.

I was sitting down with the CFO of this powerful manufacturer and in walks the head of their PC division. He was a big guy, physically, but more importantly, he was a powerful man. The company and I may have felt like we were big fish, but, the truth was, we were like minnows. I was now in the room with a couple great white sharks. I knew they could eat our lunch. I was too small to do anything to them. I mean, what was I supposed to do, sue them? They had more lawyers than I did (probably more than everyone else did), and probably much better lawyers.

No. This time I was going to have to play it cool. I was going to have to stay in control of myself and wait for the situation to swing in our favor. It's what I'd been doing for years: patiently waiting for the right moment. At this particular meeting, that pivotal moment finally happened.

The head of the PC division walks in and just starts tearing into me and the company. I knew we were only one of 5,000 distributors for them so we didn't mean much, but, from the way he lost it, you'd think I had real power over him. Of course, in that moment of his personal weakness, I did have power over him. He'd given it to me.

We're having this disagreement for the umpteenth time, and he slams his fist on the table and says something like, "I'm sick and tired of you and your little company and this rebate nonsense. We're not paying your exaggerated numbers, so just stop wasting our time already."

The old me would have lashed back. I would have exercised my temper and my ego and stood up for myself at the wrong moment.

Thankfully, I wasn't the old me anymore.

His anger was unfounded and undeserved, so I forced myself to remain calm. Instead of getting angry, I replied, "You've got to pay us. You can slam your fist on that table as many times as makes you feel good, but the facts are the facts. Now, I don't know how you treat your thousands of other retailers and I don't really care, but Pomeroy IT Solutions is one reseller you are going to pay."

We got the bulk of our money. We got it because in that moment, no matter how powerful that man was, he'd lost control. Instead of controlling his impulses, he was controlled by them. Because of my previous experiences, and the character I had developed as a result, I was able to keep control, and, in so doing, gain more control.

Now, they didn't write us a check for the full amount right on the spot, but his loss of control was the turning point. I had him after that. He'd conceded control to me, and, over the next two years, we got our money by drips and dribbles. We only ended up charging off $3 million over the next several years. The other $17 million was recovered. No one but the accounts receivables team—not even the Board—thought we could get any of it back.

The thing to remember is that, when you are aware of yourself and your emotional state, you're better at learning. You can learn what pushes your buttons. You can learn what makes you tick. When you're aware of others, you can learn what makes them tick. In other words, you can learn how to control the emotional tension of a situation, so you can diffuse it and keep working. Instead of getting mad and losing control when things don't go your way, remember that those are the very times when you have the opportunity to shine.

One time, when I was learning to play golf, I hit this beautiful shot— right into the bunker. It's not a pleasant feeling to end up in a sand trap, and I swore about it. That really upset the gentleman who was teaching me to play, so he stopped and said, "What are you using language like that for?"

"Because I hit it in the bunker!"

"Yup. But swearing won't change the stroke. You've practiced the bunker before. You know how to get back out. Instead of getting angry, look at this as a chance to show everyone how well you can beat that sand trap. Show them what a great bunker player you are"

We'll get more into turning negatives to positives in Chapter 7, but self-awareness—and self-control—form the foundation for that skill. Instead of losing control when you're faced with adversity, look at it as a chance to show how strong you can be. That's character of the right kind. That's success. When you lose control (of yourself), you lose control (of the situation). A Leader at any Level can't make that mistake. The costs are too high. Emotional Intelligence is the key to dignity under pressure.

Chapter Summary
- Personality is the combination of your predispositions to specific situations; Character is built by taking control of your personality
- Self-efficacy is the way you see your ability with respect to a given task
- Self-image is what you believe you are (knowledge, skills, abilities, physical characteristics, etc.); it is largely built from self-efficacy, personality, and character
- Self-awareness is the key to self-control and a major component of being an effective leader; part of self-awareness is an accurate assessment of your strengths and weaknesses
- Emotional Intelligence is the ability to understand the volatility of emotion and make it work for you—instead of letting yourself remain under its control
- The best way to improve yourself is to reinforce your existing strengths; build your team so that others have strengths where you have weaknesses

RESISTANCE – GO THE SPEED LIMIT

So, now that we know what leadership is, and the importance of Emotional Intelligence, let's start looking at specific issues you will face as a Leader at any Level. Probably the biggest issue you will face as a leader is that of resistance. If everyone just always did their best at everything you asked them to do, the only real 'issues' left for you to face would be ensuring strategic alignment and providing coaching. As long as you can guide the business (department, community organization, family, etc.) in the correct direction and get people the training they need, the business should grow. It's not quite that simple in reality, but the general idea is thought provoking.

Let's start off with a story. It comes to us from the New Testament of the Bible, and is found in Matthew 21:28-31. For ease of understanding and application, we'll update the language a bit and flesh out the narrative.

> There was once a business owner with two sons. One day, the man realized he needed some help with the business so he went to his first son and asked him to go and help out in the business. The first son said, "No way, Dad. I've got other stuff to do." Hearing that answer, the man went to his second son and asked him to go and do the work instead. The second son quickly said, "Of course, Dad. I'll head right down."
>
> As the day went on, the first son felt guilty. He knew his dad needed his help, so he went down to the business and started working. The second son, on the other hand, couldn't ever seem to finish up what he'd been doing so he could head down, and he ended up spending no time at the business that day.

The parable ends with: "[31]Whether of them twain did the will of his father?" Meaning, "Which of the two did what their dad asked?" For our purposes though, we're going to finish the story.

I like to think that, maybe after dinner that night, the father sat down with his two sons and said, "Boys, I wanted to talk to you about today."

Turning to his first son he would say something like, "When I can't run the business anymore, it will pass to you."

Then he would turn to the second son and say, "But you will get nothing."

The second son would reply, "What? Why, Dad? Why does he get the whole thing? I'm your son too. Shouldn't we be splitting it fifty-fifty?"

"Because he went and worked," the father would explain. "He may have told me he had other things to do, but I know where his priorities are by the work he actually did. He was willing to sacrifice for the business and put his ego aside to make sure the business was successful. You, on the other hand, told me you would go, but then you never did."

"Well, I had all this stuff come up," the second son would say. "It's not my fault."

"Save your excuses. If this business were important to you, you would have made the time for it. Your brother did, so he will be in control when I die. You will get nothing from it."

This particular parable showcases the two most common forms of resistance a leader has to face: Constructive Resistance and Dysfunctional Resistance.

Constructive Resistance

The first son is an example of Constructive Resistance. He said he wouldn't comply, but when push came to shove, he put his own ego aside and did what was best for the business. He may or may not have caught the overall vision yet, but he was willing to work for the greater good regardless of his own desires.

Admittedly, this isn't the best example of Constructive Resistance. All the same, Constructive Resistance is the acceptable kind of resistance. It may sound strange, but it's okay for people to challenge your ideas. The catch is, you want them to challenge your ideas because they've done their homework, not just because they want to be difficult. You want them to bring intelligent arguments to the table, so they can uncover potential errors before the plan rolls out. You want people to shoot holes in your ideas, so you can patch those holes and make the idea stronger. Remember "no pain, no gain"?

The key difference between Constructive Resistance and belligerence is measured by the willingness level of the person making the argument. Belligerence is also called active resistance. It's what happens when you've got a bad apple in the bunch—someone who just wants to protest and fight and make themselves become everyone else's headache. They don't want to follow the plan for whatever reason, and they're not going to follow the plan. Period. The best thing to do with this kind of person is to 'coach them out' of the organization.

Constructive Resistance, however, is someone who's looking out for the best interest of the company and just sees things a little differently. These are the people who seem outspoken against a plan at first, but, once the decision is made, they will go along with it no matter what their personal preferences are—they're humble enough to control their egos. They believe in the company and want it to succeed. These are the best people to have around because they'll work hard—and they'll make you work hard. You can't get complacent with this kind of resistance poking in from time to time.

I often had this experience with my son after he worked his way to the position of president at Pomeroy IT. We frequently saw things differently and had to butt heads over the best solution. Thankfully, though, it helped the final results; it helped to bulletproof our decisions and make them sound from more angles than just one. Constructive Resistance can do that. When you generate an idea, you naturally bias it because you only have one viewpoint and, no matter how sophisticated your IQ and EI, there will be angles you didn't consider. Constructive Resistance helps to put that bias on the table so additional angles and alternatives can be considered.

Dysfunctional Resistance

Dysfunctional Resistance, on the other hand, is something you don't want. Dysfunctional Resistance is perfectly demonstrated by the second son in our parable example. He quickly agreed to do whatever was asked of him, but when push came to shove, he didn't follow through. Rather than simply say no and leave his father in a position to keep looking for help, the son said yes, then left his dad in the lurch. This is the real problem with Dysfunctional Resistance. It's not that people are unwilling to help out—though that can be troublesome—it's that they pretend they're going to fulfill an assignment and then don't, sabotaging the project in the process.

The dictionary tells us that Dysfunctional Resistance is "opposition…by the use of noncooperation or other nonviolent methods, as boycotts and protest marches" (Random House Webster's Unabridged Dictionary 2001). Think Gandhi or Martin Luther King, Jr. Essentially, Dysfunctional Resistance is the refusal to cooperate with a morally repugnant decision. In the case of government, we claim this as a right. Business, however, is not a democracy. Proper resistance to a business decision you disagree with is Constructive Resistance. Do your homework and come ready to offer a counter proposal. If that's not an option then stop buying the business' products or, if you're employed there, start shopping your résumé for a new employer.

Ignorance vs. Defiance

There are basically two causes for why people don't do what they're asked, and those causes mean a world of difference in the corrective action that should be taken. Sometimes people will accept an assignment and misunderstand just what the assignment entailed. When it comes time to report, they report their failure, but it's not because they wanted to fail. This is ignorance, and it's an ability issue. In this instance, they need training or additional resources.

The second reason is out of defiance. These are the people who accept an assignment because they know they can't fight it at that moment. As the deadline approaches, they spend their time building a case for why the task could not be completed or looking for excuses instead of working toward the goal. These people need to go the same way as the active resistors. If someone isn't interested in helping the business progress, they have no place on the team.

Typically, Dysfunctional Resistance is a symptom of defiance and is really an indicator of a deeper problem: a lack of preparation stemming from a lack of commitment. If a person was committed to the company and its success, he would have taken the time to do his homework beforehand. He would have put in the time and effort—the hard work— required to have a real case around a researched concern. With that knowledge and preparation in hand, he could have brought up his issues and had them discussed openly—more akin to Constructive Resistance. He would have looked out for the good of the company—instead of focusing solely on covering his own you-know-what.

It sounds a little harsh, but defiance cannot be tolerated. A Leader at any Level should eliminate defiance the moment he or she can because, as soon as you start allowing it, you begin turning the organization into a cesspool. Defiance breeds defiance, or as the saying goes, "One bad apple can spoil the bunch."

I had this happen with one of our very promising managers. We recruited him from IBM, which was a major, major coup for our little business. We'll call the guy Joe Money—which is obviously not his real name—and let me just say that he had all the right training. IBM had an intensive development program at that time, and we wanted that caliber of person in our own organization. It took a long time to convince Joe to join us, so once he did, I made sure to stay close, coaching and setting expectations and making sure he understood the different nuances of how our business worked.

About a year later, the branch Joe was in charge of was running some losses. Joe and I sat down and went through his financials line by line, looking at everything he was spending and breaking it down into the greatest level of detail. Through that process, we made some decisions together about what needed to be cut and where things could be trimmed to get the branch back on its feet. Joe agreed to the plan. This had been one of our top branches, and he agreed that we needed to make the changes to stop this top branch from bleeding.

A month later I went through the financial reports again and Joe hadn't made a single one of the changes he'd agreed to. I felt awful. I wondered where I had failed that something like this could happen. I had put years of time and effort into recruiting and grooming Joe to be a remarkable leader in our company. He was from a prestigious background, and because of him, I was able to recruit others from IBM—yet he had just defied me. What was I going to do? What would you do with this highly prized business asset and close business associate?

I called Joe's boss, the Senior VP in charge of that branch, and told him to terminate Joe. At that point the Senior VP told me he couldn't terminate Joe. Instead, he repeated to me all the wonderful things about Joe and the benefit Joe could be to our organization. That was frustrating. Instead of one person being defiant, I now had two—the 'bunch of apples' was beginning to spoil. I had to terminate Joe myself, but I wanted to give this Senior VP a chance to redeem himself. Over the next few months, I gave this Senior VP several opportunities to prove that he was still committed to the organization—including the opportunity to help our distribution operations I mentioned earlier. Ultimately, I realized he wasn't committed, so I searched out a replacement and got ready. Once everything was in order, I told the Senior VP to come in the next day with his blue jeans on and clean the bathrooms. I've already told you the story of how that turned out.

In the space of a few months, we had terminated each of them. We had set expectations for each of them and they had each failed to meet their individual requirements. We had given each of them a second chance and they had each disregarded the opportunity. I believe everyone should get a second chance—a chance to redeem themselves from a mistake. This lets you fix the problem if someone is simply ignorant. It gives you a chance to teach and train them and correct the mistake. Still, business is not baseball. In business, two strikes and you're out. They were both shocked that the company would let them go, especially for such a 'small' matter as defiance. After we terminated them both, I came in with my blue jeans and cleaned the restrooms—to show, once again, that I wasn't above my own instructions.

The moral of the story is that I had fought for Joe. He was awesome, and I wanted him to join us. I wanted him on the team really badly. Still, when he began to defy the company leadership, we had to let him go. When his boss started defying us, we gave him a chance to get back on board, but, ultimately, we had to let him go too. It wasn't the ideal outcome, but, if we hadn't, what message would it have sent to the rest of the organization? Don't ever fool yourself into thinking that everyone else is ignorant to what's going on. People are too smart for that. Businesses are too well integrated for news to not travel quickly.

Besides, what could have been expected from these two in the future? If they defied the leadership and got away with it, we would only be inviting them to be defiant again. We would have been telling everyone that we played favorites, and that it didn't matter if people performed their assignments or not—that it wasn't about getting results anymore—it was about being buddy-buddy with the leadership. That was a culture we couldn't tolerate; it was a risk we couldn't take.

Both Dysfunctional Resistance and Constructive Resistance come down to the level of alignment between an employee and the organization. A person who is negatively asserting is aligned with the organization, as difficult as that may be to wrap your head around. They want to see it succeed, but they believe that the proposed idea isn't the best way to make that success a reality. They are speaking out because they are concerned that you're about to lead the company down the wrong path. Passive resistors, on the other hand, have placed themselves ahead of the organization. They have let their egos (or inabilities) become more important than the company. They are out of alignment with the vision and need to be let out of the company altogether. The great residue of all this is, if everyone knows you will not tolerate Dysfunctional Resistance, it won't happen. Failure aversion will keep people focused.

The Fundamental Attribution Error

Going back to the two causes for Dysfunctional Resistance for a moment, we need to reiterate a warning. It's important to recognize the difference between ignorance and defiance. Unfortunately, differentiating between the two is complicated by a little piece of behavioral psychology called the fundamental attribution error.

Allow me to elaborate with an example: Have you ever been visiting with a friend and they cut you off to answer their phone? You're telling them something extremely important and they just hold up a hand while they pull out their cellphone. Rude, huh? You just want to tell them to turn off the dang phone and pay attention because what you're telling them is vitally important. How do you feel about this? Frustrated? Angry? Maybe just a little annoyed? Maybe you're not even surprised because this friend does this kind of thing all the time.

Then they hang up the phone and say, "I've gotta go. My mother just got taken to the hospital. They don't know what's wrong."

How do you feel now? Sheepish? Worried? Regretful? Do you want to know what you can do to help? Congratulations, you've just been a victim to the Fundamental Attribution Error.

In the previous section, I shared an example of driving down the freeway toward an important meeting only to get cut off by another driver. Do you remember how you felt when you imagined that situation? As it turns out, that was either a drug dealer on the run from the cops or a young man taking his pregnant wife to the hospital as she went into labor. Which one is irrelevant; the important thing to recognize is how you probably feel differently depending on whether it was a drug dealer on the run or a young man desperate to help his wife.

The fundamental attribution error is, in the simplest terms, the pattern of considering environmental factors when reviewing one's own performance but failing to consider them in observing the performance of others. In other words, if something bad happens to someone, the fundamental attribution error says it's because they are a bad person. If, on the other hand, something bad happens to you, it will be due to factors beyond your control. Sounds like an ego trip, huh?

By extension, this means that if someone does something bad—like passively resist your latest initiative—they must be a bad person. Or, if someone cuts you off, they must be nasty and mean, right?

This concept is kind of deep and dark because it's a gut-reaction event. It's not even a conscious process in most cases. People don't generally go out of their way to think negatively about the people around them. Negative thoughts happen—frequently in some cases—but few people wake up in the morning wondering how they can think nasty things about other people that day. And, because the impulse originates in our subconscious—from within our own minds—we often accept the idea without really thinking about it or considering the implications.

The truth is that, as an observer of someone else, we are unable to see all the influences that play into that person's decisions and actions. Ever. Period. We don't understand all the hardships they are facing and don't know what kind of external factors are acting on them, influencing their choices and actions. Because of this, we ascribe all their acts—or even their luck—to their personality factors. Ironically, this helps us avoid an uncomfortable thought process.

The thought process goes something like, "If bad things happen to good people and I'm a good person, bad things can happen to me. However, bad things don't happen to me (because no one really wants to believe bad things will happen) so that other person must not be good after all." In this way, the fundamental attribution error serves to reinforce a specific belief in order to avoid a mentally uncomfortable situation called Cognitive Dissonance (we'll get into this more in the next chapter).

In developing your emotional intelligence and training yourself to be a Leader at any Level, you have to come to terms with a few hidden mental processes—things that the brain does without any conscious input: snap judgments. Think of them as survival instincts. Sometimes they're right on. Sometimes they're way off. The key is developing your mind and awareness to the point that you don't need to rely on prehistoric instincts. Instead, you'll be able to make informed judgments at will.

Thankfully, as a human you have the ability to look before you leap. Snap judgments are, in some respects, like running to the edge of a cliff over an unknown lake and jumping in. You have no idea if the water is clean—or if there's even any water in the first place. You have no idea what might be living in the lake either. You could be jumping in with a bunch of alligators or piranhas or goldfish. Without looking beneath the surface, you'll never know.

The fundamental attribution error shortcuts our normal processes of reasoning. Consider the instance of an extremely important business decision: a strategic plan, the choice and implementation of a new network, or the approval process for a new project. What are all the steps you go through? You probably do a lot of research, including talking to people at all levels. Once you've covered your bases with the various stakeholders, you research the actual options themselves. You weigh pros and cons. You compare features or guarantees or prices or any other relevant information. You may even run a pilot program or use a temporary sample product as a trial.

Now consider that every interaction you ever have is a potential business decision. You never know who you're talking to. Plenty of business owners don't show off their success. In fact, that's one of the reasons many of them are successful. They don't feel the need to gratify their egos by spending everything they make. The point is, though, that you never know when you might be talking to your next big client.

When we opened our second franchise down in Lexington, Kentucky, we had a huge grand opening. It was pretty successful in my view. We had a lot of people there. As I was mingling and trying to make sure everyone was taken care of, I came across an older gentleman among the rows of computers.

I went over and introduced myself, and he looked at me and said, "You know, you really have something special here." This was back in 1983. We'd only been in business for a year and a half. I wasn't sure whether things were really going to take off or whether we were just riding the front end of a short fad.

But I said to him, "I appreciate that. I think we're going to do pretty well."

"No. This is something really special," he said. "This computer industry is right on the verge of something really spectacular."

I could tell he'd been pretty successful in his own time, so I asked him one of those burning questions every small business owner has, "So, how do you know when you're successful in business?"

"Five years. You must build a strong customer base and a strong capital base. If you work hard at it, you can do that in five years."

I didn't know if I believed him, but it was enlightening just to talk to him, so I asked him what he did. He told me he was in the concrete business. I asked him where because I was trying to get a little background info so I could sell him a computer. He told me that he was going to buy a lot of computers for his business, and I promised to give him great service. He told me he was sure that we would, and that was that. It was a nice conversation, and I walked away thinking what a wise man he was.

It wasn't until later that I found out he owned a gigantic concrete company that worked with all the coal mining companies. In fact, the city he was from has one of the highest millionaires per capita out of any city in the United States. And, true to the man's word, we ended up doing a lot of business with them over the years.

If I had looked at him and thought to myself, "What's an old guy like that doing in a store full of new computers like this?" I never would have gotten the sales. It just goes to show that you can't assume anything about anyone.

Likewise, you can't see someone do something and immediately assume you know why he did it. Maybe that vender is being a jerk because he's feeling some heat from behind his own lines. Maybe he's worried about losing his job if he goes any lower, but he doesn't want to tell you that because it could seem weak. Maybe, just maybe, he doesn't even realize he's being a jerk. Maybe it's just how he was raised. He could actually be the nicest person in his immediate family. If you don't know, don't tell yourself you know. While you won't be able to stop your subconscious mind from wanting to hurl itself headlong off the cliff in hopes of clear, deep water below, you can stop your conscious mind from following after without question.

So how does one avoid falling prey to the fundamental attribution error? Well, the first step is to develop your self-awareness so you realize when you're jumping to conclusions. We need to recognize when we have a limited view of the puzzle—which is always. With only a handful of pieces, the number of assumptions you have to make in order to make a decision about the whole picture is mindboggling, yet the mind will quickly make that leap, given the chance.

If possible, therefore, the best thing to do is withhold judgment. When someone cuts you off on the freeway, don't cuss him out and assume he is a hateful, nasty, inconsiderate person. Instead, tell yourself that there might be a better reason. Remind yourself that rational people usually do rational things. When one of your colleagues accepts an assignment and then comes up short at the finish line, don't immediately decide he is being defiant and terminate him. Try to dig a little deeper. Figure out why he failed. Ask him questions. One of my favorites is "Do you need more attention?" It'll catch him off guard and probably result in a very interesting, or possibly heated discussion. Make sure you bring your EI to that conversation. The idea is to get more information though. You want to figure out if he intended to fail or just didn't understand the assignment. Unfortunately, that's much easier said than done.

Since completely withholding judgment is almost impossible for most of us, the next best thing is to try to put yourself in the other person's shoes for a moment. We need a rational subject to experiment with, and no one is more rational than you, right? Put yourself in the other person's shoes, and ask yourself why you would do whatever he just did. Why would you race up the freeway and cut someone off? If you've never done that before, it might take a little more thinking to come up with ideas. The point of this exercise, though, is not to try to guess what the person's real motivation was. That would leave us no better off than just following our initial, gut impulse. We still don't have the facts of the case to be able to make any kind of judgment.

Instead, just recognize that there are multiple possible explanations. That's the key here. The answer is to exercise your emotional intelligence and control your judgments until you realize that there is more than one reason to do whatever the person did—or at least be willing to change your judgment the moment you have additional options. He could be a drug dealer on the run, or he could be desperate to help his wife. You'll never know which it was. On the other hand, you may be able to sort out why your employee is passively resisting if you approach it right.

When you recognize that there are logical reasons for doing something which, initially, may seem illogical, you help keep control over your emotions. This, in turn, helps you to avoid bringing emotional baggage with you and potentially sabotaging your other interactions. Instead, you can choose how you want to feel. Changing the way you view the situation also helps you keep control over what you say or do toward the offending person and the people you run into later. People will recognize this ability in you and give you more respect for it.

Motivation vs. Ability

Going back to the termination decision, we need to consider the concept of motivation vs. ability. With the fundamental attribution error, we tend to assign the worst causes to any given outcome. When a colleague doesn't get you the report you need on time, we assume it's because he forgot or because he's mad at us. He must be a bad person because good people don't do bad things like turn in important reports late. Maybe we even go so far as to call him incompetent. Deep down, though, we all know it's just because he's lazy, right?

Perhaps. To say no at this point would be a snap judgment and fly in the face of everything we've been talking about. Maybe he really is lazy. Maybe he's defiant and it's time to let him walk. Then again, maybe he was on another, higher-priority task and just barely got to your report. Maybe he's having troubles outside of work and it's affecting his ability to be productive. It's not a good excuse, but it still happens. Or, here's the real kicker, maybe he's never created this report before and the template you gave him didn't make much sense to him. Maybe the reason he's late is because, after staying late every night for a week and a half and coming in on Saturday, he finally figured the thing out this morning. Or maybe he still hasn't figured it out. You'll have to go through the report yourself to know.

Some people are just scared to ask questions. Some people have a pride issue about questions. They feel like they should know everything and don't need to ask—or that it exposes them as weak or incompetent to ask a question. They recognize that they don't have the answers, but they worry that, when business slows and the pink slips start flowing, the weakest links are always the first to go. Or maybe—just maybe—you're just a scary person. I know I was sometimes a bit abrasive. I was never harder on anyone than I was on myself, but that doesn't mean I was easy-going with everyone else. We had a job to do, and a business to run. I wish I could say that none of the other employees ever worried about approaching me, but some probably did. An interesting point about understanding human nature is that the more you learn, the more you realize you don't know.

Asking questions is actually a strength, not a weakness. Being confident enough to admit that you don't know something—and then trying to find a way to learn the information—is a strength. When people come to you with questions, praise them for it. Support and encourage them. If you treat people as though they have 'stupid' questions, they will stop coming to you. They'll bury their ignorance and pretend they know what they're doing in order to avoid embarrassment. Covering up an issue only leads to worse problems down the road.

Whatever the reason, the point is that some people honestly just don't know what they're doing. It's not that they are actually mean or bad or anything, they just don't know how to do things any better. Maybe they were recently promoted and haven't finished figuring out the job yet. Maybe they are in over their heads, and they'll never figure it out. Maybe they think they've figured it out, but they're wrong. In any case, if a person just doesn't have the skills and know-how, their issue is not motivational in nature. Fooling yourself into thinking that every problem goes back to someone's motivation is a recipe for mistakes.

I remember when my partner and I were still starting out in the computer business. We were selling everything we could get our hands on—and then some. Our issue wasn't demand or finding customers or anything like that; it was supply. We couldn't get enough computers in stock to meet customer needs. I remember one exchange with the distribution rep where we did something a little foreign to him. Something a little revolutionary. Something we'd learned while selling cars.

"We need 300 computers," I said.

"You know I can't get that many for you," the guy replied. "You know that."

"But I've got to have them," I said. "So, how about this: You know those dot-matrix printers you're pushing that aren't too popular right now? How about I order 100 of those over the next three months?"

"I'll get you your 300 computers," the rep said.

It's not that the rep was a bad person. He wasn't trying to torpedo our business by not supplying the number of computers we wanted. He probably got paid based on what he sold, and he probably had certain quotas to fulfill and the like. It's not that he wasn't motivated to sell us more computers. If he'd had them, I bet he'd have sold us 500. Instead, it was an ability issue. He had to meet his quotas, and he had to try to allot things fairly. He couldn't get us the computers we wanted because he had problems of his own. Specifically, he had a supply issue and a number of different customers clamoring for as much inventory as they could get.

We could have gotten angry and cursed him behind his back. We could have cursed our 'bad luck' and just waited like everyone else. But we didn't. We changed the game for him. We made it more worth his while to do more business with us than with others. Was that fair to the other retailers? No one was stopping them from doing the same thing. Besides, who said anything about business being fair?

In negotiations, this is called 'integrative bargaining.' The normal idea in negotiations is that of distributive bargaining: that there is one pie and it's a fixed size. In order for me to get more, someone else has to get less. This attitude pervades society like a disease and destroys everything it touches. For some reason, people believe that there is only so much success to go around; if someone else is being successful, there's less success for you or me. It's not true, but it's still a common viewpoint. In reality, the easiest way to gain success is to help others be successful.

In keeping with that idea, integrative bargaining changes the size of the pie (makes it bigger), so I can take a bigger piece without stepping on toes or making enemies. In order for it to work, though, you have to believe your counterpart on the other side of the table is willing to deal—and they have to believe the same about you. If you've fallen prey to the fundamental attribution error and told yourself that he's a cantankerous, spiteful person, he's probably felt that from you, and that will make him very unwilling to deal.

Let's take another look at my experience with the grocery store rep from the previous chapter. He came in demanding some software that hadn't even been released yet. He was a customer—a very important customer—so I wanted to do all I could to make sure his needs were met. The catch is, the software just honestly wasn't out yet. It wasn't a motivational issue on my part, it was an ability issue. I didn't have the software yet because it hadn't been released yet, so I couldn't get him a copy.

Well, he wouldn't take no for an answer, and I really didn't want to tell him no and risk losing his business in the future, so we thought creatively. It just so happened that I had that prerelease demo copy of the software he wanted, so I offered it to him. I wish I would have realized that it had all those restrictions on it, but I didn't. He went away happy then, but it wasn't long before he was back and madder than ever.

At that point I fell prey to the fundamental attribution error, acting on assumptions that today I can't back up. What if I'd thought about all the other reasons why he might have been blowing up? He was from a big company that desperately needed to get up to date with the technology of the time, and from his viewpoint, I was holding him back. Who knows what kind of pressure he was under from his own company? I could have called the manufacturer right in front of him—or offered to have the manufacturer call him directly. Either way, I should have asked for help. The point is, if I'd been able to catch myself and think through it all, I might have been able to salvage at least part of the relationship, which could have translated into untold good will and possibly millions of dollars.

To recap this a little, when you stop to put yourself in someone else's shoes, pay particular attention to the "possible" environmental factors causing his behavior. Look at the ability side of the equation before assuming someone just wants to be dumb or mean. Believe it or not, people are generally intelligent. They generally try to think through their actions and pick things based on the preferred outcome. Very few people actually set out to make fools of themselves or blow deals. To put that in perspective, how often do you try to make a fool of yourself? People just do dumb, emotional stuff sometimes. Usually, it's just a lapse or weakness in their emotional intelligence.

If possible, get a second opinion (and third, and fourth, etc.) when you're trying to make a decision. You're more likely to compensate for your own biases this way. It will also help pull you away from the moment and separate your decisions from your emotions. Unfortunately, consensus isn't much help 'in the moment' because there's usually not time (or emotional bandwidth) to seek it. Still, remembering ability vs. motivation and the influence of environmental factors can help you cut through the emotions of the moment and think more clearly.

Now, to be fair, I'll admit that we've talked a lot about possibilities and 'maybes.' To be clear, decisions need to be made and tasks need to be accomplished. That's true whether you're in business, in the community or at home. That progress—and success—can't happen on the foundation of uncertainties. However, it doesn't need to happen on a bed of false assumptions either. The more self-aware you are, and the more attention you pay to your surroundings, the more accurate you can be with regard to your best-effort judgments and decisions.

If you take the time to check yourself for the fundamental attribution error, you can stop a lot of incorrect judgments before they cause problems. Just remember to ask yourself why you would do whatever the person just did. Ask yourself if it's really an issue with them wanting to do something wrong—being defiant—or if they just don't know how to do it right—being ignorant. Give people the benefit of the doubt, and you're more likely to receive it in return.

Unfortunately, there's not any one magical formula that will solve all of your resistance problems. There's no single recipe that will allow you to predict human actions. Human behavior is best understood by experience. Essentially, you have to live it and learn it. So why bother learning about Constructive Resistance and Dysfunctional Resistance? Why bother learning about human nature and the fundamental attribution error?

It's quite simple, really. Go mix baking soda and vinegar. What happens? It bubbles, right? That was fun.

Unless you have a background in chemistry, you'd never know that it's producing a gas that can kill you. That's right. Who knew? I happen to have a friend who studied a lot of chemistry when he was younger. He explained to me that the acetic acid (vinegar) combines with baking soda to form a kind of powder, some water, and a little carbon dioxide. He also pointed out that carbon dioxide is heavier than oxygen, and, in the wrong circumstances, it will displace the oxygen out of the air and suffocate you.

Now, that's not likely to happen from your kids making food-coloring volcanoes because it just doesn't release enough of the gas (unless they're going through baking soda by the ton and vinegar by the gallon and do it in the basement with all the windows and vents closed), but the principle is there. Human nature is the same way. You can watch it happen all day, every day for your whole life and may never understand what's really going on under the surface—or the potentially hazardous side effects. Once you get a little insight, however, your eyes are opened to a whole new world of how and why things really work.

The point of this section is to help you open your eyes and see what's happening around you in order to help you be a more effective Leader at any Level. In other words, we're trying to help you understand that people are smart—smarter than we give them credit—and that they can make intelligent decisions. It just also happens that, sometimes, we disagree with their reasoning. Understanding the principles here will help you to better understand the motivation of people and be a more judicious Leader at any Level.

You don't need to get mad at Max when he brings up a different alternative in that planning meeting. As long as he's getting his job done even when he disagrees with it, he's the kind of guy you want around. In fact, letting him make some decisions will help him stay committed. On the other hand, Randy—who's always been so easy going and likeable—should probably be coached out of the organization for always accepting assignments and then bailing on them at the last minute. All those amazingly crafted excuses can't be enough for salvation anymore; that defiance is setting the wrong kind of example. And Tina—the new lady on the team—isn't trying to challenge you for dominance by flopping on her projects and making you look bad. It turns out she just needs a little training because deep down, she wants to do a good job. That's why she comes to work every day.

Human psychology is an ever-changing field because humans are ever-changing creatures. Our minds are rarely still. We're always innovating, growing, learning, and challenging preconceived notions and 'boundaries.' That's what separates us from the animals: our capacity to grow and overcome. As a Leader at any Level, you need to recognize when people are trying to grow with the company and when they're trying to grow in spite of the company, then reward or discipline accordingly. In the end, it's all about getting results. Over the long haul, results won't lie.

As it turns out, going back to the case of Joe Money, the story actually has a happy ending for him. In 2001, he got the Entrepreneur of the Year award for the small-business category. He wrote me a letter about it later. He was mad at the time that I fired him, but, in the years since, he'd realized that it was the best thing that could have happened for him. Before, he'd been such a star that everything had always been easy for him. No one had ever really called him to task for anything, and, as a result, he'd been a little lazy. Getting fired had helped him wake up and get his head on straight. Believe it or not, he thanked me for firing him because now he was following his passion and having amazing success.

So, again, separate out the human behavior from the human. Someone may be defying you and need to get fired. Don't take it personally. In all likelihood, they are defying your position or organization, not you personally. But, even if they are defying you personally, there's no reason why you can't end up on civil terms. Remember, once you lose control, you lose control. Don't meet defiance with anger. Meet it calmly and explain the situation. In all my years of business, Joe was one of the very few I ever really fired. Most people kind of knew when they had broken the rules and headed out before I had to do anything. I consider that a lot of success and little failure. Even in that bit of failure though, it was a success because I learned from it and Joe ended up better off.

So don't be disheartened if you can think of a member of your team that needs to be terminated for defiance. You're probably doing them a favor. If they're defying you, they are probably unhappy with their job anyway. Cross-check your suspicions, get an outside opinion and then act on it. You'll feel better when it's done and you'll clear the way for the right people who can collaborate with you to find real success.

Chapter Summary

- Constructive Resistance can be disconcerting but should not be punished; the person is still looking out for the best interest of the company
- Dysfunctional Resistance is caustic to an organization if left unchecked; it stems from either ignorance or defiance
- Failures due to ignorance relate to training deficiencies and should be corrected
- Failures due to defiance are attitude problems and cannot be tolerated in any degree
- The fundamental attribution error makes it extremely difficult to judge another person's motivation correctly without taking time to do more extensive research; if at all possible, withhold judgment and get corroborating opinions

COGNITIVE DISSONANCE – PUSH THROUGH THE TRAFFIC

In the last two chapters we've talked about human nature and some of the things that factor into the critical awareness of emotional intelligence. The whole reason for this was to get you up to speed on what really makes people tick, both yourself and others. As you learn to really embrace these principles and take control of your emotions, you'll find it easier and easier to become a true Leader at any Level.

Before we finish our crash course in human psychology, there is one more concept that you need to understand. In the previous sections, we've talked about how people are intelligent, and how they typically think through their actions so they can pick an outcome they like. Understanding this concept will help you understand human behavior most of the time. Unfortunately, there is one huge exception to this rule. Something that almost invariably causes people to act in unpredictable, often irrational ways: Cognitive Dissonance.

First, we need a couple definitions. According to the Random House Dictionary, the word 'cognitive' means "of or pertaining to the mental processes of perception, memory, judgment and reasoning, as contrasted with emotional and volitional processes." In simple English, it means it's something that's going on inside your head as opposed to in your heart or somewhere around you. Dissonance means, "inharmonious or harsh sound; discord; cacophony" (Random House Webster's Unabridged Dictionary 2001). Or, in other words, a number of things that don't fit together. It's two bullies meeting on the playground and only one of them is going to leave.

The way this usually plays out is that a person has two perfectly acceptable ideas. Each one has merit and is supported by evidence. On its own, each idea is reasonable and rational, and a normal, law-abiding citizen could entertain the idea without much difficulty. Unfortunately, these two ideas are also mutually exclusive. Kind of like dogs and cats in cartoons, they can't coexist. You can have one or the other but not both. Boiling water or ice cubes. You can't mix them and have them stay the way they are.

I'm going to apologize up front but my goal for the next little bit is to put your mind into a dissonant situation. It'll be uncomfortable but, in all likelihood, strangely familiar. The reason for this is to help you understand and recognize the feeling so that, as we move through the rest of this chapter, you'll be able to identify it. Additionally, I want you to experience it under a 'controlled condition' so you can learn not to fear it. More on that later though. For now, here we go with the example:

Good people do good things, right? That's how we know they're good people. Good people don't do bad things, right? That's also how we know they're good people. So are you a good person or a bad person? I'm glad to hear that. Now for the dissonance: have you ever done something bad? Good people don't do bad things. Are you a good person or a bad person? Are you sure?

Now, most people would agree that they're good people. And they'd be right. Most people are good people—and intelligent too. Yet, at the same time, most people have done something bad in their lives. Not necessarily a felony or anything extreme. Maybe just the occasional white lie to a customer about why a shipment was late. Maybe they cheated on a test or two in high school. The point is, people sometimes do bad things yet still believe they are good people. Are they wrong?

Psychologists would call this effect cognitive dissonance. When these two conflicting ideas are in the mind at the same time, the brain has to reconcile them. Trying to hold them together is as I said, like trying to hold ice cubes in a pot of boiling water. It just doesn't work. Unfortunately, truly dissonant ideas are actually more like oil and water: they can't just be mixed, brought to a common temperature and put away. Instead, the mind has to do some 'creative accounting' to make things balance. And, in the interim, a person will feel usually very uncomfortable with their situation. Hopefully you got a taste of that earlier. You need to understand this because, as a Leader at any Level, you will see people around you suffering through this condition, and you need to be able to identify with what they're feeling.

This emotional discomfort stems from the fact that, as humans, we tend to define our worlds in absolute terms. In order to learn and accept something, we want to test it extensively so we can feel confident that it's true. However, once we accept a principle, we tend to believe that it is sound and immovable on a scope far beyond the bounds of any testing we may have done. It's easier to operate this way. If something can be accepted and filed away as fact, we don't have to consider all the different ways in which it could actually be wrong. We don't have to waste time trying to shoot holes in our own paradigms. We don't all have to sit on the street corner and philosophize all day. We all like rules. We don't like it when there are lots of exceptions to the rules. What's more, this process of learning something, accepting it as fact, and internalizing it as an immutable rule allows us to be efficient—and it usually works.

The issue arises when new information calls the 'fact' into question. The phrase 'cognitive dissonance' has its roots in the 1950s book When Prophecy Fails by Leon Festinger (Festinger 1956). He was investigating a UFO cult and trying to figure out how they went on with life after 'the apocalypse' was foretold and then didn't come. Without going into the gritty details, the basic idea was, "How did they operate on January 1 when the world was supposed to end the night before?" When the world as you know it is suddenly called into question, it can be a bit alarming. This is why cognitive dissonance tends to be accompanied by feelings of dread, guilt, anger, confusion, and disbelief. Feelings very few of us look forward to.

Types of Cognitive Dissonance

While the emotional response tends to be similar in all cases, other elements of a person's reaction—including coping mechanisms—can differ depending on the circumstances in question. Differentiating in this way, psychologists recognize four main types of cognitive dissonance. They are: Belief Disconfirmation, Induced Compliance, Free Choice, and Effort Justification.

Belief disconfirmation is the idea that a long-held belief has suddenly been proven wrong. This plays in with major change efforts in organizations. For instance, when I first started out in car sales, a lot of the other employees felt like our dealership was a dump. They felt like our location was bad, our clientele base was poor, and our inventory selection was skewed in the wrong direction. Many of them believed that we couldn't make it—that our dealership was worthless. To be fair, we were ranked 95th out of 105 dealerships in our zone. We were pretty close to the bottom, but the general manager had a vision—and he had determination.

When the general manager and I set out to become number 1 in our area, we didn't announce it at first because we knew we'd take flak from some of the long-time salespeople. They wouldn't believe the dealership could make it. They were set in their old beliefs, and to accept that we could be the best would have been in direct conflict with that paradigm. They had adopted the self-destructive belief that our dealership was just the bottom rung, and, in their minds, it had become an unchangeable, invincible fact.

Belief disconfirmation can be looked at like resistance to change, whether active or passive. It took a lot of time and effort to get those salespeople to come around—and some of them left because they just couldn't come around. For the ones who changed, it took showing them the results a little at a time, slowly working them through the curve to where they didn't feel as anxious about giving up their old belief in order to grasp onto the new one. The new belief that we were going to be the best. The good news? We did it. It wasn't easy and often it was uncomfortable but we did it anyway.

The solution to getting past belief disconfirmation is to make the old belief seem more frightening than the new one. In some circles, this is called creating a 'burning platform.' Picture yourself standing on a safe, sturdy platform over the Grand Canyon. There's not a lot of reason to go to the edge, much less jump to a different platform. That is, until someone sets your platform on fire. Now you can either burn up or you can make the jump. If you stay put, you're dead for sure. If you jump, you might just make it.

The second type of cognitive dissonance is induced compliance. The theory behind this is that people will come up with their own reasons to justify their behavior if the external rewards aren't enough, or vice versa. The idea is that, if a person does something but then receives an 'insufficient' reward for his effort, he will come up with additional justification in his mind for why he did it.

No one likes to believe that they've been short-changed. We don't like to feel like we've been taken advantage of. As a result, if we do feel short-changed, we often come up with additional reasons why we performed the action in the first place, thus alleviating the discomfort. However, while this type of dissonance is well documented in research, the practical application is more limited. Typically, in the workplace, if someone feels insufficiently compensated, he'll make it known or reject the task.

The risk with this type of dissonance is that people will imagine all kinds of different reasons. In rare cases, the reasons they dream up can later come into conflict with a new strategic direction—especially if a poorly planned pilot program is later canceled. The people 'induced' to participate in the pilot program may have a lot of difficulty letting go.

The third type of dissonance is that of free choice. This comes into play when a person has two or more options, and more than one are acceptable. In researching and making the decision, a person will identify the various characteristics of the different sides of the decision and choose which aspects he likes and dislikes for each side of the choice. Because he hasn't made the choice yet, he isn't in a dissonant situation yet, so he has no problem liking all the alternatives on some level. After the person makes the decision, however, he will go back and unconsciously reevaluate the decision criteria, up-rating the points that support his decision and down-rating the ones that are in conflict with his decision.

This is like the iOS vs. Android question. Each operating system has a unique set of strengths and weaknesses. Each can accomplish any number of tasks. Glamour and everything else aside, either one is acceptable for all but the tiniest minority of the population who need a very specific, unique feature. However, once a person purchases into one system or the other, he is more likely to subconsciously downplay the features of the 'losing' system that initially attracted him. For instance, people might downplay Apple's selection of apps after choosing an Android phone. On the other hand, someone purchasing an iPhone may downplay the level of customization and variety available in Android phones.

The point is that the rejected choice may still have some appealing aspects, and that concept doesn't sit well in a person's mind. It goes something like this: "If I really like the iPhone so much, why did I buy this Android?" To reconcile the mental turmoil, we convince ourselves that we never liked the other option in the first place. In other words, "I bought the Android so I must not have actually liked the iPhone as much as I originally thought."

This can be dangerous in the work environment because, once a person makes up his mind about something, it gets harder to see the positives of the other options anymore. If a person goes into a meeting having already made his decision, he can be irrationally stubborn about sticking to it.

Migrating to a new system architecture, for instance, means making a big decision between any number of equally acceptable options. That happened to me after retirement while I was on the Board of Pomeroy IT Solutions. The Board wanted to upgrade to a certain infrastructure and I dissented. I felt an alternative platform was the better way to go. They moved forward with a majority vote and began the implementation.

Over time, it became clear that they'd made a mistake. Budget overruns crashed the whole project. Unfortunately, the Board had made their decision and wouldn't look back the other way. Their decision shifted from trying to do what was best for the company to trying to prove themselves right—and me wrong. They ended up losing their credibility and having a tough time getting anything done after that—to such an extent that I pushed to take the company private again. This happens on a smaller scale too though.

We often undertake smaller projects and, once we make our decision, we convince ourselves that the other options really were worse options. That just makes it harder to change directions if the current course of action turns out to be the wrong one. Even when presented with hard evidence. Don't be afraid to cut your losses and admit that you were wrong.

Closely associated with free choice is the fourth type of cognitive dissonance: effort justification. This is similar to the concept of 'throwing good money after bad' and has the same potentially negative effect. The idea here is that, if someone makes a herculean effort to get something done, he will sell himself in the process. In fact, people will even sugar coat the final results for themselves in order to justify their efforts to themselves. This is similar to 'drinking the Kool-Aid' in an organization. If you're going to put a lot of effort into something, you want it to be worthwhile, right?

The dissonance here is that we're intelligent people, and intelligent people don't waste effort on pointless things because that wouldn't be intelligent. Instead, we fool ourselves into believing that the lackluster outcomes are much better than they seem, so that we don't have to feel guilty about all the time and effort we put in. Where free choice refers to selling ourselves in the process of the decision, effort justification refers to the selling of ourselves on the outcome even when it's worse than projected.

So, when things don't turn out to be as spectacular as they were supposed to, we exercise our confirmation bias to look for the handful of things that support our view and ignore all the signs that indicate the opposite. This is also a logical fallacy called selected instance. Unfortunately, it clouds our judgment and prevents us from learning from our mistakes. In effect, we've brainwashed ourselves to believe we had success.

For examples of this, look no further than politics. Every time a new, huge program is announced, it's accompanied by grandiose promises of all the things it will do. Then, in the day of reckoning, the supporters will cite the handful of evidences that show success and ignore the landslide of proof against them. Look at the stimulus packages following the meltdown of the financial system in 2008. We were promised jobs and a rebounding economy. Instead, someone figured out how to make up a number called 'jobs saved,' and that was touted as a huge success as the economy slumped into a rut nearly as bad as the Great Depression while unemployment continued to climb.

Let me ask you this: How do you know if a job was saved or not? Especially if the economy still has fewer jobs than it did before the stimulus? I mean, how do you honestly know? I understand that there are mathematical formulas for predicting nonsense like that but let's be serious here. Still, after all that money and propaganda, no politician on either side could let the stimulus look like a failure until they were sure they wouldn't get blamed for it.

The problem caused by cognitive dissonance is that people behave irrationally when they're under its spell. We already know that people are actually intelligent. We know that, in general, they work toward some obvious, rational, positive goal. It might be the betterment of a family, a community, a business, a team, etc. and it might cause some unforeseen collateral damage on the way, but it's a rational goal. It's something that others would understand and support them on.

With cognitive dissonance, a person will essentially brainwash themselves into thinking a bad course of action is the right course of action because the right course of action is too uncomfortable. This is a dangerous situation because it generally involves a person not realizing the self-destructive path he's on—yet staunchly believing in it all the same. When you really look at what's going on (especially from the outside), you realize it's delusional.

Alternatively, when someone is confronted with a dissonant situation, it can cause him to feel shaken. He can feel blindsided and disoriented. He may feel confused and, until he can resolve the feelings, it can adversely impact his performance. He may feel lost or guilty or any number of other negative emotions. So how does a person get through the uncomfortable experience of cognitive dissonance?

Rationalization

Let's set the stage by doing a little role-play. You have an important meeting with a client. You're going to pitch them your latest product—a product you know they'll love. You've had your team working on the presentation for two weeks solid. They've assured you that everything is lined up and ready to go. Then, the morning of the presentation, your team leader admits that they haven't finished the presentation.

Your initial reaction is probably anger that the team would lie to you. And justifiably so. Of course, you should have been inspecting the materials along the way, but this is Dysfunctional Resistance—possibly defiance. All their progress reports and promises were falsified. Whatever the reasons, they've set you up to fail. Once you get beyond that, however, you face the cognitively dissonant situation: you have a presentation to make but you don't have a presentation. You're an organized, ever-ready Leader at any Level who is disorganized and unprepared? Your world is thrown into disarray. You feel dread. You know your own manager is going to be expecting good news from this pitch, and you doubt that you'll have much good news to tell him.

You had the idea that everything was on track and running smoothly. Now that's been train-wrecked with the idea that nothing is ready. But the situation gets worse because you have to tell your own boss something. You know that he'll be waiting to hear the news of how big of an account your team just won. So what can you do to fix the mess? There isn't time to create an effective presentation, but that doesn't mean you have to let the fallout get out of control (the conclusion to this dilemma is found on page 108, but be patient).

The knee-jerk reaction in this type of circumstance is to blame someone else. To place fault on another party. Unfortunately, where you're the manager of the team, you can't really do that. It was your job to make sure they were doing their jobs. You didn't solve the problem or appropriately track the team's progress, so you're the one that deserves the blame. Regardless of who merits the blame, you're going to keep control of your emotions so you can keep control of the situation, right? You could fire them all but that just leaves you without a team and still doesn't help you make the presentation or explain things to your own boss.

The second typical reaction is one called rationalization. This is the process of taking two opposed ideas and shifting how we view the importance of them, or adding some new piece of information to them, to make them fit together. It's like putting the ice cubes in the boiling water and letting them melt away. But what should you do?

Consider one of Aesop's fables entitled *The Fox and the Grapes*. It reads like this:

> *Driven by hunger, a fox tried to reach some grapes hanging high on the vine but was unable to, although he leaped with all his strength. As he went away, the fox remarked, 'Oh, you aren't even ripe yet! I don't need any sour grapes.'*

In this story, the fox decides he'd really like some grapes. It's only after he realizes he can't get them that he decides they weren't ripe—or possibly were too ripe. In other words, he's trying to comfort himself in his failure by telling himself that it's better to have failed. He's telling himself that, if he had gotten the grapes, they would have been sour and gross, possibly making him sick. The truth is that he changed his mind, and, rather than simply move on, in his pride—his bad ego—he had to turn his failure into a victory of sorts. He brainwashed himself.

The dissonant pieces of information here were wanting to eat the grapes and not being able to eat the grapes. In order to resolve this conundrum, the fox downplayed the importance of the grapes by saying they were sour. It's interesting to note, though, that the fox was still hungry. His stomach probably disagreed with him as he left. There is a saying that 'to rationalize is to tell rational lies.' Certainly the fox was telling himself a lie—and that's regardless of whether or not the grapes really were sour. He was deceiving himself because he had no way of knowing whether the grapes were sour or not.

For better or worse, the human mind has an amazing ability to rationalize things in order to help them fit with that person's overall perception of the world. This effect of rationalization is so powerful, in fact, that it's entirely possible for a person to commit a felony and then reconcile it inside his head. He's able to justify his personal misdeeds even while accepting the overall prohibition on the action. He can feel perfectly honest in denying the commission of a crime when he knows that he committed the act upon which the crime is based.

As it turns out, the UFO cult Festinger was studying rationalized away the world's failure to end by deciding they had been spared to continue preaching the word. The aliens had seen their efforts to spread the good word and rewarded them with more time. Ironically, their proselyting efforts actually increased after an event that, in reality, should have debunked their belief system. Instantly, the idea that "the world was supposed to end but didn't" is no longer bothersome. It's been rationalized. It makes sense and it relieves the mind of the previously incongruous ideas by adding a new piece of information. It's like walking into a dead-end in a maze and cutting a hole in the wall so you can keep going—or like realizing you can't win a game so you change the rules instead.

On a more minor scale, cognitive dissonance and the process of rationalization allow us to remain at peace with the world. Otherwise, we might run the risk of going crazy the next time we heard about something good happening to a bad person or, vice versa, something bad happening to a good person—particularly if that good person is a friend. On some level, we all accept that bad things happen to good people, but, on a more personal level, it's a very difficult pill to swallow.

Usually, the circumstances that bring on this feeling aren't so extreme as the end of the world. Still, regardless of the cause, few people find guilt, dread, or confusion to be pleasant feelings. As a result, we are likely to try to avoid situations that would place us in a dissonant state. This is important to note because failure typically puts us in a dissonant state.

In general, people don't think of themselves as failures. So what happens when they fail? They try to rationalize the failure away—they brainwash themselves—so that they can keep thinking of themselves as successes. A Leader at any Level can't do that. Leaders at any Level don't allow themselves to rationalize, which means, by extension, that they can't allow themselves to fail. This means that you have to do whatever it takes to succeed. This is the whole idea behind igniting the Fourth Gear. True leaders have to figure things out when other people would just give up and quit.

When we were fighting for our $20 million in rebates, everyone except the receivables team thought we were crazy. They all knew that little David could never beat Goliath. Imagine the surprise when Pomeroy IT was able to recover the vast majority of that debt. I couldn't let us fail by just taking the charge-off, so the team and I had to pull through and make something happen. After that, we knew we couldn't be stopped. Instead of giving up and rationalizing a failure, we ignited the Fourth Gear and earned success. We let the dissonance of knowing we were not failures drive us rather than giving up and then repeating that failure again and again until it ultimately brought down the business.

Aside from failure, probably the most common way cognitive dissonance occurs is when an organization (a business, a community group, or a family) tries something new—specifically a new process to accomplish an old task. Developing a new process to accomplish something new is less likely to have the same dissonant effect because people are unlikely to have an established thought process in their head yet; i.e. there's no belief disconfirmation. However, trying to build efficiencies by streamlining old processes can often stir up these negative feelings—like when a few of us decided that our little dealership was going to go from number 95 to number 1. So how do we deal with the negative feelings within ourselves?

Confronting Dissonance

First of all, recognize that the feelings are normal and natural. It sounds almost cliché but accepting the anxiety is better than trying to resist it. Besides, 'resistance is futile' anyway, right? No matter how hard we try, we won't be able to avoid all the dissonant situations we might face, so it does no good to try to run from them. It's also important to realize that it doesn't make you a bad person or inferior or unintelligent or anything else when you're experiencing dissonance. It may not be healthy to try to maintain a dissonant state, but that doesn't mean that you're mentally ill when you experience such a situation.

The next step is to investigate the causes. What are the two dissonant ideas? What are the conflicting belief systems? When did they end up in your head? What put them there? Next, start looking for ways to reconcile the conflict. Thankfully, this process will happen more or less naturally, and your brain is already exceptionally effective at getting this done. Unfortunately, if left to chance, your brain will probably come to a less-than-ideal rationalization, instead of a true reconciliation. Self-awareness and emotional intelligence are required in order to guide the formation of your new belief structure.

The key in this is to let go of your pride. Think back to our discussion on ego and what it means to be a Leader at any Level. It's important to remember that "pride goeth before the fall" (Proverbs 16:18). The most prevalent form of cognitive dissonance is when one of our existing beliefs is challenged (belief disconfirmation). The easiest way to overcome the dissonance in this instance is to just let it go. Instead of stubbornly believing that we're right and anything new is wrong, we need to try to learn from every situation. Even the theory of gravity has been changed and superseded by current physics research. Be willing to investigate new ideas, and avoid judging them before you've had a chance to understand the ins and outs of how the idea might interact with your current belief structure.

As Henry Ford said: "If I had asked people what they wanted, they would have said faster horses." Sometimes, disruptive, revolutionary things seem a bit strange at first. When computers were first coming out—back when they still filled warehouses and ran on vacuum tubes—Thomas

Watson, then president of IBM, is purported to have pegged the worldwide market for computers as a total of 5 or 6. Contrast that with the emergence of the smartphone—technically a computer. Nobody knew they wanted an iPhone, but its launch and successive iterations have rocketed Apple from serious difficulties to become one of the biggest companies in the world, as measured by capitalization (# of stock shares x stock price).

New ideas, especially new technologies, often cause us to experience cognitive dissonance. They don't make sense to us because they don't fit into our current paradigm. They're like blind spots on our mental lenses. Still, being able to look at those dissonant situations and push through the discomfort can bring some pretty spectacular growth and opportunity.

If I hadn't listened to my friend's radical idea to sell computers, I might still be financing cars today. My self-image at the time didn't include computer sales. In fact, back then, there was no such thing as a personal-computer salesperson. Computers were no longer the size of a warehouse, but they were still something of a business luxury. However, rather than clinging to my old beliefs and fighting back against any new perspectives, I gave the idea a chance. I thought my friend was crazy—and I kicked and screamed part of the way—but I still gave him and his idea a chance. It was that decision which led me through the career that taught me the points I'm trying to convey now in this book. How different might life have been if I allowed cognitive dissonance to overrule my rationality?

So how do we help others avoid cognitive dissonance? Or, at least, how do we help them get through it when it's unavoidable?

One thing to look at is the way we present new ideas and concepts. If we present a new concept as directly opposed to an old one, we are more likely to induce cognitive dissonance. By presenting that way, we're emphasizing the dissonant parts of the new idea. If, however, we encourage the people involved to come up with the particulars about how to implement a new idea, we can help them begin the process of conversion and minimize the cognitive dissonance they might feel. In essence, the idea is promoting 'buy-in' with regard to a change initiative. By getting people on board, they have a chance to change their belief structure slowly before it comes in direct conflict with the new system, allowing them to evolve rather than make a leap of faith. You'll have to lead by example in this change too. You need to walk the steps first so you can then be a Leader at any Level.

So, going back to our earlier story, what are we going to do about the boss now that the presentation is shot? Well, first thing's first. Go and do the best job you can with the client—or reschedule with them, if possible. If you've built a great relationship with them, they may be understanding of the technical difficulties. Just don't try to give them excuses, they'll see right through that. Be honest, up front, and sincere. Be an example of grace and discipline under pressure.

Next, visit with your team to figure out went wrong. Don't prejudge them. Don't assume that their Dysfunctional Resistance was based on defiance. Gather the facts before you make a decision. If there was defiance involved, take the appropriate action. If there was a training or workload issue, learn from it and make sure your team gets the coaching and support they need.

When you go to report to your boss, bring honesty and ideas. Don't try to cover up anything. Thankfully, you weren't betting everything on this one client, right? You have a pipeline of additional opportunities, right? Go and talk to your manager about how it's unfortunate that this client fell through for now, but you've learned a lot of things that will help you land the next one. Maybe you even did a good enough job to earn a second chance with the client today. In any case, focus on the positive, forward movement to help your boss keep momentum on the project instead of falling into a rut. Don't give him excuses or rationalize or exercise your ego; give solutions and ideas for improvement and outline your next steps.

Recognize that the potential dissonance here is that of a successful sale versus a complete failure. In order to mitigate the failure side of the equation—thereby mitigating the dissonance for your boss—you need to point out the portions that were still successes—but don't grasp at straws or embellish for this; you don't want to lose credibility for the future. You suffered a setback, don't try to pretend it didn't happen. Just make sure you have a plan to save your momentum and keep moving forward.

So why go through all this? If cognitive dissonance is so uncomfortable, why talk about it? Why not just plan ways to avoid it entirely? Well, mostly because complete avoidance is impossible. No matter how hard you try, you will get blindsided by it at one time or another.

Additionally, your coworkers are going to experience it too. As a Leader at any Level, you need to be ready to help coach them through the dissonance and its unpleasant, emotional responses. Your customers may experience it too. You need to be ready to help them work through the "buyer's remorse" stage of the purchase process. You must be able to help and support them as they wrap their minds around their decision—you need to make sure they're happy. They need to know that, if they aren't happy, they should come back to you—otherwise they'll be going to your competition instead.

The fact of the matter is, understanding a concept eventually leads to acceptance. Since you can't escape from cognitive dissonance, don't waste the energy trying. Rather than wasting time trying to avoid it, confront it head on. Embrace it and use it as your time to shine. It's your chance to show how strong you can be.

There was a point in my career when Pomeroy IT was growing fast enough that we'd topped out our credit with the bank. We needed more capital to continue growing, but, despite putting every possible penny back into the business, we were basically maxed out. This was a death sentence because we were in a growth industry. It was grow or die, and we'd been put in a corner that would force us to slow our growth. This was a dissonant time for me. We were trying everything in order to reconcile the idea that there was no more money contrasted with the idea that we needed more money for growth, and we needed growth to stay alive. Not a pleasant situation.

Then we got lucky. I met a gentleman who suggested we go public. We listened carefully to his pitch and then talked with our banker about the idea. Our banker warned us that it was impossible—that we were too small to go public. Now we were faced with another dissonant situation: we could go public to get the money to stay alive, but the company was too small to go public, yet we needed more money to grow bigger. So we kept working at the situation, trying to reconcile a way through.

To make a long story a little shorter, we did it. Through research and the help of a consultant, we faced down the misconception that we were too small to go public. We accepted the discomfort and doubt and moved forward. It was a lot of effort over long months, but, with the help of a smaller investment bank, we successfully went public and got the capital we needed. We were victorious, and it showed just how strong our little Pomeroy IT really was. We weren't going to drown in the current like so much of our competition. We were going to swim upstream.

I share this example not so you'll think we were better than anyone else. Lots of little companies go public behind the scenes. I share it so you'll realize that, in facing the dissonance, you can test yourself and prove how strong you are. Mark Twain[11] told us that, "Courage is resistance to fear, mastery of fear—not absence of fear. Except a creature be part coward, it is not a compliment to say it is brave." In other words, we can't show how strong we are without an appropriate challenge. Cognitive dissonance is a deeply rooted, psychological challenge against which we can prove ourselves time and time again if we'll just have the courage to be a Leader at any Level and do it.

Cognitive Dissonance as a Tool

One final note about cognitive dissonance: it can be a powerful tool if you understand it properly. This is an advanced concept and not one to be trifled with, but I present it here as a possible tool for unlocking success in some rare circumstances. My father understood this concept whether he

---

[11] The pen name of Samuel Langhorne Clemens, a bestselling author sometimes considered as the father of American literature

realized it or not. I remember a few occasions as a child when I did something stupid. He never got angry or yelled or anything. He would simply pull me aside and let me know that "a Pomeroy wouldn't do something like that." Suddenly my behavior was incongruous with my identity. Needless to say, the behavior stopped.

My high school football coach used this on me too; some would call it reverse psychology. In a way, I guess it was. Still, it was a cognitively dissonant lesson, and it stuck with me my whole life. I went to him to quit the football team fairly late in the season my junior year. I wasn't trying in school at that point, so I was academically ineligible to play anyway. Instead of just accepting my resignation, that man had the audacity to tell me that, "Son, if you quit now, you'll be a quitter for life." It's only forty years later that I understand how profound those words really are.

Don't ask me why I believed him then, but I did—and believing him introduced cognitive dissonance to my young mind. I was a Pomeroy, for one, and Pomeroys weren't quitters. More importantly, I was young and headstrong and invincible. I was going to be a success in life, not some half-baked quitter. How could I reconcile this in my head? If I quit, I was a goner. All my dreams and ambitions were crushed. My self-image would be torn to little pieces and buried out back. So I did the only thing I could: I didn't quit. I stuck with it. And, trust me, that coach made it the hardest decision he possibly could. He replaced the tackling dummy with me. He made things as miserable for me as he possibly could. I spent only a fraction of the time on the field that I spent on the bench. Still, I wasn't a quitter, and that meant I couldn't quit. At the end of the next year, after a season and a half of very limited play and nearly unlimited abuse, he named me the MVP.

He said I had earned it by refusing to quit—no matter how bad things got. I didn't realize it at the time because I was still so mad at him, but I had been an example of what everyone on the team should have been: determined. In a small way, I'd been a Leader at any Level. In retrospect, I owe him thanks. Much as we all hated him then, he'd been spending his time trying to toughen everyone up. That's what he did to me. He put my head in a situation that I couldn't escape from easily and, as a result, I faced things head on. It was a valuable lesson for the struggles I would face in business over the next forty years.

So cognitive dissonance can actually be a useful tool if it's employed carefully. However, it's very strong medicine and best saved for dire circumstances. It puts people in a very uncomfortable spot. It's also somewhat manipulative when used this way. It forces people into, theoretically, a paradoxical situation. You remember that uncomfortable feeling I put you through earlier? You'll be putting other people through that same, uncomfortable emotion set. Think about that carefully before you go using this particular tool—and keep in mind that its use is very focused. This is a scalpel, not a broadsword.

In an article about pushing change efforts in organizations, John P. Kotter[12] cites a lack of urgency as one of the major reasons that those changes fail. Companies have detailed plans and initiatives, but people are too comfortable with the current situation (Kotter 2000). If this sounds like a situation you face, cognitive dissonance can be a powerful tool to push the change forward. This is the 'burning platform' concept we introduced earlier. In effect, you have to make the current direction of the business seem out of synch with the intended direction of the culture and vision. One reason this tactic is so dangerous is that culture is a powerful thing, and, if you aren't exactly sure what direction the culture will drive things, you will find change happening, but you may find that it's not the change you hoped for.

Cognitive dissonance is akin to psychological warfare. Usually, it's a war we wage against ourselves in the privacy of our own heads. Usually, it's counter-productive. On occasion, however, it can prove invaluable.

As a Leader at any Level, you can cultivate the ability to identify the signs and symptoms of dissonance and help coach people to reconciliation, instead of rationalization. You don't have to fear the discomfort anymore because you recognize that it's normal and natural. What's more, you can lead the way and be the example, helping others along the journey in smaller, easier to accept steps, rather than making people face the full force of dissonance at one time.

Chapter Summary
- Cognitive dissonance is an uncomfortable mental state wherein a person is trying to reconcile two or more opposing ideas
- Cognitive dissonance can lead people to brainwash themselves and act in irrational ways
- Rationalization—the act of lying to one's self—will lead to recurring failure and must be avoided at all times
- When used carefully, cognitive dissonance can be an effective tool to push change through an organization

---

[12]A leadership and change management guru, author, and former Harvard Business School professor

SET EXPECTATIONS – STAY AWAKE AT THE WHEEL

One of the ways you can help people stay on track and avoid cognitive dissonance is to make sure they understand what's expected of them. If they know what they're supposed to be doing—in detail—they're less likely to be surprised and thrown off track by the effort it takes to do their jobs properly. Taking this thought a step further, if they know what their target is (the mission statement and vision), they can anchor to the overarching goal, instead of the specific procedures required by their job. That way, as the job evolves with the company, they can always look back to the overall targets as a guiding star, instead of clinging to obsolete processes and becoming dissonant.

However, believe it or not, this is more difficult than it sounds. In general, the difficulty arises because management teams think they can hand over a sheet of paper with a job description and consider the expectation side of things fulfilled. As a Leader at any Level, you know better than that, right? You know that you must teach and model the expectations and provide clarification as often as necessary. In this chapter, we'll talk about identifying specific, line-item expectations for you to share with the people around you. We'll start by talking about what constitutes an expectation.

As an example, it's tough to evaluate someone on the expectation of 'be organized.' My desk might be immaculate or stacked three inches deep with papers and reports; how do you know whether I'm organized or not? As always, we need to get deeper into the human behavior and nature of things.

Instead of measuring the weight of the paper on the desk, consider something that does imply organizational ability, like submitting progress reports on or before deadlines, attending meetings on time, maintaining client relationships through follow up, or cross-referencing new information with old ideas to look for better opportunities. A possible 'gold standard' would be something like 'how does the person do with managing multiple deadlines across multiple projects?' That's an organizational nightmare, and performance on a task like that indicates an organizational ability that far surpasses any extrapolation based on desk clutter.

When it comes down to it, this is about establishing precedents and patterns and developing trust. Take the simple example of punctuality. If I show up five minutes late for the first three meetings we ever have, what will you be thinking with regard to our fourth meeting? Do you honestly believe I'm going to be there on time? You've already sensed my lack of respect. What if I have really good excuses each time? Will that matter? If I really value my time to meet with you, won't I be there on time?

The idea is that establishing—and meeting—effective, appropriate expectations is a fast way to build trust. Setting those same expectations and not meeting them is a fast way to violate trust and destroy credibility. This is because of the simple fact that, in most cases—the stock market being a notable exception—past performance is an indicator of future performance.

Now, I'm not trying to say that people can't wake up one morning and turn over a new leaf to become a new person. What I am saying is that it's unlikely to happen. What's more, in the event that it does happen, that person is likely to face a lot of opposition from their acquaintances. This opposition occurs even if the change is for the better. It's not that people don't want their friends to improve and grow; it's just that it triggers cognitive dissonance. It's belief disconfirmation to change your opinion of a person from being lazy to dependable. Military training helps people change for the better all the time—it makes responsible, respectful, dependable adults out of reckless, self-centered children. Positive change can happen; it's just sometimes hard to believe that it will happen.

If you are habitually, pathologically late, it's a sign of a lack of respect. If you realize that and decide to change one morning, it's going to take time for people to catch on. You can make the change and stick with it, but—even though you've decided to be on time from now on—people are still going to have a firm image in their heads that you're always late. Until you've been showing up on time for a long time—months, maybe even years—people are still going to think back to the image you've already established in their heads. That's why first impressions are so critical.

We talked about how the fundamental attribution error makes snap judgment a dangerous way to do things, but, in the case of first-time meetings, it's kind of the only way. At least for the first little while. You can try to do some research ahead of time—visit social-media sites, review a résumé, contact references, etc.—but, when the meeting comes, your first impression will still be comprised overwhelmingly of what you see, hear, and experience in your initial meeting. If things go well, you're unlikely to form a bad opinion no matter what your research indicated, and vice versa.

This isn't to say that then you'll want to hire the person. You can form a favorable opinion and still recognize that he doesn't match the culture of your organization. Still, if you leave your first meeting with a bad taste in your mouth, you're unlikely to call him back no matter how perfect a fit he would have been. After all, you're going to have to work with the person. No one wants to hire someone they don't think they can get along with.

Establishing Expectations for Yourself

This brings us to the first half of the concept of setting expectations. This first half is the expectation you set in others with regard to yourself— and, by extension, what they set for you, consciously or otherwise. As a Leader at any Level, you want to make sure this is a positive thing. Showing up late, dressing too casually, or trying to fake expertise instead of doing your homework are not options; the impression you leave behind will ensure that the person is uninterested in contacting you again.

Prospective clients will worry what would happen if they were trying to do business with someone who obviously didn't care. Prospective employers will be thinking the same thing. No one wants to employ an unmotivated person. You may actually be the best possible candidate, but you push people into a position that triggers the fundamental attribution error and leads to negative repercussions. The way you present yourself is also an extension of your ego, so you need to be cautious about that too. Make sure you're presenting the right kind of ego.

The age old axiom of 'dress to impress' certainly holds true. As does the idea of 'dressing for the job you want, not the job you have.' But it's deeper than simple outward appearance; it's your mannerisms and how you portray your understanding and level of emotional intelligence. It's being polite and polished. It's the way you think and act and how well you control yourself and your ego.

If you take the time to be serious about setting the right impression, you'll find that you leave favorable expectations in the people you meet. They will expect that they can count on you to get things done right from the beginning. It's not even necessarily a conscious effort on their part. However, it's only fair to warn you: that's when the real work begins. Maintaining and improving someone else's expectation for you is more difficult than setting a high, positive expectation to begin with. This means two things: First, the higher the initial opinion you establish, the better your prospects will be—so long as you work to meet the expectation. Second, trying to set up a low expectation so you can surprise someone with your true ability later is a losing strategy.

It comes down to the idea that no one can actually ever give 110% at anything. If you think about it, 100% represents all a person's ability. If you ever give '110%' at something, all you've really done is reset your 100%

level to a higher mark. If you want to consistently impress people, give them your all with consistency. The problem with cruising at some lesser level and then bursting out in a surprise is that people will—after their initial, pleasant surprise—wonder why you've been holding back all along. They'll wonder why you lied about your ability in the first place. As we talked about in the last chapter, it's uncomfortable to be wrong. It's uncomfortable to have to update an opinion about a person, place, or procedure. It's also uncomfortable to think that someone has been holding back when they could have been helping so much more all along.

So how do you make sure to establish a good, solid impression right off the bat? The most obvious—sometimes most overlooked—tip is to do exactly what you say you'll do. It comes down to basic, personal integrity. Do you control your ego well enough that you don't need to cut corners or look for shortcuts? Can you be completely open and honest with your customers and your colleagues? Or do you have to keep secrets because of mistakes you've made in the past? If you do, the time has come to clear the air.

There's an interesting correlation between the perceived severity of a mistake and the elapsed time since it happened. As time goes on, the mistake will seem worse and worse until it hits some critical threshold and passes almost instantly into the realm of things people don't care about anymore. That's when it becomes old news. Unfortunately, that threshold tends to be much further out on the clock than the day when you are inevitably discovered.

In other words, if you screw up, try to make it right as quickly as possible. Like we talked about last chapter, don't try to cover up the error; get it out in the open and present your plan to fix it. Don't try to hide behind excuses. If you cover things up in hopes they will go away, you are only making the problem worse. Eventually, the mistake will come out and you'll be on the hook for not only the problem but the cover up as well. Unless you manage to string it along long enough that it becomes irrelevant—and there's little chance of that, so don't try. Just show your integrity as a Leader at any Level and keep your ego under control.

In the rare occasions where you give your word to get something done and then realize you can't get it done, be honest about it. Immediately go and tell whoever gave you the assignment. Let them know the situation and see if there's a way to restructure things so you can meet their expectation. Don't let yourself become a passive resistor who shows up unprepared. Don't ruin a promising opportunity by putting yourself in defiance. That's not what a Leader at any Level does.

Another thing that shows your integrity—and something that should be expected of you—is submitting proper notice when the time comes that you need to leave one organization for opportunity in another—and keep in mind that it can take six months or more to recruit and train your replacement, depending on your position. Also, to be clear, the only reason you should leave an organization is if you don't have any opportunity for growth anymore. If there is still opportunity for growth, the best place for you is to just stay where you are. Jumping jobs for a minor bump in pay is not only an exercise in unhealthy ego, it's usually unnecessary—and looks bad on a résumé. If this instruction seems excessive, just remember, do you want to be ordinary or extraordinary?

Normally, you'll make what the market thinks you're worth. You might think you can cheat things over the short term—and you might be right—but, over the long term, the market will win. If you think you can make more somewhere else, you need to be looking at why your current organization isn't valuing you the same way. It's hard to start over in a new place with a new culture and be as efficient and effective as you were before. You'll have to learn the new ropes and build your network within the new organization. Why would a company pay you more to come and be less effective for them?

On the other hand, if you honestly feel like your set of strengths and skills isn't valued in your current organization, and you've seen all the growth you're going to see, you might start looking elsewhere. The only real reason to leave a company is to go to one where you can have the challenges you need to see the growth you expect.

What's more, moving from one company to another paints a story on your résumé. It sends a signal for future employers—it sets an expectation. If you can't seem to hold down a job for any considerable period of time, hiring managers are going to wonder what kind of problems you have under the hood. Are you too entrepreneurial and need to just get out on your own? Are you a bad apple with an outrageous ego who is going to offend your team? Are you just lazy? Are you unwilling to put in the dedication and effort necessary to increase your responsibilities, so you're hoping to short-cut the process by jumping from one employer to the next? If you're getting results and working at an organization that values those results, you shouldn't feel a need to leave that organization because, in theory, they should be valuing you.

Setting Expectations for Everyone Else

We've talked about how you need to set yourself up with the proper expectations for your employer in terms of being rewarded for success, and we've talked about how what you say and do—and even how you dress— can generate expectations for you in the people around you. There's another aspect of expectation we need to look at which, for a Leader at any Level, is even more critical. This is the aspect of expectation that you set in your employees and how you keep them on track. For something as critical as this as this principle is, it gets surprisingly little attention from normal management. As a Leader at any Level, it's your job to fix this problem.

Before, we talked about how you set expectations through everything you do. These are smaller, more incidental, and almost accidental. They are unavoidable but, if you're aware of what's happening, the expectations are controllable. You may not be able to plot them out on a chart, but you can guide and cultivate the expectations so that they work for you instead of working against you. Now we're going to move on and talk about what people normally think of when they consider expectation. These are the expectations that are clearly mapped out and planned: the expectations involved in things like job descriptions, project assignments, meeting agendas, and leadership.

The whole process of setting expectations with employees begins at the beginning. And, of course, by beginning, we mean during the hiring process. It amazes me how little time, effort, and attention so many managers place on the hiring process. So many of them want to be able to wave a magic wand and have a position filled. They want to pass a requisition to HR and be done with it. There's no thought about the future growth and fit of the candidate. There's no thought about whether the person actually understands what's expected of them or not—and that's a serious problem.

You see, one of the primary things you want to accomplish during the hiring process is determining whether the candidate will be a fit for the organization and whether he will have the skills to effectively complete the various tasks and assignments you'll give him. In order for you to learn this, you have to first have a clear understanding of what you want that person to do in specific. You can't fill a generic job description and hope for the same success as you could get out of a customized position.

It doesn't do much good to hire a top systems architect if he knows SAP and you're on Oracle. Sure he has the skills and intelligence to learn the new system, but it makes much of his experience irrelevant and causes inefficiencies in the integration process as he joins your company. But there's more to it than simply knowing he can handle the raw technicalities of the assignment. You have to know that he'll fit the culture.

Back when I was starting out, I learned an interesting practice from a friend. Whenever someone would come to interview at my friend's company, he would send someone to the parking lot to check out the candidate's car. The idea was that the candidate was likely to treat the company the same way he treated his car. If your life is a mess, that will probably show on the floorboards of your car. If you can't take care of simple things like cleaning of the back seat of your car, why should anyone expect that you can handle the much more complex tasks of managing multi-million-dollar client accounts or leading cross-functional teams? It goes back to the idea of testing someone for true organizational ability.

I loved the idea and incorporated something similar into our hiring process. Rather than just checking out the car, however, when we hired a new executive, I used to have him treat me to dinner in his home. I was happy to provide the food—via catering, if necessary—but I wanted it to be in his home because I wanted to see how he treated the things he was already responsible for. How did he treat his spouse, children, or pets? How did the house look? Some scattered toys or old appliances weren't the issues I was on the lookout for; I was looking for better indicators. Is the grass dead? Unmowed? How is the exterior paint? Has the kitchen been swept? Are there spider webs in the ceiling corners? Are there bits of trash in the carpets? Is the kitchen table clean?

What I was really looking for was an impression of how the person treated his most valuable assets. Similar to checking out a person's car. We were in the asset management business, in many regards, and the idea is that he isn't going to treat anything of yours any better than he treats his own living space—not over the long run, anyway. Additionally, you don't want them bringing personal problems to work.

Another recommendation for the hiring process is to clearly outline every single expectation a candidate will be subject to. This goes beyond the job description and making sure he can handle the specific tasks; this gets into the culture side of things. You want to know if he will commit to the various aspects of your company's culture that make it a great place to work. Is he willing to do his homework? Will he study the business?

An interesting way to test this is to give candidates a case study a day in advance. Let it be about something totally unrelated to their field of expertise. The idea isn't to test what they already know; it's to test what they can learn—to test their commitment to learn whatever they need to in order to succeed. When I started in credit and collections, I knew nothing about credit or collections. When I started selling financing and insurance, I knew nearly nothing about financing or insurance. When I started selling computers, nobody knew anything about selling computers. In each case, I had to put in the long, hard hours to learn the material. And, for one not predisposed to studying, it was no easy task. You want to know if the people around you will have that kind of drive. Will they be willing to study something outside their normal interests if it helps the business succeed? Will they be willing to ignite that Fourth Gear?

Hard Work isn't Long Work

The first expectation to set is one we've talked about already: hard work. When we discussed leadership, we discussed that it meant leading by example—and setting an example of failure aversion and Fourth Gear ignition. You want to make sure that each person understands the real definition of hard work: the need to do whatever it takes to wrest success from the jaws of failure; the ability and determination to study, do homework, and innovate in the face of what seems insurmountable or impossible; and the understanding of human nature that will allow you to guide, coach, and effect change. You need to have that inner fire personally, and you need to make sure that everyone else understands that the same fire is expected in them. If you get everyone else to ignite their Fourth Gear, but fail to ignite your own, they will quickly leave you behind.

Related to the concept of hard work is the idea that nobody should need overtime. For most professions, with real hard work, a person should be able to do their job in a normal, 40-hour workweek. Too many people waste valuable time during the day when they should have been working—putting themselves in a position where they have to clock more than 40 hours to get their jobs done. If you've assembled the job responsibilities properly and set expectations effectively, overtime should be unnecessary—and people need to know it, or you run the risk that they might try to take advantage of the system. Let everyone know that you don't believe in overtime pay and that they will be sent home at 40 hours. Interestingly, at its core, this policy shows respect for the employee and his private life because you are encouraging them to be more internally balanced and take time for interests outside of the workplace.

The Customer Comes First

Another clear expectation to set is that the customer needs to come first. This seems like another of those obvious things that shouldn't need to be said, yet, if everyone knows that the customer comes first, why do people still put themselves first? Consider companies which have been brought down by accounting scandals in the past decade. Or what about the infamous relationship between collections companies and consumers? The issue isn't whether or not people will put the customer first; they are intelligent enough to know that they need to put the customer first or they'll be out of a job. The real task for a Leader at any Level is to make sure that everyone knows who his or her customer really is—and the complicated part is that the customer might be different for different parts of the company.

With HR, for example, the customer is probably the leadership team; that's who they are supposed to serve. The accounting department is in the same situation; their information is designed to help leadership run the company. The IT team has customers all over the company as they try to unify and streamline the information systems. The sales team's customer is the most obvious one—and the customer in the traditional sense—but, unless that's made clear to them, they may think that management is their customer. The leadership team is supposed to be serving the shareholders or owners.

Let's play a quick game to demonstrate why this is important to know. Let's say there is a huge dinner party going on. All the guests have arrived and you're part of the serving team. The chef hands you a big tray of food and tells you to go give it to your customer. As a member of an organization, that's your job: to serve your customer. Now you take your tray out into this room. To one side, you see your sales team, to another is your purchasing manager. Across the way are the CEO and the Board. Right in front of you is the accounting team and, just past them, are some clients of the firm. Then you see your venders off to the left. You only have enough food on your tray for one table. Which table will you go to?

In order to make sure that every table gets served and no table is forgotten, everyone in an organization needs to know who their customer is. Are your salespeople supposed to be working for the end consumer or for the leadership team? That will make a big difference in the work they do. If they're working for the consumer, they'll sell what that customer needs most. If they're working for management, they'll sell what makes the most money. Those two things may not always be the same.

This doesn't mean that you're doing special favors for your customers—or breaking the rules for them—it just means you are getting the right results. It means you know where your focus should be, and you are going to push with all your ability to get there. It gives you a direction to go in as you ignite your Fourth Gear.

There are any number of ways to decide who a given division or department should be serving as their primary customer, but, unless that distinction is made, you run the risk that no one really knows. Everyone knows that the customer comes first but, let's face it, which customer? When I've got my clients asking for one thing and my boss telling me to do something else, who do I listen to? That expectation needs to be made clear up front and it needs to be made clear by a Leader at any Level setting the example. The gradual accumulation of examples will establish the culture and clarify who the customer really is. Understand that, be aware of it, and take advantage of the knowledge.

The Importance of Initiative and Integrity

When you're hiring, you also need to be clear that initiative and integrity are expected. People need to know that, while the overall goal and expectation will be crystal clear, the methods won't always be so easily charted. People need to know that you expect them to take risks, update procedures, and streamline processes—and then take ownership for their actions. They need to know that you expect them to find new, innovative ways of doing things, but that you expect them to stay inside the bounds of the law. They need to know that you expect them to act when they see opportunity and that you expect them to fix things when they screw up—and that you have zero tolerance for dishonesty. In order for this to happen, you have to build a culture that forgives mistakes but expects improvement in the wake of failure. If you allow risk taking, you will inevitably have sinkers with your successes. Not everything will stick to the wall. Recognize that and move on.

Perhaps most importantly, people need to know that, when they join your organization, the managers are not going to be 'answer gurus.' In other words, candidates need to know that they'll be expected to confront their own challenges, not run to their manager for help every time something new or different happens. They need to know that their leader is there to work with them to provide coaching and training. You don't want people to think they'll be left out on a limb, but you don't want them to think their manager is there to replace their mommy. That's not the point of leadership. People need to take the initiative to find answers to the problems they face and report back to their leader accordingly.

Leaders at any Level learn how to work to find solutions with people, not for them. This is because they understand that they don't have to know everything. They just have to be willing to put in the hard work and learn. They learn how to leverage networks to discover where similar issues have been faced to get new ideas and possible solutions. They allow people to brainstorm solutions and face those challenges rather than simply handing over a quick fix on a silver platter—one that, often as not, won't work.

Believe it or not, people are happiest when they're challenged. It's true. People are fiercely competitive by nature. They may come to work because they need that paycheck, but they stay at work for the opportunity to experience new and interesting challenges. They stay for new and exciting opportunities. This goes back to the heart of the matter: people are smart and they go to work to work. The idea that people fight through the interview process to earn the right to a job only to sit around and be incompetent is ridiculous and untrue. Any manager who feels that the people around him need to be managed really needs to wake up and realize that, if you hamstring people long enough, they'll learn to stop leaping.

Setting all these expectations is hard work. Making sure they're understood takes time and practice. You must learn—starting now. As a Leader at any Level, you can master setting the right expectations. Your past performance may have established a pattern, but that doesn't mean you can't change—especially now that you know what kind of resistance you might face.

The bright side is that, if you do the hard work during the hiring process, the firing process will be easy. This is because, once people know and understand the expectations, they will self-select out of the organization if they can't—or won't—meet the expectations anymore. Better yet, if you truly focus on communicating the expectations of your organization during the hiring process, you'll screen away those who don't fit before they ever join up and become a problem. In this way, having clear expectations can help you keep the people who are aligned with the vision of the business and shed the ones who aren't—those people who are most likely to become active or passive resistors.

Now, the key to really explaining expectations isn't simply giving a list of assignments to a person, it has to do with explaining the 'why' behind those assignments. If you want people to truly understand the vision of the company, you can't simply program them with tasks like a robot; you have to show them how those tasks integrate with the overall plan. You have to show them that their responsibilities, however large or small they may seem, are a critical part of the whole. People have to know what to do, and they have to know the importance of what they do.

This requires that they learn the reasons behind things. People are intelligent. They want to be a part of something bigger than themselves and they want to make meaningful contributions. If you'll treat them with respect and treat them as the smart, talented people they are—that is why you hired them—then they'll perform better for you. Part of that treatment has to be the background. The 'why.'

Instead of acting like a dictator and telling people what to do and when to do it, harness their creativity and brainpower. Give people the chance to prove how good they can really be. In order to set them free on projects, though, you'll need to make sure they understand the expectations. To do that, you'll have to explain the strategy. Be a Leader at any Level by helping the people around you understand the overall vision and goals. As they come to understand the direction of the company, they can focus their efforts in that direction. Then they can correct inefficiencies and problems on the fly.

It's like in so many movies where the 'leader' of a group dictates what the people are going to do but never has an open discussion with the people about why they're doing it. Then, when bad things start to happen, no one knows what to do and things start to fall apart. The manager has crippled them by prohibiting autonomy. That's why there's a term 'micro-management' but no analogous term for 'micro-leadership.' And that's the difference between a leader and a manager. A manager feels the need to control things. A leader doesn't worry about controlling everything because he or she is setting the example and can trust their intelligent people to follow along or get off the train. The most important thing for Leaders at any Level to control is their own ego, not the flow of information or the activities of the people around them. Leaders at any Level have trust in themselves, allowing them to have trust in their colleagues as well.

Accountability to Expectations

The final key to setting the expectation is to follow through on it. Without accountability, expectation is nothing. It doesn't make much difference how clear I am on what I expect out of you if there's no punishment for violation; all that demonstrates is that I don't really expect anything. That's not leading—on any level.

People need to know they'll be held accountable. Interestingly, this stems from a need to be recognized for their accomplishments. People don't need to get bonuses for their hard work because the reward is in overcoming the challenge; however, they still want to be noticed. If they aren't held accountable, they'll have reason to believe that their work is unimportant: if their work was important, someone would notice the result.

As a Leader at any Level, it's your job to make sure you notice people's efforts and hold them accountable. When they do a good job, let them know. When they fall short, let them know quickly. The whole idea behind setting careful expectations is that everyone needs to know that you all sink or swim together. Everyone needs to know that, when the business is successful, they will be successful. Equally important is the need to know that, if the business fails, you all fail together. In a business that effectively sets expectations, the only difference between success and failure will be the direction of the strategy. In either case, everyone will be doing the hard work necessary to earn success—they'll be igniting their Fourth Gears.

Related to this is the idea that hard work is expected, not rewarded. This is an interesting relationship in most companies. Most people apply for a job knowing they're going to have to work hard to succeed. That's common sense. So why is it that, after these same people work hard, they should need something special? It's like management believes people apply for the job with an expectation of hard work but, once those same people have the offer, they expect to be able to coast by. When management takes this point of view, all they are really doing is encouraging employees to turn complacent. You, however, need to set the clear expectation that hard work is expected, not rewarded.

Now, this isn't entirely true because hard work is rewarded in the sense that people keep their jobs by working hard. Additionally, employees experience success, receive more opportunity, and greater challenge when they demonstrate a willingness to work hard. The thing to really be careful about is giving 'bonuses' for hard work. This sends the message that a person has somehow done more work than was expected of them. By extension, this means they can get away with less work in the future without any kind of penalty. After all, people can only 'bonus' by doing 'extra' work.

This doesn't preclude bonuses in their entirety. An overall company success can still be communicated via a bonus. What it precludes are bonuses for 'hard work.' It precludes bonuses for landing an extra account or recovering a higher percentage of the receivables. That idea is similar to giving a cashier a 'bonus' for ringing up more customers. That's just their job.

Going back to the principle of cognitive dissonance, remember the idea of induced compliance (page 95, if you want to review the concept). This was the brand of dissonance that stemmed from the external rewards being unequal to the task. Psychologists have actually done studies on children in which they rewarded the kids to play with a certain, highly-desirable toy (Lepper and Greene 1975). After a time, they stopped paying the kids to play with the toy. Now, to be clear, this was the best toy in the room. There were other toys around, but none was as much fun as this one. Think of the toy that would be at the top of every kid's Christmas list. What do you think happened after the researchers stopped paying the kids to play with this toy? You guessed it. The kids stopped playing with it.

Even though the toy was supposed to be the best one, once the kids were rewarded for playing with it, their perceptions shifted. Instead of seeing the toy as intrinsically rewarding, they started looking for the extrinsic reward. When that external reward vanished, so did their enthusiasm for the toy. This is because induced compliance tells us that the reward will balance the effort. If something should be intrinsically worthwhile (playing with a toy) then it needs no extrinsic reward. Once an external bonus is applied, the brain will naturally start to let go of the internal reward system. It doesn't need it any more. After a while, the extrinsic reward will completely supplant the intrinsic reward, and, as a result, people's behavior and perception will change. If you 'bonus' hard work, you take away the intrinsic reward people have for overcoming a challenge and replace that inner victory with an external reward. Are you sure you want to perform a psychological experiment on your coworkers?

The point is that giving people a bonus for doing hard work implies that the hard work isn't expected. Worse, giving them that bonus will actually train them to seek the bonus in the future, and, if or when the bonus is withheld, people will start to withhold their discretionary effort. Christmas bonuses are just as bad. They have nothing to do with Christmas—which is for kids anyway—and people learn to expect this kind of bonus very quickly. Then, if you ever can't or don't pay a Christmas bonus, people will turn resentful.

In Chapter 9, we'll talk about the pros and cons of a salaried vs. commissioned pay structure. For now, we'll just get a little teaser. If you want to reward hard work, use a commission structure. That way, the more effectively a person works, the more they make—but it's never a 'bonus' for their effort, it's just a fulfillment of expectation.

If you've been ineffective at setting expectations and / or following through on them until now, it's not too late to change. You can start by outlining exactly what you expect from your team—down to the little details. Even if it seems like it should be an obvious expectation (like showing up on time to meetings) make sure it's written down. Then commit everyone to follow the guidelines. Follow up with them. Be open to updates and changes.

Make sure your expectations are founded on things that are measurable and specific. Punctuality is easy to measure. You're either on time or you aren't. Efficiency is harder to pinpoint, though. People are all intelligent but some will be more creative than others. As a result, what's easy for one may be more difficult for another. Over time, they can share best practices and narrow those gaps but efficiency is still difficult to track. Instead, set specific, behavior based expectations—like completing reports on time. The key is to make these expectations easy to follow. That means observable behaviors. After all, as a Leader at any Level, you're going to be an example of all these things at all times, right?

If you can't demonstrate it, it's not a behavior. For instance, what does it mean to 'manage' someone or something? Set aside the book for just a moment and 'manage' something. Difficult, isn't it? Learning is similar. Or building a relationship. Having integrity is almost hard to measure until someone doesn't have it. Each time they falsify something, it will show. An expectation to not gossip is easy to monitor though; people either gossip or they don't. There are enough challenges to go around already; don't make deciphering expectations another, unnecessary one.

Set the expectations in such a way that everyone can succeed. They're all intelligent, but that doesn't mean they can't misinterpret something if you keep it vague. Setting the expectation is like calling a play for a football team. Once the play is called, the players just have to trust that they can carry out their individual parts, and, together, they'll make something happen. If any member of the team violates the expectation and performs a different play, you're going to get sacked. Think about it. You're a Leader at any Level. That means you're not the coach, standing over on the sidelines. You're the quarterback, standing in the middle of the play and leading by example.

You can do it. It might take some practice but that's okay. You're smart enough to learn this principle and, in so doing, you'll help the team head in the same direction: toward success.

Chapter Summary

- You control the expectations that others develop toward you; be sure to set positive ones
- It's easier to set a good first impression than recover from a bad one
- Don't hold back in order to be a last minute hero; you'll only end up doing more harm than good to your reputation
- Don't just test what people already know; test what they are willing to learn
- Well-established expectations become the foundation for the culture in an organization
- Hard work is study, homework, and an aversion to failure; it's a drive to do whatever is necessary to succeed; it's not necessarily long hours
- People need to know who their customer is in order to put that customer first
- People are happiest when they are successful through a challenge; they need _recognition_ for success—not a 'bonus'
- Managers try to control everything; leaders set the example and expect people to follow
- Without accountability, expectations mean nothing; people need to know they will be measured against the established standards, or the standards will be ignored

Financial Reporting – Watch the Dashboard

Now we're going to change gears a little and give you a break of a sort. Up until now we've been focused on human behavior and cognitive psychology. We've been learning why people do what they do (motivation) and how to make sure they are doing what's best for the business (leadership). We're not done with those topics yet, but, in order to get deeper into the principles of leadership, we first need to cover some nuts and bolts of how to set a strategic direction—how to decide what expectations to set. If you don't know where you're going, does it do much good to step on the gas?

In Lewis Carroll's masterpiece, *Alice in Wonderland*, he approaches the same concept in a different way. The following exchange takes place between Alice and the Cheshire Cat while Alice is lost in Wonderland:

"Would you tell me, please, which way I ought to go from here?"

"That depends a good deal on where you want to get to," said the Cat.

"I don't much care where—" said Alice.

"Then it doesn't matter which way you go," said the Cat.

"—So long as I get somewhere," Alice added as an explanation.

"Oh you're sure to do that," said the Cat, "if you only walk long enough."

I doubt any of us is overly eager to end up like Alice—lost in a strange world. In her defense, it was undoubtedly difficult to figure out where she needed to go when she had no idea where she was. That's why we've spent so much time on ego and self-awareness. In order to plan a strategic direction, we need to know where we stand. You can't plan a route from A to B without knowing where both A and B are. Thankfully, if you understand the financials of a company—truly understand them—you'll be doing well on both location and destination.

Back when I was in car sales, I would sit down and do something that was, perhaps, a little revolutionary in comparison to many of my colleagues. I would figure out what I needed. By that, I mean I would sit down and figure out how much I had to make in a month in order to reach the various goals I had for myself and my family. Then I would work backward. How many cars did I need to finance to reach that magic number? This is called a Breakeven Analysis and, in business, it is a critical skill to master.

If I wanted to make $5,000 and I averaged a $40 commission per car, I knew I needed to finance 125 cars or more—preferably more. Complicating that was the fact that some customers came ready to pay cash. If I just sat back and waited for deals that needed financing, I would have been in trouble. I had to sell customers on the idea of financing their vehicle. So, estimating a 50% penetration for financing, I needed the dealership to sell 250 cars a month if I wanted to reach my personal goals.

Calculating the number of sales I needed was simple, but I didn't see many of my coworkers doing that analysis. Thing is, then I could look at each car that came through as another tally mark against my total. Each little sale was just one more piece out of the overall total. Even better, I knew when I had cleared my needs for the month. I knew when all the bills were paid. I knew exactly what I needed to do to make ends meet and have success. I had my specific, measurable expectation.

To do this required discipline. I had to be able to sit down and budget out what I felt I was going to need. I couldn't just make up numbers and hope to stick to them later, I had to be realistic. I had to know the business inside and out. In this case, the business was actually my family. The concept is the same, though, and applied later.

The skill served me well when I got out of car sales and into computer sales. We were in a very low-margin industry by the end. At the beginning, we were selling $1,100 machines for $4,000+ each, but margins like that attract notice and competition. In our first year, we had a 40% gross margin. That dropped to 20% pretty quickly. We knew even that wouldn't last. And, soon enough, reselling hardware just wasn't lucrative on a per-item basis. The industry average net profit margin hit bottom somewhere between 1 and 2%. I knew we were better than that at Pomeroy IT though. I knew we were a better company than the rest. We had better people. We were more dedicated, more intelligent, more driven, and I knew we could spend less. I set the fairly ambitious goal that we would get a 3% net profit margin. Implicit in this figure was what we needed to be able to grow.

You see, growing a business is like walking a razor's edge. Grow too quickly and you'll burn up your capital, run out of inventory, and choke yourself to an early grave. Grow too slowly and the market will destroy you.

It's the proverbial rock and a hard place. What's more, you can only borrow so much to fuel that growth. The rest has to come from within (retained earnings). Because you can only borrow a certain percentage of any given asset (called a 'loan to value ratio,' or LTV), you have to grow those assets faster than you can grow your debt liabilities. That doesn't sound so bad until you've had some rudimentary accounting.

We won't go into depth here—find a good financial consultant for that—but we'll give you a crash course so we can all speak the same language. For those of you already familiar with accounting, you can skim this part.

The basic idea behind everything in accounting is that the sum total of your assets is always equal to the sum total of your liabilities (debts) and equity. In algebraic terms, it looks like this: $A = L + E$. Unfortunately, the variables themselves are intensely intricate, making the equation far less simple than it appears on paper.

For instance, a moment ago we were talking about the difficulty of growth. In most cases, growth is indicated by an increase in assets. Whether that's buildings, cash, inventories, accounts receivable—the point is that the Assets are growing. Now, according to our equation, Liabilities and Equity have to grow at the same rate in order for the equation to balance. We've already established that banks won't lend on your assets dollar for dollar. That means that your liabilities will grow more slowly than your assets. The only way to keep the equation in balance is to grow your equity. In other words, you've got to put more of your own money in the game.

Thankfully, it doesn't necessarily have to come directly out of your pocket. It can come out indirectly by simply taking less money out of the business than 'your fair share.' Every dollar of profit you don't take out to pay your salary or bonuses or draws or whatever becomes a dollar of shareholder's equity.

This illustrates a point that will pervade this section. The scope of what we'll be talking about in this chapter is just the basics. You will need to go beyond the scope of this discussion or you will fail. You may get lucky for a while but, ultimately, you will fail. The key to understanding the financials of your company (and your competition) is that every line item is a roll up of underlying items. Your inventory may have a certain 'worth' attached in dollars but, when you look at the underlying assets, what are they really worth? Because of the way they do their accounting, Caterpillar has tens of millions of dollars of unrealized—and therefore untaxed—gains hiding in their inventory. Then again, their assets don't lose worth at the same rate as computers or food. In your industry, inventory may be more of a time bomb and less of a savings account. You need to know which you work with in order to make intelligent decisions.

Financial Reporting

Let's begin by talking about the six main financial reports that you, as a Leader at any Level, want to understand in detail. Before we do that, however, there are some cautions you should know about financial data. The biggest thing to be careful of is that financial data is like a snapshot; it doesn't really tell you a story over time. This can end up being a serious problem because it's entirely possible for a company to pad their numbers. Over time, that pattern will become obvious and bring the company down—as in Enron—but, in any given quarter, it's possible. That's why public companies have to have a third party come in and audit them. In other words, they have to have someone else come in and check their math. The hope behind this is that it will keep companies honest and make the market more accessible to the average investor.

Remember, these financial reports are really the only hard evidence a person can get when trying to make an investment decision. In all likelihood, if you're willing to do the hard work to drill down and read between the lines, governmental regulation requires enough reported detail that you can learn far more about a company than it wants you to know. As a Leader at any Level, these reports will also prove critical to you as you lead people toward success through the iceberg-infested waters of business.

I was rigorous about reviewing these reports for Pomeroy IT. In fact, I would spend my Sunday mornings going through them in detail. I remember one time when I noticed something odd about our receivables numbers. As I went back through the historical reports and compared them to the current ones, I noticed a trend that bugged me. There was just something off about it. Finally, I went to the accounting team, and we looked into it more deeply. As it turns out, the CFO had been hiding a delinquency in the receivables. A fairly large delinquency.

We had to take a three million dollar charge off because the CFO had made a mistake and, in a panic to cover his ego and keep it hidden, had not aged the receivables properly. We were like the Titanic, cruising at full speed ahead. If I hadn't been reviewing these reports, we'd have crashed right into an iceberg. The dominos were all set up and ready to topple. The charge off itself was only a few pennies per share, though our share price took a bigger hit, but we were able to survive it because we caught it and fixed the problem—and that CFO left the company. If we hadn't, we would have gone from being a great company on a course for healthy growth to being sunk in the blink of an eye.

That's why it's so important for a Leader at any Level to understand these reports and to read them frequently. It can be time consuming and difficult at first, but it is absolutely critical to gain this mastery. You can save money for the company and steer it away from destruction. Understanding the reports will also help you speak more intelligently about the strategic direction of the business, and it will give you instant credibility with every stakeholder for the company—the bank, investors, managers, mentors, your supervisor, coworkers, etc.

Balance Sheet

The first of these reports is the Balance Sheet. This report is probably the most deceptive because it appears to simply be the fundamental accounting equation on paper. The truth is, the information provided by this report goes much deeper. The balance sheet is a list of all the assets of a company in opposition to all the liabilities and equity of a company.

For a brief overview of the most commonly considered items from the balance sheet, see Appendix B at the back of the book. Again, to get in more depth on this topic—like you must if you want to be successful—you should consult a finance or accounting professional. Conveniently, you can do this by visiting with the accountants at your own company. Despite the undeserved stereotypes, accountants are people too, and they will understand these concepts inside and out based on years of training and experience. In order for you to master the P&L and other financial reports, you'll need to get in touch with these experts and apprentice yourself to studying their peculiar world.

Using the Balance Sheet report, a person can calculate any number of useful ratios, including the debt-to-equity ratio. This particular ratio shows how much of the company is owned by the shareholders and how much is owned by the bank and other debtors. Banks pay particular attention to this number when they are considering whether to extend new credit or not. Their concern is that, in companies with a high debt-to-equity ratio (lots of debt, little equity), the individual owners will decide that their risk is low enough that they can cash out and walk away, leaving the banks to run the business—something banks don't want to do. Because of this, the debt-to-equity ratio is one of the more important ratios in the financing side of business—at least when it comes to banks. As we mentioned before, banks want to see that plenty of money is being funneled back into a business. They want to see indications that management is committed to growing the business and not simply drawing the money out of it.

Banks have a vested interest in seeing a business grow because the alternative is for the business to fail—and that means bankruptcy proceedings, charge-offs, and uncollected loans. Banks are businesses too, and that means they exist to make money. What's more, when you exist as an intermediary for holding and transferring money (like a bank), you won't last long if there's no money to be held or transferred.

What all this means is that, if you're growing, the banks are willing to lend to you to fuel that growth and earn a return, same as any other investor. The place people get hung up is when they are already failing and want to borrow just to fuel their failure. This happens most often when people go to the bank and get a loan before the business is really viable. Then, over the next year or so, the business continues to lose money and, before long, the person is back at the bank trying to get more money. They can't accept their failure because their ego gets in the way, so they desperately try to find another way out.

There are some businesses and industries that have significant start-up costs to get running. However, far too many entrepreneurs think that they need a fancy office and a new car in conjunction with their new business venture. This is not the case. You have to make it before you spend it; any other attitude is a plan for failure.

When we started the company that would become Pomeroy IT, we had a tiny, single-room office. Not a suite, not a building. One room. It was just big enough for an address and a phone. That was it. Once we started going, we used the money from our first operation to fund the development of the second, and so on. We only brought the bank in for our meager down-payment on the franchise agreement and then as necessary when organic growth was insufficient to fuel the actual growth.

Ultimately, we realized that mergers and acquisitions were the only way to attain the growth necessary for survival, so we went public to gain access to even broader capital markets to fuel that growth. Still, we only borrowed money to fuel growth—and then provided a return on that capital. We didn't borrow to keep ourselves afloat.

If your business isn't making money, it's a failure. Consider the fairly recent case of Solyndra. The company's products weren't selling, yet they went to the government for a massive loan to keep them afloat while they continued to not sell. While a loan through the energy department may have more favorable terms than that of a loan through a more traditional bank, I also think it's unlikely that Solyndra would have qualified for more conventional credit. Banks are very skilled at examining the financials of a company, and they will see your weaknesses even if you don't. If you want to look like you care about your business, you need to make sure you understand the financial side of it when you go to talk to the bank or any other potential investors. Your financial reports will give you that understanding.

The Balance Sheet report will give details about inventory levels and cash on hand. You can see if the company buys its properties or leases from someone else. You can compare outstanding receivables to outstanding payables (money people owe to you vs. money you owe to your suppliers). You can see how much cash the company is holding in contrast to how much debt it is floating. In this way, the balance sheet provides a lot of insight into a company.

The key to understanding the balance sheet is to make yourself aware of the realities that underlie each of the broader categories. You can't just accept the numbers as they stand on the paper. You need to know the 'why' behind them. Know who the clients are in your accounts receivable; are they likely to pay you or not? Know who the vendors are in your accounts payable; how patient will they be if you get in a short-term bind? Know the age and size of the buildings in your property/plant/equipment account; are you on the verge of needing to replace something? Do you have excess capacity? Know their locations too; if real estate skyrockets or plummets, you need to be aware of how that will affect you. You also want to understand your depreciation schedules and the tax implications those entail. Know who your larger shareholders are, if you're public, and make sure you pay attention to their histories and the way they do business.

Another key principle is knowing the breakdown of your inventory and the age of the assets. A 386 Compaq would only be worth anything today as an antique, but there were times when we were moving hundreds of them and selling them for thousands. If we hadn't been turning that inventory, we'd have been left holding a lot of outdated equipment that devalued our inventory numbers. Ultimately, we had to make use of a time-adjusted inventory model to accurately record our inventory on the balance sheet.

However, no matter how useful the balance sheet is, it doesn't tell you the whole picture. No report can. Not in isolation. That's why there isn't just one report to look at. The balance sheet, for instance, can't tell you if a company is making money. Even if you compare cash levels year over year, you can't really tell whether the company is truly profitable or simply bringing in enough new financing that their cash reserves are growing in spite of the business.

Income Statement (P&L)

The second report is the Income Statement, otherwise known as the Profit and Loss Statement (P&L). It's designed to tell you whether a company is making money or not and where their money is going. It generally starts with the overall revenue of a company. There are a few other items that come later which can contribute to the profits of a company but those items are traditionally very small in comparison to the whole picture. The next item is typically the cost of goods sold (COGS) which indicates your raw material and assembly costs for what you turn around and sell.

Two of the most commonly reported figures from the income statement are EBIT and EBITDA. EBIT (Earnings Before Interest and Taxes—also known as Operating Income or Operating Profit) tells you how much money the business made before it had to pay for financing activities (Interest) and the Government (Taxes). This number is particularly useful to gauge the long-term viability of the company. If it doesn't have a positive EBIT, a company isn't generating profit through continuing operations. In rare cases, a company can be generating a profit as reported by EBIT yet still post a loss once interest and taxes are accounted for.

EBITDA (Earnings Before Interest, Taxes, Depreciation and Amortization) is a similar reporting convention. In this case, the business operations are looked at for profitability without factoring the degradation of plants, lease-hold improvements, etc. In theory, this allows you to look at the profitability of the company in isolation from its current capital structure. Using these numbers can help you get an idea of the best way to finance a business—whether to lean more toward debt or equity or split them evenly—and help you better compare the profitability of similar businesses with different capital structures.

The income statement will also break down the different areas of operations and show you the effects on the profit of the company; it will allow you to calculate your margins, and that is one place where you can create a lot of success. Most people think about either growing the top line (revenue) or growing the bottom line (profit). While both of those numbers are important, the margins might be even more important. For instance, you may grow profit from $10 to $20 but, if your revenue went from $100 to $500, you've likely got a problem. In this case, your profit margin dropped from 10% to 4%. You're still making money and you're still making more money but you're becoming far less efficient. If you'd maintained your previous margin, you'd have made $50. That's 250% of what you actually made. Does that help explain the power of margins?

To show the same issue with a focus only on revenue, consider a company that sells one-dollar bills. They think they can be so efficient that they sell them for only $0.90. Sounds like a great deal for the consumer. Every year, their revenue shoots up like a rocket. I mean, everyone wants what they're selling. But how much money are they making? They lose ten cents every time they make a sale. That doesn't show in the revenue. It would show in their cost of goods sold though.

Even cleverer, what if a company doubled their sales staff? They could increase their revenue but, without the appropriate customer base, those salespeople might be doing a lot less on an individual basis. That means higher overhead costs in the form of people costs, which would be going up much faster than the revenue. That results in reduced profit margins in spite of what may be increasing profits and revenues, like the example before. That's why it's important to understand margins and keep them in mind when making decisions. Anyone can make any sales goal if they can just lower the cost of the product enough. That doesn't help the company find success though.

Success is found by digging in to the line items and being ruthless about cost controls so that margins don't shrink in the face of growth. I remember one time going down to our receptionist and giving her the phone bill and a challenge. I asked her if she wanted to make a little extra money and, unsurprisingly, she said yes. I told her to look through the phone bill and find ways to cut it. Then we set up a bonus structure that tied back to how much she cut the phone bill. The idea was that, back then, long-distance calls were charged by the minute, and they weren't cheap.

That young woman—a 'mere' hourly employee—found ways to cut the phone bill by something like 20%. That experience taught me to never underestimate people just because you think they're in an entry-level job. They're still just as driven to succeed as anyone else. In any case, she instituted a phone bill audit that tracked the destination and purpose of phone calls and fined employees who were making personal calls from work. If you made a personal call on the company's dime, you were charged to replace those funds. She also instituted a practice of calling vendors collect! I never would have thought of that. The idea was, if they wanted to do business with us, they could pay for contact with us.

The changes she made saved a lot of time for the company too. Previously, when we were paying for our own phone calls, our reps were spending a lot of time on hold. Once we switched to the collect-call model, vendors had a vested interest in getting down to business and taking care of things quickly. All told, that receptionist saved the company more than $100,000. All because I thought the line item of the phone bill was too big, and she took the initiative to make some serious, innovative, cost-cutting changes.

Despite its advantages and the wealth of information, however, there is one important flaw of the income statement: it doesn't tell where the hard currency is. Lots of companies are profitable on paper and yet their bank accounts are slowly drying up. Why is that? Poor asset management, to be honest, but the point is that the income statement won't tell you whether the cash is coming in or going out. For that, we need our third critical report.

Statement of Cash Flows

The Statement of Cash Flows is usually broken down into 3 different types of activities: Operating, Investing, and Financing. These three categories are structured to account for all the activities where cash would go into or out of a business. The biggest thing to recognize in the statement of cash flows is that it tells you whether you'll have enough cash to make payroll at the end of the week—or payments to suppliers, tax payments, etc.

When we talked about a company being able to grow itself to death, this is the report we were referencing. The income statement may tell you whether or not a company is making money, but it doesn't actually tell you how much cash is changing hands. A contract for future services and applicable payment can be secured and, in special cases, recorded as income, showing through as profit on the income statement (though it really ought to be going on the balance sheet as unearned revenue—a liability). However, if payments are delayed or timed wrong, the cash from that sale might not be available for use in the company to cover expenses.

Additionally, the purchase of capital assets would go on the balance sheet, not in the income statement. That means we could spend a million dollars for a new building and not show it in the income statement. Now, in all likelihood, we got some form of financing for that purchase. The balance sheet will reflect that financing. So will the statement of cash flows. The income statement won't necessarily reflect either right away and likely not in their full amounts. This means that a company can be hemorrhaging vast amounts of cash and yet still appear profitable on paper. If a company starts spending all its cash on improvements, it can end up running out of cash even though it still has ample profit reflected on the income statement. Then again, a company could start selling off assets as it liquidates itself and show positive cash flow while posting losses on the income statement.

This report helps you to monitor and account for things like seasonality and cycles. It is especially important in mergers and acquisitions when you are trying to blend two different sets of accounting books and trying to make sure everyone still gets paid when they need to. When I was younger, I saw the effect of not making payroll. My dad had a man who had been working with him for fifteen years. We had done a lot for this man in giving him a place to stay and steady work and the like. Then, one day, my father fell on hard times and missed payroll once. My dad wrote the man's paycheck but it bounced. The guy quit after that one error.

The thing about the statement of cash flows is that your suppliers have their own bills to pay. Your employees have their own bills to pay. The government definitely has bills to pay. The point is that money never sits still. It is constantly flowing and, the moment you have no cash, you put a stop in that whole river. People won't tolerate that. It's a serious violation of trust and you will instantly lose credibility.

These three reports tend to be the most sought after for people trying to guide or valuate a business. While none of the reports in isolation can give an accurate picture, together they work like a three-legged stool. By learning to cross-reference between the reports and read between the lines, you can learn a great deal about the financial health of a company. You can help steer your company or division or department around the icebergs and keep your momentum and growth.

Even more important in this regard is learning to track the reports over time to look for the trends. Seeing a snapshot of a person tells you only what they look like right then. It tells you nothing of how they act over time. Nothing of their personality. If you'll be faithful about watching these financial reports over time, you'll gain a deeper, more meaningful understanding of the business and how it operates. You'll have a clearer vision of how to align with the strategic initiatives of the company and where to spend your efforts in order to provide the most value and earn the most success.

The next three reports are typically more internally targeted, but they will help you immensely as you fine-tune and track the vision and direction of the company.

Projections and Forecasting

The fourth report is a record of your forward-looking projections (forecasts). These are typically based on your past achievements and trajectory and are melded with a good deal of fortune telling and educated guestimating. This report is especially difficult to prepare because it is based on trying to predict the market trends overall, industry-wide, and within your specific markets. And, while trends tend to follow patterns in the long term, over the space of a year or two things can seem random at best.

One of the hardest tasks I had at Pomeroy IT was taking the company public and then having secondary and tertiary offerings. One of the reasons for that difficulty was because we had to prepare a prospectus and a five year plan. Preparing a plan is easy; people do it all the time. The issue is that they often fail to recognize their assumptions and, by that failure, doom themselves to further, future failure. If your projections don't make sense, you will lose credibility. Preparing a careful, detailed plan complete with appropriate exit strategies and contingencies is, therefore, difficult.

Preparing real projections requires careful analysis of the industry and the competition. It requires you to understand what aspects of the market other companies are targeting so you can structure your own strategy accordingly. In some ways, it's like playing chess with a master. You aren't playing the current move; you're trying to play five and six moves down the line. By far the most difficult part, however, is that you have to perform a sensitivity analysis on your projections so you can get a feel for which aspects carry the most clout. Then you have to prepare multiple plans to cover the most likely predictions and set them up as contingencies. In other words, if you prepare your projections the right way, you'll have to prepare more than one set in order to cover the range of possibilities.

The idea here is to maintain updated projects based on any new information you may find. You want to have your forecasts running out three years at the least. Each month, you want to look at those projections, update them and extend them out another month. This set of reports becomes the roadmap for your strategy; you know what your targets are and how you will act in the market. Best of all, having accurate forecasts will help you avoid looking ignorant when you are conversing with your various stakeholders.

Budget

Additionally, the more researched and well-planned your projections and forecasts, the more accurate and useful you can make the fifth report: your budget. Now, most people look at budgets from the wrong angle. Most people start with the top and work their way down. Or they start in the middle and work their way out. They use the projections to guide them on how much revenue they think they can make and then try to calculate everything through from there. That may result in something resembling a budget, but there's a better way.

I already told you about how, as a car salesman, I would figure out what I needed and then work backwards. The same kind of break-even analysis is possible in a business. Instead of deciding on some magic number you'd like to achieve and then budgeting for that number, figure out what margin you need in order to provide for growth. That's why I set the net profit margin for Pomeroy IT at 3%; that's what we needed in order to be healthier than the competition, so we could grow effectively and stay on top. As hardware margins slowly worked their way below 7%, we kept looking for other ways to earn money. We turned a greater focus on services. If we'd just set revenue or profit targets, we wouldn't have seen the trends and altered our business strategy to compensate.

The thing about managing to the margins is that they don't lie. It's easy to pad a revenue goal by simply lowering the price and encouraging sales now that would have come later instead. This is common enough it actually has a special term: sandbagging. Unfortunately, sandbagging is a very short-term solution because, at the end of the next quarter, you'll just find yourself even worse off than you were this quarter. It's basically stealing from your future to make yourself look better now. It's driven by the wrong kind of ego.

It's possible to pad a profit goal by capitalizing expenses that should maybe be taken as immediate expenses or alternatively, again, by sandbagging. Profit is a more difficult number to play with than revenue because there are so many other variables in the mix but, again, lowering prices—thereby putting pressure on the margins—in order to make more sales can create in volume what you didn't create through individual sales. Capitalizing expenses or delaying repayment on liabilities can, in some circumstances, temporarily make profit numbers look a little bigger as well. Again it'll catch up to a company, but the tactics exist all the same.

However, lowering prices will crush your margins, sending up a red flag. Delaying repayment or capitalizing expenses will inflate your margins because, on a relative basis, your sales are supporting less expense, sending up another red flag. In either case, a revenue or profit target that is 'hit' through accounting acrobatics will become obvious when considering the margins. When numbers start creeping above or below the budget, that tells you that something is not going as expected and deserves a closer look.

Budget to Actual

In order to track that variance, we have the sixth report. This one is, perhaps, the most valuable tool you have internally as a Leader at any Level: the Budget to Actual report. If you've done your job in building accurate forecasts and used them to establish an intelligent, workable budget, the budget to actual report will act as the GPS of how you're doing compared to how you thought you would be doing.

In essence, this report compares actual earning and expenses of the company to what the projections were, letting you know whether you're on target, falling short or shooting high. Knowing how you are doing in relation to your budget is important because your budget should have established the ideal outcome. Beating your budget is good but beating it excessively will make analysts wonder why your goals were so low in the first place—just like trying to set a low expectation for yourself and then blowing it away later. If your budget was prepared correctly, it will account for the things that need to happen in order for the company to have success. To beat the budget by any significant amount means either you failed to do everything that was prescribed in the budget or the projections themselves were way off in the first place. Either way, it's a problem that bears researching.

The key to this report is knowing exactly where you stand so there are no surprises. If you've set the expectation properly, people will know exactly what they have and don't have access to in terms of funding. They will know that their supplies budget is all they have for supplies. When they know you're monitoring the reports, it will help them stay honest to their budget by removing the temptation to get out of budget. This, in turn, will have a sort of snowball effect throughout the organization. As each team or department or division recognizes that it's actually accountable for staying on track, the end result will be that the whole business stays on track.

The other advantage to this for you as a Leader at any Level is that it will help you earn the respect of your coworkers. They are most likely getting paid for their results—including profitability. By holding people accountable to their budgets, you are helping them stay profitable, thereby avoiding future failure.

In 1998, in setting our projections and forecasts for 1999, we realized it was going to be a very profitable year. Y2K was coming and every business was frantic to get ready for it. Our position as an IT consulting firm meant that we were going to have a huge jump in sales. At first, we were thinking about the logistics of it and the difficulties we would face based on our current sales and service staff. However, our projections on into 2000 and beyond didn't support the same heightened sales numbers—Y2K was a one-time event.

A lot of the managers at the time wanted to gear up for the sales explosion, but I refused. I told them that we'd make do with what we had, or we'd have to pass on the additional business. I wasn't willing to put us in a position where we increased our fixed costs one year to harness a wave of sales only to find ourselves eating those same fixed costs in the years to come. Ultimately, we all agreed that giving up a little business in the boom year was preferable to carrying excess weight every other year—or mass layoffs.

Instead of relaxing our budget and unfurling our sails to take advantage of the one year, we tightened our belts and stuck to our guns. Our sales went from $750 million in 1998 to almost $1 billion in 1999. I'm sure we could have done more if we'd hired the additional staff and put money into additional infrastructure. Here's the moral of the story though: in 2000 we dropped back to around $800 million in sales. Essentially back where we would have been based on projections that ignored the Y2K effect. Could we have blown our growth targets away in 1999 by growing with the industry? Sure. But where would that have left us in 2000? When our sales dropped 20% to put us back where we were, what would we have done with all the added fixed costs? If we couldn't make 3%, we would die. I was sure of it. Instead of risking our 3% in 2000, we sacrificed a little business in 1999 and made a 7% margin that year.

By harnessing what we already had on hand, we were able to make far more money on the same fixed costs. That's what I call economies of scale. If we hadn't been monitoring all these reports, we never would have pulled in a margin like that in 1999. We also would have likely found ourselves in serious trouble in 2000.

The point is, you have to make it before you spend it. Our forecasts didn't have the market growing at the 1999 rate over the long term, so we stayed conservative. Instead of jumping onto the growth wave of the internet and buying ourselves new homes and Ferraris, we stayed true to our budgets and projections. We stayed disciplined and checked our egos at the door and, as a result, had great success.

You may find, as you begin to truly study and understand these reports, that you uncover potential weaknesses in your business. That's okay. Just like with people, businesses all have different strengths and weaknesses. As long as you know what they are, you can work on them. If you don't master these reports, however, you run the risk that someone else discovers your weaknesses first and exploits you for them. Don't put yourself in that situation. Be aware of your business in the same way that you are aware of yourself.

By doing so, you will be able to navigate the treacherous, ice-berg strewn waters of business. You will have a better understanding of where you stand in the industry, where you came from, and where you project yourself to go. Having this information will boost your confidence as a Leader at any Level and give you more credibility with the universe of varied stakeholders with which you interface. Having this mastery will also help you immensely with the next set of skills we are going to discuss. Understanding the P&L and managing to it will help you keep tabs on progress, allowing you to give people the trust they want. Knowing the territory will help you know what should and shouldn't be done in your current environment. Having all that under control will also help you be more nimble and more able to tackle surprises and problems as they arise, allowing you to truly be a Leader at any Level.

Chapter Summary

- Financial reports are a vital way to keep tabs on the health of the business; if you don't learn how to monitor the financials, you will fail
- No business report in isolation can tell you everything; using the reports together can tell you more information than a business might care to admit
- You have to make it before you spend it; don't finance your ego with your business, thereby sacrificing future success
- The budget to actual report is a guide to success when created properly

---

NEGATIVES BECOME POSITIVES – TAKE ADVANTAGE OF DETOURS

It's an unfortunate reality that everything doesn't always work out perfectly. We don't all win the lottery, and, sometimes, our best ideas turn into our biggest flops. When we discussed emotional intelligence (EI), we brought up the point that, without experiencing the bad, we wouldn't know how good the good really was. As a Leader at any Level, you've probably come up against a number of difficult situations—things that made you appreciate the good times—particularly in the past decade or so of boom and bust and boom and bust. None of this makes it any easier to swallow the pill of adversity though.

So what would make it easier to swallow the difficulties? What would make it less stressful to be faced with failure? To be faced with a situation that, on the surface, seems almost insurmountable?

What if there was a way to refocus your world-view lenses to hone in on the silver lining to every grey storm cloud? Because, as we all know, there is always another storm lurking over the horizon. No one ever escapes from all the challenges of life. Not without escaping life entirely. So how do we train ourselves to look at the good points to the bad situations? How do we pull the good news out of the bad?

Well, it goes back to our earlier discussion of cognitive dissonance. When we discussed dissonance, we explained about how it usually resulted from being confronted by a surprise that didn't sit with our current belief system. I think it's fair to say that a surprise challenge is a violation of expectation; if you'd known it was coming, you'd have taken care of the problem before it became a problem.

So the first thing to do is recognize that the feeling you're having is cognitive dissonance. That uncomfortable, stressful emotion you're experienceing is normal—maybe not pleasant, but still normal. It's nothing to be afraid of, and you shouldn't really let it affect you. You've felt it before and you'll feel it again, so don't waste any time or energy dwelling on the discomfort now. Instead, focus on what you need to do to move forward. Remember that the key is trying to retain your momentum.

The other thing that we talked about was how the trigger of cognitive dissonance was also the trigger for your time to shine. It's your chance to show just how strong you can be. It's your time to prove to yourself that you really are a Leader at any Level. That discomfort should kindle in you a desire to hit a home run. Remember, "If it doesn't hurt, you're not getting stronger."

So, with that in mind, I'd like to relate a story to you. This happened a number of years ago. At Pomeroy IT we were, to be honest, kind of a small fish. We were world-class at what we did but there were so many larger fish in the pond. We were a little enterprise trying to compete with the IBMs, HPs, and Dells of the world in the computing industry. They defined the industry; we just worked in it. Still, the fact that we were able to hold on meant we were doing something right. It meant we had something going for us.

One of those things was our tenacity. My partner and I were both car salesmen before we were computer salesmen—that's how we met each other—and, let's face it, car salesmen don't have their take-no-prisoners reputation for no reason. We were determined to take—and keep— customers however we could, and we were pretty creative and effective about making that happen.

Well, one day, one of our largest customers called and said they had decided to "go direct." In other words, they were large enough that they were going to start purchasing straight from the hardware manufacturers instead of buying through us. The idea made sense for them; they were going to cut out the middle man and save a little money in the process. Only, on their scale, those 'little monies' were going to add up fast. It made sense for them, but it crippled us. They were a huge account—easily one of our biggest. Not to mention the fact that they were a source of cheap, easy credibility for when we approached other customers. We used to point out that we did this company's work, and they were a huge, multi-national corporation. If we could handle their needs, we could handle anybody's needs. Only, now they were saying that we couldn't handle their needs.

Have I set the stage well enough yet? Can we all agree that losing one of your largest clients is a big negative? Good. So what did we do about it?

Well, after crying to ourselves for a little, we got to work—hard work. We researched the information for the hardware manufacturer and taught ourselves the terms of the agreement that our client was entering into. We weren't willing to give up without a fight, and that meant we had to know what we were up against. We were sure there was some way we could add value—some way to retain at least a portion of the business—but we needed to research everything to find out how.

Then we found an answer—well, the first answer of several. The manufacturer was going to charge something like $50 per box to ship the computers directly to our client. Additionally, the client didn't really know where to put all the product once it was received but before it was installed. Lastly, our client had never taken delivery of their own computers before. They didn't know what process to follow for loading, unloading, or inventorying, and they didn't have the technical team to perform the process anyway.

So we stepped in and offered to get the computers for them for the same shipping cost. No loss to the client on a comparative basis but, when you consider the hundreds and thousands of computers they were getting, it was something of a coup for us. So we got a tractor-trailer and drove down from Cincinnati to Texas to get the computers for them.

Then we asked the client about how they were going to do their setup and disk flash. Back in those days, computers didn't ship with a pre-loaded operating system and easy-to-follow installation and upgrade instructions. What's more, sometimes computers that shipped were defective (DOA or "Dead on Arrival"). Components sometimes broke during transit or were just manufactured incorrectly from the beginning. New computers needed to be tested to make sure everything worked properly before they could have all their software loaded. The client didn't have anyone on their staff knowledgeable enough to be capable of doing what we called the 'burn in and test.' So we offered our services at a fair price. Coup number two.

Lastly, once we'd brought everything back and delivered it, we had to ask how they were going to get everything set up and activated on their network. How were they going to configure their intranet protocols, migrate system information, and the other technical things that would actually make the system operate the way the client needed it to. Again, they didn't have anyone who could do that on staff. We offered to do that for them too. Coup number three.

See, the beauty was that we no longer had to order the computers. We no longer had to deal with potential inventory obsolescence or product that was damaged during shipment. We also didn't have to shoulder the cost of holding accounts receivable on our books. All of that was between the client and the manufacturer. They had dropped us as the middle man but, because of our value-add prospects, we were able to turn things back around and strategically reposition ourselves. As it turns out, the services we were providing all along were far more valuable to the client than any given piece of hardware.

Because we were able to take a step back and look at the situation without giving up, we were able to find that silver lining. By the time everything was said and done, this extreme negative had been completely turned around. We'd been able to retain all our value-added services for the client while dropping the accounts receivable expenses. We weren't charging them any more for anything than we had before they switched to buying direct but our risk had fallen off. It cost less for them to go direct, and, under the new arrangement, it cost less for us to have the client go direct. Once everything was figured out, we were better off than where we started.

It was a potentially disastrous situation but we were able to turn it around by taking a step back and looking at the whole picture to see where we still added value. One of the most important things we learned from this experience was to not get emotional.

We've talked about keeping control of your ego to keep control of the situation. This is a prime example. If we'd have given in to our panic with the customer, we may have tried slashing prices or promising free perks or some other nonsense. Had we done so, we would have looked desperate, and it would have hurt business instead of accelerating everything toward the service-centered business model we wanted anyway.

Anything Can Wait a Day

Another of the key lessons here was that anything can wait a day. Unless it's a customer complaint, let the problem sit for one day (if it is a customer complaint, you need to fix it ten minutes ago—more on that later). The purpose for this delay is that, when you're first confronted by a problem, an ancient instinct kicks in: the sympathetic nervous system and the fight or flight response. Whenever you're faced with a new, sudden stressor, your body automatically triggers a physiological response that limits your mental strength and speed to focus you on being physically strong and fast. This is a holdover from the days when hesitating to think or reason in the face of a challenge meant becoming lunch for a hungry animal that wasn't about to pause and give you a chance to "talk it through."

Probably very few of us face ravenous animals in our offices or homes, but the instinct is reinforced in other ways too. Think back to the bully on the playground when you were in elementary school. Think back to all those times you parents almost caught you doing something you shouldn't have been doing. Think back to the last time you were cut off on the freeway and had to react quickly. Think back to the last boss you had who came storming out of his office one day, yelling your name. The fight or flight response allows for those instant, gut reactions which keep us safe and alert in the face of potentially dangerous situations. Under the right conditions, it's designed to save your life; under the wrong conditions, it just makes it hard to do anything emotionally intelligent.

However, we've accepted that cognitive dissonance will happen, and that, though it will make us uncomfortable, we can handle it. Now we need to push the limits on that concept and recognize that we can handle it for a while. Again, unless a customer calls in with a problem, let the issue wait for one day. The thing about the fight or flight response is that it is short term. If your body were to maintain that state of alarm for a whole day, your heart would probably give out. Instead, that panic response only lasts a few minutes, maybe half an hour. By waiting a day, you allow your mind and body to recover so you can face the problem with all your wits around you.

The next thing to do is gather your team. Get their feedback and input. They're smart people, and they'll have ideas you never considered. You need their insights to help you look at a broader range of possibilities. They'll be able to help you refine your own ideas to increase the chances of success. They can also help you do the research and gather the information you need to put together an implementation plan when the time comes.

Next, go to the front line. Go to the source. You may be a Leader at any Level but they have their hands in the problem directly. Go join those people and get your own hands dirty. Experience what they do. Ask lots of questions and be ready to listen carefully to the answers. Get a feel for their opinions and perceptions of the situation. They're the ones who will end up living with the decision. Do they work for you, or do you work together? Make sure you've got their input, so you'll know they can live with the final outcome.

While you're there, make sure you spend plenty of time with the star performers. You want to find your MVPs and talk to them. Find out what they're doing right. Figure out why they are the best. How do they do what they do? Are they following the same protocol as everyone else? Have they adapted and streamlined it? Are they more charismatic? Do they spend more time in the hard work of studying and learning? Do they make more client calls? What is it that puts them ahead? Is there a way to teach those concepts to the other people on the team? Can everyone else be brought up closer to that level?

Using what you've learned, go back and refine your original plan. Make sure you're looking at potential synergies, and that you're preparing contingencies in case of unfortunate surprises. The more research you do, the more prepared you'll be, but you have to balance that with the need to act. You want to wait one day on the problem, but you don't want to go putting things off for a week. If you wait too long, eventually, you'll end up violating the expectations of the people around you. They'll get the mistaken impression that you don't care about them or what's going on. You don't want to do that because it violates trust, and that becomes an even bigger problem than whatever you were already facing.

So do the hard work—your homework—and then make the plan. Look for how the problem will change things. Are you losing a major client? Why? Are you having repetitive equipment failures? Why? Do a root cause analysis and dig down a few levels so you can get a better feel for what the heart of the negative really is. Jumping to conclusions would be like putting a Band-Aid on a snake bite. It might look nice and make people think something's been done, but it won't fix the problem.

Once you know what the root cause is, start to brainstorm what you can do address it. What is the range of solutions? Is the obvious answer really the best answer? All too often, in our haste to address a bad situation, we jump on the first solution that presents itself and hope we were right. All too often, we weren't.

In the example, we couldn't just argue that the client company was wrong to go direct, we had to agree that they were right—and then consult with them on the best way to go direct. If we had used the obvious approach with our multi-national client (and argued), we would have lost their business and lost our good relationship. Their management was already determined to go direct. There was nothing we could really do to stop that; not without selling at a loss—and you can't make up for that in volume; if you can't maintain your margins, you're just putting yourself out of business anyway—but that was the obvious answer: to go back and try to negotiate something more favorable for them so we could keep the status quo.

Only by looking beyond the easy 'solution' were we able to identify the alternatives we ended up using. If we'd allowed ourselves to get emotional, or lost our self-control, we'd have lost the chance to maintain such a critical account. So take the time to get your bearings right before you start trying to move again. Let me share another example about how this can work.

One day, while we were growing pretty rapidly, I had the purchasing manager come in and ask for permission to hire another person. On the one hand, it made total sense. Our growth was explosive, and it followed that we'd need to add headcount. However, I was following the P&L closely, and I decided to push back a little. In my mind, hiring another person was a negative. My problem was that another person meant another paycheck going out of the business; hiring another person also meant equipment and supplies and benefits—the costs add up at a frightening rate. I recognized the necessity of hiring people in order to support past and future growth, but I preferred to avoid it as long as possible, so that I could channel that money back into continuing that growth.

I sat down with the purchasing manager, and we reviewed some things. We talked about what was going on in his department. We discussed what was going well and what wasn't going well. We talked about the people in his department individually. We talked about who was doing well and who wasn't. Basically, I was trying to make sure I really understood what was going on in the situation, not just what the purchasing manager had told me was going on. I wanted to do the research to strip away as much of the bias as I could; then I could get the background information necessary to make the really creative kind of decision that turns negatives to positives.

Next, I called in his best producer. I found out that some of them felt bored by their jobs. They wanted more responsibility, more challenge. I asked the star performer who the worst performer on the team was and then followed up by asking if this star thought he could do his current job and the job of the worst performer.

In the end, taking the time to go through everything with the purchasing manager resulted in some pretty big changes for the department. Instead of simply hiring a new person, as would have been the obvious decision, we actually fired one of the existing people—the poor performer who wasn't getting anything done anyway. Then we took those responsibilities and divided them up among the remaining people, giving most to the star performer. We also gave that producer a healthy, well-deserved raise. By learning from the top producer, we were able to roll-back some of his best practices to the other employees in the department, improving efficiency.

The net result was that we improved morale in the department; gave people the challenges they wanted; avoided growth-related, unnecessary headcount; and saved the company more than $80,000 a year in 1990s dollars. How's that for a message that we wanted to stay fit, trim, and nimble in spite of our phenomenal growth?

On the one hand, it's a good thing that people come to you with solutions to their problems; you want to see that kind of initiative. The purchasing manager felt he needed more headcount; that was the obvious answer when the team was starting to seem overloaded. I was glad he brought a solution to me; however, rather than simply take things at face value, I wanted to dig in and look for alternative solutions. To be clear, I was willing to hire another person if we needed to. I didn't like the idea, but I would have done it to maintain our growth.

Before I went with the easy answer, though, I wanted to check for other possibilities. I wanted to check the bias of the purchasing manager and look for things he might have missed. I wanted to look for those opportunities that people miss when they let themselves get driven by their emotions. That meant I needed to verify whether the purchasing manager's solution was rooted in emotion or not. And, after everything was said and done, the other managers knew what to expect. They knew what to look for to increase efficiency in their own departments.

So, the first thing is to take a step back from negative situations and give yourself room to breathe. You need to have a clear head to be able to strip away bias and emotion. Give yourself a day and then engage your team to help you find a way through the issue. Another key to remember is that, as a Leader at any Level, you are leading, not going it alone: trying to exclude your team so the 'visionary solution' can be all yours is an exercise in ego. A true Leader at any Level doesn't need to take the credit from a success.

Change the Agenda

Another technique for turning a negative into a positive is a little more complicated. Again, the idea is to diffuse the emotion from a situation, so, instead of facing the negative on equal ground, simply change the agenda. Sometimes, as a Leader at any Level, you'll be suddenly confronted by a negative situation that requires some form of immediate address. This could be a controversial question in a staff meeting, a confrontation in your office, or an employee complaint. The idea is that you want to keep yourself out of the emotional arena, and you can do that by redirecting the topic of discussion.

Now, to be clear, this doesn't mean that when someone brings a concern to you that you start talking about the weather. You need to keep things relevant to the person and relevant to their concerns—concerns you need to address. It just means you need to be doing your homework so you'll know what subjects you can turn the conversation to.

Here's an example from my days financing cars. The sales manager was holding a sales meeting. He was a country guy from the sticks, but this guy was good. He knew sales and leadership. He was amazing about staying on topic and focusing on the reason for a meeting. He didn't get sidetracked or lost in the conversation; he stayed on task in sharing tips and best practices. Well, apparently there was an issue with the service department, and one of the salespeople decided to bring it up.

The sales manager jumped on the question and said, essentially, "That's a great point. Why don't you see me after the meeting. In fact, I've been needing to talk to you about your numbers anyway."

In just a couple sentences, the sales manager was able to head off a potentially tense situation and get the meeting back on track. By telling the salesman to meet with him after, the manager was able to acknowledge the concern but put it off to a more convenient time, allowing the manager to keep control of the situation and the emotions in play. Then he offered a not-so-gentle reminder of the where the salesperson's focus should have been: selling.

This is a short but effective example. We've talked about ego before and how people who aren't controlling their ego will often try to shield themselves and redirect attention away from their weaknesses. People who are in control of their ego will still have problems, but they will have more of a tendency to approach you about them at the appropriate time and place. A sales meeting is not the appropriate time or place to bring up an issue with another department.

By accepting the issue and offering to look at it, you stroke a person's ego and let him know that you do care. However, rather than leaving the negative there, you need to also remind the person that you won't let him shield his ego. You need to let him know that you're aware of his shortcomings and look forward to helping him work through those problems too.

In this case, the sales manager was able to do all these things. He promised to give a listening ear to the salesman's concern but also made it clear that, in a sales meeting, sales was going to be the topic of discussion. The manager also made it clear that the salesman wasn't going to be able to hide his lackluster performance behind a complaint against someone or something else. When people give in to their egos and try to use emotion to dominate a conversation, just remember that the one who maintains self-control retains true control of the discussion. You only lose the floor when you lose your cool. Whether the other person's actions are intentional or not, don't let yourself be suckered into an emotional debate. Especially not in a public forum like a meeting.

At Pomeroy IT, we had an annual sales meeting where I would usually get up in front of all the sales people and go through the business report and our strategic plan. The idea was to make sure that all the sales people were on the same page and working toward the same goals and success. As part of the presentation, we would always open the floor for questions.

I remember one time in particular where we opened the floor and a hand went up. It was a young man—we'll call him Jack—and he had a question for me. I looked over at the VP of sales and could tell this wasn't going to be pretty. Then Jack asked me about our hospitalization policy and compensation structure. It was irrelevant to the topic of sales but, more importantly, I knew this was a situation that could get very emotional very quickly. Benefits are like people's children. You can't really talk about them without stirring up strong emotion, and, in this situation, it was likely to be negative emotion and most of more than 300 salespeople vs. me. Not an experience I wanted to have. So I changed the agenda.

"Let me ask you this," I said, "are you the number one salesperson at Pomeroy IT Solutions?"

Everyone already knew who the number one salesperson was—we'll call him John. Jack had the decency to shake his head.

So I said, "John, how are you doing?" He stood up and I continued, "Congratulations on being number one in sales. You don't have to come to these events if you could be out there making a sale, by the way. You're my boss, in a manner of speaking."

There was some laughter before I got back down to business.

"Tell me, John," I said, "are you happy with the pay and benefits plan?"

"I can honestly say that I don't have a problem with it," he responded, smiling. "My paycheck is making me pretty happy these days."

I smiled back and said, "That's what I thought. You see, Jack, I feel for you. I do. But, in sales, it's all about results. Compensation and benefits are just a form of the business. When you get down to the substance, it's all about performance. Real success is in getting real results. Nothing else matters."

I changed the agenda by taking what would have been an emotional disaster and turning it back to the real issue. We were at a sales event to get on the same page about achieving sales success, not to talk about compensation and benefits. I acknowledged his concern and calmly reminded him of the real reason we were there.

The best part of the story is, a few years later, Jack was at another of the annual events. This time, he'd taken my advice and put it to the test. By changing the agenda, I had motivated him to prove himself. He was now the top salesperson in our organization. I congratulated him and asked, "So, did you want to talk about compensation and benefits polices now?"

He laughed and told me, "No, sir, everything is great."

It may seem a little harsh to change the agenda in this way but it's sometimes necessary to get people back out of an emotional minefield. In this case, Jack had opened a can of worms that could have crippled the sales force. Instead of focusing on company strategy and sales techniques, we would have spiraled down into an argument over what was fair and what wasn't. We would have lost everyone's enthusiasm.

I may have put Jack on the spot for bringing up an emotional topic at the wrong place and time, but I didn't throw him under the bus. I didn't sacrifice him. I calmly changed the agenda and redirected everyone back to the task at hand. It wasn't my intent to humiliate him or get public revenge or anything else; I just wanted to make the expectation clear: the policies are set by the people who can get results. If you don't like the policies, either get the results and change the policies or go somewhere else where they cater to the lowest common denominator. At Pomeroy IT, we wanted people who would do what it took for success, not people who just wanted to sit around and wait for success to find them. We needed success like we needed air—we weren't in it just for some money. I took the negative of Jack's off-track question and tried to turn it into a positive opportunity to reinforce the culture of the company.

The idea of changing the agenda to turn a negative into a positive is sometimes difficult to employ, but it is a skill that will set you apart as a Leader at any Level—and you must practice it. When you feel yourself starting to get emotional, think back to the real purpose of the company.

What's the strategy? What's the mission? How do you measure success? How can you redirect the conversation back to those things? All too often, we lose sight of the vision and that's when we start to get discontented with our surroundings. By staying focused, we can keep earning real success and keep moving forward.

I recruited at college campuses a lot. Mostly it was because I wanted people who knew how to study and do homework. The other reason was that, in this new, emerging industry, there wasn't really a pool of talent out there I could go to. We had to build our own pool.

One of these college recruits picked up some pretty good success pretty quickly. I remember, one day, when he and one of his coworkers came to talk to me. Now, my first mistake was letting them come together. Never let people raise a complaint in a group if you can help it; don't put yourself in a position where they can gang up on you. Like I mentioned earlier, you want to stay out of the emotions, and that's hard to do when you've got more than one person intent on heading straight into the most controversial, emotional issues they can find—but we'll talk about that more in Chapter 11.

These two young men come into my office to talk and start off by telling me they want ownership in the company. These were guys that had come in with no relevant experience. One had been making maybe $30,000 before he joined up and the other was fresh out of school. We had turned them into something. They were producers now; they accounted for millions of dollars of business, and each of them was making close to $200,000 in early 1980s dollars. They were producers but, at the same time, neither had been with the company very long. I'm not sure where they came up with their plan, but they demanded partial ownership.

I asked them just how much they thought the business was worth. They were floored. They had no idea. They hadn't done the hard work of homework to get their numbers straight. They had this crazy idea that they were somehow owed ownership and that's all the 'research' they were going on. Just emotion. It was crazy.

Still, I managed to keep my head—even though I wanted to pitch them out of my office onto the street—and asked them how much they were worth. As I said, they were making around $200,000 each already, which, at that time, was a great living.

They replied, "We're worth $300,000 each."

"And just how much of the company do you think you should own?" I wondered.

"We deserve 50% ownership," they answered.

I sat back and looked at them. I didn't know how they'd ended up so strung out on their own egos that they would come to me like this—not yet, anyway—but I didn't find it amusing. I'd taken a lot of serious, personal risk to build the business. I'd given up a very promising career in car sales, and these kids thought they deserved a piece of what my partner and I had built out of nothing?

Finally I said, "50 percent? This is a four million dollar business you're talking about."

"Then we want two million."

"But you just finished telling me that you're only worth three hundred thousand each. Now you want two million?"

"We deserve 50 percent of the business. Look at all the success we're having."

"Tell you what, I'll give you 1 percent of the business and you can build from there."

They declined, and ultimately, I lost my cool and fired them both. Now, I figured I'd settled the issue by getting rid of them and their egos, but I had no idea how negative the situation was about to get. A new startup had hired both of those young men and given them everything they wanted. In hindsight, I'm almost certain they'd been wooed by the company before they ever came to me. Otherwise I can't see how their egos could have gotten so big so fast. They'd had success, sure, but not that much success. What hurt was that they took their accounts with them. The customers they had relationships with followed the reps, robbing Pomeroy IT of a big chunk of valuable business—another lesson learned.

Then, as if that wasn't bad enough, half of the staff in the Tri-County office defected. That's right, the negative got a lot more negative. I felt like we'd been stabbed in the back. All these people we had trained and brought up, and they had all turned against the company overnight. It was fairly early in my career and, rest assured, I learned a number of lessons from the experience. I learned to always have a backup plan and an exit strategy—the subject of the next chapter. I also learned what it means to cut the deck—the subject of Chapter 9. One of the biggest lessons, though, was turning this huge, gaping, negative pit into a positive situation.

For the next few years, the remainder of the team and I worked together to get our customers back. It brought us together as a team, and, amazingly, we did it. We recovered every account we'd lost. It took years of hard work, but it showed us that we could do anything. It taught us just how strong we were to overcome so much adversity. It also taught me to stay closer to the customers so no sales rep was their sole point of contact.

While it's not necessarily a positive, we also saw this upstart competitor flounder and go out of business, taking the two hot-shots with it. In fact, shortly after it went out of business, the two young men had the audacity to come back and ask to have their jobs back. We didn't take the risk.

In retrospect, I probably did everything wrong with these young men:

I didn't split them up and meet with them one on one; I didn't wait a day; I didn't change the agenda. If I'd have done things correctly, I could have come back the next day and explained the risks they wanted to shoulder. To pick up 50 percent of the business would have meant a $400,000 tax event—for each of them. It also would have meant that they, and their spouses, would have been forced to sign on a $60 million bank debt—personally and individually. They wouldn't have had voting rights (since they hadn't asked for them), so I still would have had control over the direction of the business. All that liability just to split $2 million of ownership between them. I don't know that any of these facts would have changed their interest or brought their loyalty back to the company, but it would have given me time to prepare—time to call customers to let them know what was happening and time to head off the mutiny in the office.

The point is, what doesn't kill you makes you stronger. Losing all those accounts hurt. It hurt a lot, but it didn't kill us. We came back stronger; we came back with the confidence of knowing that we could overcome some pretty insurmountable obstacles. We also knew how to win over difficult customers—skills that proved useful in the coming years.

Who Is Your Real Enemy?

One other element about turning this negative into a positive is that it taught me to learn who the real enemy is. The pre-programmed answer to this question is that the competition is the enemy but, in reality, that's just not true. Or, at least, not true enough. The competitor that these kids defected to was certainly a thorn in our side but that's not enough for someone, or something, to be an enemy. 'Enemy' is a strong word. That's why we normally call the competition 'competition.' We're in contest with one another—like trying to win the gold medal at the Olympics—not a war—trying to destroy each other completely. It's about personal victory, not another's defeat.

An enemy, on the other hand, is someone who, by definition "feels hatred for, fosters harmful designs against, or engages in antagonistic activities against another; an adversary or opponent" (Random House Webster's Unabridged Dictionary 2001). Your competition probably doesn't like you very much, and, depending on their company culture, they may be quite vocal about it, but they aren't your most dangerous enemy. There are laws regulating what they can and can't do against you. Again, you're in a serious contest with them, but they aren't trying to kill you.

The analogy could maybe be best described as bumping into a fellow hunter in the woods. You're both after the same trophy game and, whichever of you finds it first, gets it. There's only one, so you want to make sure you find it first. Just to make it interesting, there's also a bear chasing you. In other words, you're each trying to find the trophy before the bear finds you. That's what your competition is like. He isn't about to help you but he isn't actively working against you either. Your enemy, on the other hand, is like the other hunter who just turns his gun on you.

When we talked about Constructive Resistance, we pointed out that the guy who wants your job isn't your enemy either. He's actually your friend because he'll force you to stay on your toes. He'll push to you learn and grow and be the best you can. He'll push you to seek your limits and ignite your Fourth Gear, instead of letting you just sit around while you hope success will wander into your lap.

No. Your real enemy is rarely the one you're staring into the face of. It's not the person that antagonizes you during meetings but still gets their job done; those people are too obvious and everyone sees through them—they're not going to do you any real damage. The most dangerous enemy is the one that pretends to be on your team. The most dangerous enemy is the insider who's turned bad. It's the bad apple—the rotten tomato. It's the salesman who complains about the company at lunch every day—the secretary that brings personal problems to the office and expects everyone else to solve them. It's the distraction that draws your focus away from the core of the business. Or, worse yet, it's your own ego.

The people in your company who have no control over their egos are the real enemies—especially if that includes you. These are the young, inexperienced people who want more than they've earned—and have no scruples against bending some rules if they think it'll get them further. These are the old, dead-woods who are just hanging on until retirement, unwilling to give anything to the company but expecting it to carry them on its back to the end. These are the middle-managers who think that they have gained omnipotence and lord their so-called power over the unfortunate souls who work around them.

In short, anyone who lets the form of things become more important than the substance—the success—is the enemy. The two kids who came to my office to demand ownership of something they hadn't built were the enemy. The salesmen who bad-mouthed the dealership at lunch when I first started working car sales were the enemy. I was the enemy when I lost my cool with the representative from the grocery store and started returning his swears and threats. When Jack brought up a controversial topic in the middle of a sales meeting, he was the enemy.

If you have enemies, they are actively seeking your downfall—whether they realize it or not. Thankfully, you don't have to let your enemies stay as enemies. Most of the salesmen from the dealership came around when I confronted them about their behavior. We turned that negative into a positive. Jack didn't stay an enemy. He caught the vision and came around to be the number one producer in the company. That was a negative that became very positive.

And I don't lose my cool like that anymore. I still have a temper, to be sure, but I don't let it rule me anymore. I've studied and learned how to control my ego and it has paid dividends. That's a negative that became a positive. You can do the same. You can help the people around you catch the vision by being an example of that vision—by being a Leader at any Level.

You see, many of your enemies are working against you but don't consciously know it. The two young men in my office had already made up their minds before they ever came to see me, but the rest of those examples were salvageable. Just because someone is working against you doesn't mean that you have to cut them off. First see if they can be reclaimed. Check to see if they're truly defiant or just ignorant. Turn that negative into a positive. Harness your emotional intelligence and approach them about their actions. Often times, they don't even realize what they're doing. Enlighten them. Lead them.

And it's good news that you can help people turn around because you could be on the 'enemy' list. The absolutely very worst enemy is your own ego. Thankfully, that means your worst enemy is most likely under your control—or, at least, should be. Stop letting it out. Train yourself. Enlist your team to help you keep your ego under control, and you can turn the negative of your most heinous enemy into a positive that will serve you for the rest of your life.

Chapter Summary
- The key to overcoming negative situations is to keep your forward momentum
- Negative situations cause cognitive dissonance; see them as your chance to rise above difficulty and shine
- When facing a bad situation, first step back and give yourself room to breathe; you need a clear head to avoid emotionally based bias
- When people try to hijack a meeting, acknowledge their concerns and then change the agenda to get the conversation back on task
- Your true enemies seek your downfall; your competition generally doesn't qualify
- Uncontrolled ego is the very worst enemy and the root of most business problems; control your ego or fail

What's the Backup Plan – Carry a Spare Tire

Still, no matter how much you plan, there will be problems that you just can't solve; mistakes that can't be entirely corrected, only gotten over. My experience with the two kids that wanted ownership is a perfect example. They had already set their minds before they ever came to talk to me. I'm convinced that they already had the offer from the other firm in their pocket before they came to me. In their hearts, they had already abandoned Pomeroy IT; they were just trying to see if they could get a consolation prize as they went out the door—and this is a common problem. If you're doing well, the competition will be talking to your colleagues. You need to understand and accept that. No matter how loyal your coworkers are, the competition is going to keep grinding on them and wearing them down. I know that because I did that to the top talent at the competition's companies.

Now, that can be turned into a positive in terms of the lessons learned, but, at the same time, it's a problem that just can't be solved. Not right off, anyway. No amount of creative thinking and consulting with your team is going to magically replace two top producers and the book of business they've built over the (short) years. That just takes time and work. Hard work.

Still, you can minimize the damage by being prepared. With some study and planning, you can put yourself in a position to perform impossibly fast damage control and get back on your feet. Again, like dealing with cognitive dissonance, you may not be able to stop the pain, but you can maintain your momentum through it.

You'll never be able to avoid getting blindsided by things. It's a fact of life. No matter how carefully you word your non-competes and non-disclosures, people are still going to leave you. That amazing woman down in accounting will have her baby and, after a few months of maternity leave, decide she doesn't want to come back. All you can do is wish her well and move on. She's not the enemy. She's not trying to bring down the company. In fact, she's doing you a favor because her vision no longer aligns with the vision of the company.

Or that top producer over in sales. He's been with the company a long time and he's starting to lose the fire in his belly. Your employment contract won't mean anything to him when he finds out he's got a terminal disease and only has a matter of months or years to live. He'll quit and leave you to find a replacement while he deepens his bonds with his family and says his goodbyes. He's not the enemy; his priorities aren't the same anymore.

And then there's that bright young man you just recruited out of Stanford's Ph.D. program. It's not like he meant to get hit by that drunk driver. He might come out of the coma and come back to work, but no one knows how long it'll be. He's not the enemy either.

These are all somewhat extreme examples, but they happen. These and worse. And then there are the more common problems or concerns that lead people away from a company. It can be anything from more opportunity to a bigger paycheck—all depending on the ego of the person leaving. You can try to contract them in so that people can't leave you but, even if you have a very carefully worded employment contract, sometimes it's better to let people go than try to keep them around against their will. Sometimes, the only difference between a top producer and an active resistor is attitude.

So what's the solution? If you can't stop people from leaving—if you can't stop some negative situations and can only mitigate them so far— what can you do? My favorite phrase in this is "backups to backups." What I mean by that is best demonstrated by considering a sports team. We'll look at football because it's a great example.

Filling the Bench

An NFL football team can have up to 53 players on it, yet only 11 can take the field at any given time. That's almost five times as many people on the roster as are actually going to be involved in the play. The reason for this huge ratio is to allow for specialization and injury substitution. Football tends to be a risky game and, as a result, injuries are almost commonplace. These are usually only minor, but even a minor injury can result in a player sitting out the remainder of any given game—possibly more games down the line.

This is a serious risk because the sport requires fairly specialized players. A defensive tackle (huge guy who tries to stop anyone from getting past) isn't usually a runner in the same way as, say, a wide receiver (fast guy who is supposed to get out far and catch the ball, then run it to the end-zone and score). There are few, if any, players who can switch between such different roles.

It follows then that an injury to the quarterback needs to be filled by someone who has a similar skill set to that of the quarterback. For this reason, a team will maintain a 'bench' of trained players who just aren't out on the field yet. In this way, the bench can be deployed to fill holes as they form, minimizing the downtime for the team and smoothing the transitions as much as possible.

Businesses nowadays need to operate much the same way. In a small, at-home enterprise, a mom and pop operation might be able to get by on their own wits and plenty of hard work—no specialization. With a larger business, however, you quickly begin to fill the roster with ever more specialized players. I remember a few of our first hires at Pomeroy IT. One was our accountant. My partner and I couldn't keep up with everything else and the back-office operations. Business was exploding too fast and we needed someone with more experience and specialty than us. The larger the business gets, the more specialized the positions will get because the scope of each individual task will increase. Our accountant couldn't handle all the accounting for the whole business forever. Eventually, he had to build a team of specialists to help him.

And I've already shared the example of the two young men who walked out of my office and took half the staff from that location with them. That was a lot of talent that we needed replaced in a hurry. Building a team to meet growth needs and recovering from an 'injury' are different in some respects but very similar in others. Thankfully, if you are a vibrant, growing company, that growth can actually help protect you from an injury situation.

What I mean is that, as you grow, you can anticipate the new positions you'll need. Because you've been studying the financials and reports of the business, you know how many techs it takes to support the sales team. You know how many reps it takes to support the customer base you're targeting. By working backward from your projected business, you can figure out how many people you need in different positions based on your stages of growth. You'll know that you're going to need three more techs over the next year because you already know how many repairs an average tech can do in a single day. Once you know that, though, the hard work begins.

You see, the solution to being ready for growth or injuries is to have a solid bench. You want to have backups that you can transition in whenever an opening appears, regardless of the cause for the opening. Sometimes, you'll have surprise openings in the form of turnover, sometimes it will just be the natural extension of growth. The bench is the list of people you want to bring into your organization who aren't already in position. It can include people already in your organization who are ready—or mostly ready—for a new opportunity. It can also include external candidates—people from outside the organization—who are ready to sign up. The key is that they have to be qualified for the potential opening, and they have to want to join you. It doesn't do any good to plan on recruiting someone if they have no interest in being recruited by you.

So you have to start early. You can't wait until the need arises and then go out and get someone; that's not enough time to do your due diligence and really check them for fit with the company. You need to know they're going to want to be part of your team, and, better yet, that they want to be part of it for the long haul. You don't want to be faced with the same situation in three to six months.

When we were really ramping up, one of the positions we had the hardest time filling was for computer technicians. It was such a new field that these techs were hard to find and even harder to recruit. We were competing with the Xeroxes and IBMs and Ph.D. programs of the world—not to mention the countless government and military jobs—and getting new technicians was becoming a harder and harder task.

The answer came to me one day while I was at the mall. Getting people with college degrees in computers was so hard and so expensive that I had to find another way. I was walking around—doing I don't even remember what—and saw one of those little arcades. Video games are just dedicated computers. I'm not talking about pinball machines; I'm talking about Pong and Pac-man and Tetris. Real video games. I was looking at a room full of purpose-built computers that gobbled up pocket change, and, with all the abuse they took, somebody had to be keeping them working.

It took a little searching before I finally found the young man who kept the machines running. We talked for a while, and I asked him where he'd learned to be a game technician. He explained that he'd tinkered with computers in shop class in high school, and that he was taking some classes over at one of the local technical schools. It wasn't much, but it was enough to keep a room full of purpose-built machines running. It was enough for what we needed. But there was a catch: we didn't need him yet. We couldn't afford him yet, and I told him so—but I also told him that I wanted him in the company when he was ready. Then I gave him my card and told him to call me in 90 days.

Three months later, I got a phone call. He was checking to see how things were going. He'd started getting bored of video game repair and was ready to come join Pomeroy IT. Unfortunately, we still didn't have a place for him. We wanted him on our team, as a field technician, but we couldn't put him there yet. I kept him on the bench and asked him to call in another 90 days.

Another three months later, he called again. Now I really knew we wanted him. He not only had the technical ability, he had the tenacity to keep calling me. He wasn't giving up. I liked that. And, better yet, I finally thought we had a place for him. By keeping him on a string—keeping him on the bench—he was ready to go when a spot in the field opened. We had him waiting in the wings and ready to go. It was almost perfect.

It doesn't always work out so nicely though. Sometimes, it takes a lot of work to excite someone's interest and get him to consider you. Sometimes it's hard to get him on your bench. I had that experience with Joe Money from our example about defiance. He was a tough nut to crack. He had all the right training and the right résumé. He was exactly what we wanted, but we had to get him to want Pomeroy IT. Hard to do when he already works at a big, established company. You have to convince someone they'd rather have the high risk / high reward structure of a smaller startup. We made sure to hammer on him every time we saw him. Luckily, he was our account rep with the big firm so we interfaced with him regularly. He knew how we were doing and he knew our business—at least in general. Every time we met with him, I would tease him about coming over to join us.

Finally, it happened. He called one day and said he was ready to make the switch. I was ecstatic. There was just one little problem: we didn't have a place for him yet. We wanted him, but the business hadn't grown to that point yet. I was forced to tell him to hang on for a bit. I explained the situation and let him know exactly what was happening. We wanted him on our team, and that meant that we needed to treat him as part of the team even though he wasn't on our payroll yet.

You know how that story turned into a tragedy but then ended well. We covered that in our discussion of defiance. Regardless of how things turned though, he was a pretty brilliant hire and getting him was a coup that took a lot of hard work. Thing is, if we hadn't started well in advance, we never would have been able to put him into the position we wanted to. We had to wear down his resistance and then grow the opening in our business. If we had tried it any other way, it wouldn't have worked. It took too long to wear him down to wait and try to woo him after the position was open. We would have had to fill it with someone else.

So you have to have a bench and you have to be working on it at all times. Always be looking—particularly in the places where you're experiencing the most growth. Those are the spots you really want lined up with backups for your backups. That way you're ready for growth, and you're ready for turnover.

Something to remember about loading your bench with high potentials is that, if you overload it, you'll find those potential candidates moving on before you can get them on the field. This basically stems from the fact that no one wants to sit around and wait forever. You can only string a person along for so long before he'll find something else. People are intelligent and they'll move for opportunities that make sense for them; whether that opportunity is with you or some other firm. Logically, in order to get them on your bench, you have to be breaking their loyalty to their current organization at some level. That leaves them more vulnerable to getting picked off by another firm.

You also want to be careful in the process of loading your bench because you don't want money to be the reason for people to switch to you. As we discussed before, opportunity for growth should be the only reason a person is switching organizations. If he's done his homework, he should be joining a company where he likes the culture. You want to be careful about people who jump from company to company; you run the risk that they are simply exercising their ego and trying to shortcut the road to success. You want to see stability whenever possible—just like we talked about in setting the expectations.

With that in mind, you want to sell the company when you go recruiting, not yourself or your product or industry. You may need to explain the product and industry to an extent, but you want your bench to be in love with your company more than anything else. This will make people more willing to wait for an opening with you and, to some extent, inoculate them against offers from rival employers.

If they love the industry, there is a huge selection of acceptable employers. If they love the product, the field narrows some, but everyone has competition, and the competition will be hunting for talent too. You don't want to put yourself in a position where you're recruiting for your competition. It's too much hard work to go wasting it.

You also can't be selling yourself because there's no guarantee that they will be interfacing with you on any kind of a regular basis once they join the organization. You don't want to get people on board only to have them change their mind because they don't work directly with you. This is especially important for executives to realize and especially when they're hiring for more entry-level type positions. When your bench is in love with the company, they'll be more loyal before, during, and after the 'benchwarming' period.

With this in mind, the best candidate is someone who's satisfied with his current position but would love the chance to take on something new. This will also help make him more resistant to being courted by the competition because he doesn't really feel a need to move on. Plus, if he likes what he's doing, you know you can have him do the same thing for you without him getting bored and moving on again right away.

Lastly, you want people who have all the qualities you have identified as expectations, and you want to make them aware that those are the reasons they've been selected. You also want to make sure you understand their expectations—doing this will help you understand their motivations for deciding to join you, so you can filter out the people who are letting their egos do the driving.

So keep these things in mind as you work at keeping the bench filled in order to prepare you for turnover and growth. The nice thing is, as with all the principles in this book, if you haven't been faithful at doing this in the past, it's not too late. You can start now with building your bench and cultivating interest outside your organization. As a Leader at any Level, this will come through the example you set and the way you speak favorably about your company. If you go to the pool with your family and bad-mouth your job, you will be destroying your bench, not building it. Instead, spend time talking about what you love about your job and the things that draw you in day after day. Be an optimist and you'll be able to start awakening interest in the people around you.

Building an Exit Plan

Now, there's still something we need to discuss about strategy and direction as it relates to the business cycle. The most basic stages of business are growth, perfection of the task, and release. Release can be selling the business, dying as the owner and turning it over to someone else in your will, or failing to keep up with market forces and going bankrupt. In short, release is the point in the business life cycle where, one way or another, you give up control or affiliation.

We've spent a lot of time so far talking about how to harness the "growth" stage in the business. This is no easy task. If you'll think back with me to the section on financial intelligence, we also talked about Alice in Wonderland and her exchange with the Cheshire Cat. In that exchange, Alice is taught that, unless she knows where she wants to go, she'll never reach her destination.

The same thing holds true with business. Unless we have an end goal in mind, we'll never really get there. Instead, we'll end up lost in Wonderland searching for an ever-more transitory 'somewhere'—always hoping the grass will be greener on the other side. As Alexander Meiklejohn[13] puts it, "There is, I think, nothing in the world more futile than the attempt to find out how a task should be done when one has yet to decide what the task is." Yet how often do we try to do this? In the name of efficiency or success or some other equally valid, valuable concept, we throw logic and intelligence to the wind and just start moving. I almost said moving forward, but, let's be honest, if you don't know where you're going, how do you know whether it's forward or back?

In any case, the end destination we're talking about is business success and knowing when to quit. At some point, all businesses die; some are

---

[13] A philosopher and Presidential Medal of Freedom recipient

simultaneously reborn with a new direction and purpose, but no business that prides itself on hundreds of years of history is the same today as it was hundreds of years ago. The reason is simple: the world has changed and continues to change. Technology advances; baby boomers grow up; wars begin and end; natural disasters happen. Whatever the cause, no company can stand still and stay successful; you're either growing or dying. Even when the nature of a product may not change much, the techniques to create the product probably will. Unless maybe you make French wine.

More realistically, everything lives and dies. Heraclitus[14] tells us "The only constant is change." Eventually, this means your organization will change too. The key is understanding where that change will take it and guiding the change along the way—like a ship on the shifting currents of the ocean; who will you put at the helm?

Pomeroy IT started as a Computerland franchise. It started as a hardware retailer. As time went on, we moved up the supply chain a little and became a factory direct retailer. We shed the Computerland franchise name and went out on our own as Pomeroy IT. Then, as the margins on hardware continued to fall and the industry continued to mature, we had the choice of going out of business like so much of our competition or evolving. We chose the latter.

We evolved ever further into the service side of technology. Instead of monitors and dot-matrix printers, we focused on network architecture and tech support. The first things to go were the retail outlets. With the change in the marketplace, dedicated computer stores were a thing of the past. We gave up our consumer presence and focused on the corporate side of the equation. Over time, as with our multi-national client from the last chapter, we downplayed hardware sales, switching to a more service-based business model. Ironically, there was a brief time in that span when we couldn't get quality inventory fast enough so we actually built our own manufacturing plant and began assembling our own brand of computers. It didn't last but, in order to stay on top of the market, it was one more thing we tried.

Still, all good things must end. We recognized that, if nothing else, eventually I would get too old to run the business effectively. There had to be a way out for me or, inevitably, I'd drag the business into my grave with me. I needed an exit strategy.

Now, in some circles, the term 'exit strategy' is considered a swear word. It's an unmentionable. Entrepreneurs want to look like they believe in their business idea so fully that there is no need for an exit strategy. They want to put up a façade that failure is impossible, so there's no reason to spend time thinking about a way out. As a potential investor and a successful businessman, I want to put that myth to rest. Not planning an

---

[14] An ancient Greek philosopher who predates Socrates

exit strategy is like taking your car down to the race track without any brakes; sure you can still get up to speed, but you're destined to crash.

First of all, the statistics bear out the idea that far more ideas fail than ever take off. Of the few that don't fail, most become simply lackluster, basically returning what was put in. Venture capital firms are banking on the one out of ten deals that really hits a home run (after looking at hundreds and thousands of deals to find just those ten). If the firms could find a way to avoid the other nine ho-hum companies, they would. Here's the thing though, even in the home runs, the financiers want to get their money back at some point. They want to be able to pull out that windfall and reinvest it in a dozen more home runs. That's the nature of venture capital. That's how they make their money to pay their bills.

What does that mean for you? It means that, even if you think your business could never fail, you need to plan the way out for the venture capitalists (or the banks, angel investors, mom and dad, anyone who helps finance you). If you don't, they are going to be that much more worried about funding you. So, for you entrepreneurs out there, let me just drill it into your heads: have a clearly-defined, well-articulated exit strategy; if not for yourself then at least for your investors. Tell them how and when they will get their money back. This may require you to build several scenarios based on the best, worst, and most likely outcomes, but, if that's the case, do it anyway.

Think of it like going to your best friend for money. In some respects, your investors will be like your best friends—your new best friends. You will have a lot of their money. You're either going to be their best friend or they're going to be your worst enemies. In any case, if you borrow money—even from a friend—they're going to want to know how and when you're going to pay them back. I mean, if you're borrowing $20, your friend might not care enough to need it back. On the other hand, what if you're borrowing tens of hundreds of thousands of dollars? There aren't many people with the financial resources to throw around that kind of cash without a care for getting it back.

Now, for your friend with the $20, you might write him a check on the spot, turning him into your personal ATM instead of a real lender. Maybe you tell him you'll pay him back next Friday when you get paid. Maybe you just need to get back home from the vacation you're on together. In any case, you're making arrangements to get him the money back.

An exit strategy is just that. It's a way to get someone his money back in order to end his tie to you and your business. Investors want to see a well-defined exit strategy in place as a matter of courtesy and respect. Otherwise, you just look like another bad ego begging for money. Turn it around and look at it for a minute.

Let's say you go into the bank and your banker is pitching you this great new market security. It's tied to the growth of the stock market but you're sure to make way more than the market return. Let's face it: the product has been designed so brilliantly that you can't go wrong. The only place it's going is up, and, if you want in, you'd better do it now because, pretty soon, it'll be too expensive to buy into. You'll have missed the boat.

You've seen the numbers, the spec sheet, the research, and the projections. Everything looks pretty decent. It's nothing overly special in comparison to other products you've been offered, but it's nothing to scoff at.

If the numbers play out like expected, you could multiply your money by ten times or more. If they play out worse than expected you might not make anything though. In fact, you could lose every dollar you put in. Still, overall, it looks like a pretty good bet, so you ask the banker one last question:

"How do I get my money back out again?"

The banker just looks at you and says, "Huh?"

"How do I get my money back out again?"

"Back out again? Why would you want to do that? Didn't you see the growth chart? This thing is just going to keep going up."

Now you're starting to see the issue. Nothing can keep going up forever. It might go up for a very long time and then plateau but, eventually, the entire world will be saturated with the product or service and there will only be maintenance opportunities left. Nothing can go up forever unless you manage to hit a home run on the first outer-space shipping company. Even then, technically, there will be a limit to the size of the company after every star and galaxy is covered.

But, unlimited growth opportunities aside, what good does it do you to double or triple or even quintuple your money if you can't ever access it? Does it matter that your $1 is now worth $10,000 if you can't get any of that money back out? What's the point? You've basically given up your money to make someone else rich and, because you can't get it back out, it's like he's now stolen your capital. Where's the consideration and respect for the help you gave?

That's why you need an exit strategy. A well thought-out, carefully-designed plan. "We'll go public" is not an exit strategy. In fact, it might be worse than no exit strategy because it shows that you thought about having an exit strategy but didn't care enough to craft a real one. Going public can certainly be part of an exit strategy—sometimes the key to it—but without a timetable and expected valuations, it's not a real plan. Planning to go public without actually planning all the details is like leaving a handful of coins on the table for a tip. If you leave nothing, the server can pretend that you just forgot. If you just leave a little change, they know you didn't forget and the tip becomes an insult. "Going public" is the same. It tells the investor that you didn't value them enough to spend any real time on their wellbeing and interest. It's a hallmark of a bad ego. At least if you had no exit strategy, they could pretend that you just hadn't thought through that far.

How Will You Cash Out?

But, aside from showing your potential investors an appropriate level of respect, there's another reason you want an exit strategy in place. You want it in place to protect you too. Let's imagine an example. You're driving on the freeway with someone in the passenger seat. However, for whatever reason, your car is more like a plane. It has redundant controls which allow your passenger to steer, accelerate, and brake at will: pilot and co-pilot. Your controls will override his, for the most part, but it will still affect the handling of the car any time the other guy does anything.

At first, everything starts off great. Your passenger basically kicks back and takes a nap. However, as you start to pick up speed and move faster and faster, your passenger starts to wake up and make tiny course corrections. It's nothing huge and you can pretty much steer over it but, eventually, the inputs start getting worse. Pretty soon, your passenger is arguing with you over the course you've set. He wants to go a different direction than you. He's smashing the brake when you're trying to gas it, and he's stomping on the accelerator when you need to stand on the brakes. And that's to say nothing of how he seems to always want to go left when you want to go right and go right when you want to go left. In fact, things are getting bad enough that it's getting hard to control the car anymore and the vehicle itself is at risk.

Enter the beauty of an exit strategy. Without an exit strategy, you're stuck in the car, hurtling ever-faster down the road and fighting the whole time. With an exit strategy, you can pull over and one of you can get off. This happens when either you buy the venture capitalist out and send him off to find another car to hitchhike in, or you sell out and he takes your car—your brainchild—and goes where he wants with it. While that might feel painful, sometimes it's the only option you have. In either case, you can't both drive the car to different places at the same time. It just doesn't work that way, and a pre-planned exit strategy provides a clear, agreed-upon way to sever the relationship without causing offense or ruining a relationship.

An extension of this concept applies to the relationships within partnerships too. As a sole proprietor, you make all the decisions for a business. The full weight of the responsibility rests squarely on your shoulders, but, on the plus side, you have no one second-guessing you or trying to take the company in a different direction. This is the only business entity type that enjoys this kind of control and 'freedom.'

In any form of partnership—be it a true partnership, a limited liability company, or a corporation—there will come a time when some of the ownership needs to stand aside. At some point, there needs to be only one vision to follow. Initially, you and your partner(s) may have similar enough visions that you can work together but, the further down the road you get, the more divergent those views are going to seem. As the company grows, the little things that seemed like no big deal in the beginning are going to start seeming bigger.

This is because, each time you hit a milestone, you're going to realize that the company is that much closer to fulfilling your craziest dreams. In the beginning, you're willing to put the wilder parts of your dream aside and focus on the core—the part where you and the partners all agree. You'll focus on building the fundamentals of the business and firmly rooting it to build something strong and lasting. Eventually, however, those differences are going to start to show. Wait long enough and those differences will tear the organization apart just like having several people all try to drive the same car to different destinations at the same time.

Let's consider an example of three doctors in practice together. They've been operating for a few years and one of the doctors is starting to look a different direction than the other two. He wants out of the partnership so he can go and do some specialized research. He approaches his partners and politely asks them to buy him out. He wants them to pay him one million dollars for his share of the business. Here's the critical question though: what is the business worth? What if the whole business is only worth two million dollars? What if it's worth ten? And that's before we throw in complicating factors like how the doctor's research has pretty drastically affected the time he spends on clinical treatment already, affecting the amount of revenue he brings in. In fact, he's only contributing about 10% of the firm's revenue now instead of his fair share of 33%. In this murky situation, how do you figure out what's fair to pay him?

So let's back up. The doctors set up an agreement—either when they started the practice or sometime after they read this book—that outlined the exit strategy. Now, when the doctor goes to his partners and asks them to buy him out, there's no question. There's no ambiguity. They look at the revenue he generates and buy him out based on a three-year projection and a predetermined percentage of that revenue. There's no uncertainty. No argument. He thinks he deserves more for his portion of the business, but, ultimately, he agreed to the exit strategy and he agrees to the price; he agreed to the formula. There's no need for lawyers or court or long, drawn-out arguments. The doctor is able to leave and follow his dreams; the other two doctors are able to maintain the practice without much of an interruption.

To be clear, you'll need to discuss with your partners what the valuation formula will be. The one used in this example is just that: an example. Where and how you pin the exit strategy valuation formula is up to you and your partners and your collective best judgment. And remember, you could end up on either side of the equation when the time comes for someone to pull the trigger. You might be the partner that's staying or the one leaving. Let that drive you to making sure the strategy is fair for both sides of the equation.

When my partner and I bought our Computerland franchises, our vision couldn't have been more identical. As time went on, though, my partner started to get tired of the growth. The frantic pace of things and all the stress were starting to wear on him. He was more content to just establish a solid retailer, kick back, and enjoy the ride. I wasn't willing to stop there though. I was convinced that we would either grow or die, and I wasn't excited about becoming another bankrupt tech startup. Besides, I wanted to push the limit and see just how big we could get. I wanted to keep growing.

At first, we had the same expectations for the growth of the business, but, as time went on, the minor differences in our visions began to show; they became more and more important until, by the end, they cast a dark cloud over the office and threatened our very friendship. Thankfully, we had the foresight to build an exit strategy into our partnership agreement. We had a simple, mathematical formula to determine the payout for either of us to buy out the other.

Taking the exit strategy to the next level, we had a built in tie-breaker and a motivation clause. The tie-breaker was our CFO. If my partner and I ever couldn't agree on something, our CFO was the decision maker. We both trusted him and it gave my partner and I a way to disagree on things yet still let the business move forward. In effect, a tie-breaker is an arbitrator. It's the person(s) you set up to make decisions when the partners can't agree. How much latitude you give them is up to you and your partners. You can force them to pick a side or you can give them full decision-making authority or anywhere in between. The idea is, when things get bad enough that you need to exit a partner, you are likely to be having a lot of disagreements. You want to minimize the impact to the business, and that means someone needs to be able to make the decisions. Someone neutral, preferably. If you have an advisory committee of other business owners, that works too.

The other key piece of our agreement was a motivation clause. I call it this because it motivated us to come to an agreement and move forward. Ours was simple: neither of us could get a paycheck or take a draw from the business until we had resolved the issue. You can't disagree for very long before your stomach will drive you to find a solution.

The final key ingredient was willingness. I wanted to buy my partner out. He argued that the business was worth more than I had calculated and, therefore, he felt that his 50% was worth more. Once we were locked out of paychecks and drafts, we were living on savings. The CFO verified the numbers I had worked up and, in so doing, verified the valuation of the business. The real key, though, was that I believed the offer was fair. In fact, I believed it so much that I was willing to take it. I wasn't happy to take it, but I was willing.

I didn't want to be bought out, let me just say that up front. I had big dreams for the business. I had huge aspirations for our growth and trajectory. However, based on our exit strategy, I knew what half of the business was worth, and, if my partner wouldn't accept it, I would. I knew the business was doomed if one of us didn't step down, and the company was more important than my ego.

Ultimately, that willingness won my partner over. He knew, in his heart of hearts, that he was done. He knew he didn't really want to stick around. He knew he didn't want the stress of the growth. He exercised the exit strategy we'd built into our partnership agreement and walked away. The company was back to one driver and it continued to flourish. In his defense, I'm sure the business would have done well if I had been the one to take the offer and walk away. I'm sure it would have been a different business, but it would have survived.

So, if you're planning on entering a business enterprise with someone(s), make sure your preliminary discussions include an exit strategy. If you're already in a partnership, it's not too late; sit down and hammer out an exit plan now before your views start to diverge. Figure out who your arbitrator or tie-breaker will be. Put it on paper. Figure out the formula for valuing the company. Decide on the critical measurements. Will it be based on profits? Gross sales? Some other key measure? Make sure to record the facet to which the business valuation will be tied.

If possible, perform the valuation now and save that mock-up with the rest of the documentation. That way, when one of the partners inevitably wants a way out, it's already planned out. You'll just need to re-crunch the numbers through a simple, mathematical formula and move on—hopefully with your friendship intact. Again, if you don't have an exit strategy already, the time to set it up is now. If you wait until someone needs an exit, you'll have waited too long and things will be inevitably messier.

Chapter Summary
- You need to have succession plans in place for every position in order to prepare for inevitable growth and turnover
- Balance the depth of your bench with your rate of growth, or the people on your bench will get tired of waiting for you and find opportunity elsewhere
- "A failure to plan is a plan to fail"; the exit plan is the ultimate goal of a business; failure to create on is to embark on a business venture without a vision in mind
- Create your exit strategy now to avoid competing egos in the future

TRUST EVERYONE BUT CUT THE DECK – WHO'S RIDING WITH YOU?

As a leader, you want to believe that people are honest. You want to believe they have the best interests of the company at heart. You want to believe that they would never cut corners or cheat on anything just to pad their bonus or commission. You want to believe they would never intentionally mislead a customer for any reason. You want to believe that people are dependable and honest and good. Most of the time, you'd be right.

See, the nice thing about people, in general, is that they go to work wanting to do a good job. They want to be successful and be part of something greater than themselves. People who go to work to sabotage the place—the true enemies—generally don't last long. Humans are hardwired to want to accomplish things, be successful, and be recognized for their success.

In fact, certain centers of the brain activate when a person achieves a difficult goal or overcomes a challenge. The activation of those centers contributes to a pleasurable feeling (and helps to strengthen self-image and self-esteem). Those neural centers are the reason that humanity has accomplished so much in what geologists and evolutionists would consider so little time. Comparatively, the dinosaurs were around for millions of years and we don't have so much as a flint arrowhead or Styrofoam cup from them.

This mental trigger also means that, even on a completely self-centered, amoebic, stimulus-response level, people want to perform. They want to do their jobs and do them well. So why is it that people sometimes turn jaded or lazy? Why is it that Lee Iacocca had to remove the personal phone lines from the desks of many of Chrysler's employees back in the late '70s and early '80s? It wasn't because those people originally signed up

130

to be lazy.

Social psychologists and organizational behavior theorists have come to understand a number of group-related psychological, social issues. These are things like groupthink, social loafing and entitlement. Thankfully, with the proper training and precautions, these things can largely be avoided or overcome. But first, what are they?

Groupthink

Groupthink is one of the side effects of group homogeneity. It occurs when the members of a group become more concerned with supporting and encouraging one another and less concerned with finding a true good answer to the problems they face. In their interest toward maintaining good relations, team members unconsciously grow more like one another, hiding the traits which don't fit as well in the overall group dynamic.

When the members of a team are all fairly similar—or have worked together for a long time and thus have become similar—they tend to mirror one another's thought processes. This happens because, in the quest for efficiency and teamwork, groups actually unknowingly push themselves toward this state—by unconsciously suppressing dissent and divergent opinions. As they spend more time together, groups begin to function more and more like a single individual. This is good for efficiency and quick responses but very bad in a few key aspects.

First of all, teams suffering from groupthink become much less creative. Because they are all thinking the same way, they have ever greater difficulty in coming up with new solutions for problems. Normally, the biggest advantage of a team is that a divergence of opinion and experience will lead a group to look deeper into the issue and come up with a better solution than any individual would on their own. We hinted at this concept when we talked about getting assistance from your team in Chapter 7 on turning negatives into positives.

Teams experiencing groupthink get very good at administrating existing programs—but only as long as those programs don't experience any new, big problems. As their thought processes more closely mirror one another, team members become more like an individual and begin to lose some of their ability to evolve and change over time. This ties back to their desire to preserve the status quo and the comfort and camaraderie within the group. In other words, they stop adapting because they stop thinking about ways to adapt.

Groupthink's second—and more serious—problem is that of consensus. One of the most famous examples of this occurred in the 1960s with the Bay of Pigs fiasco. There have been numerous studies on what went wrong but the general idea is that a handful of powerful men were convinced that a plan was going to work, and, with their power and persuasiveness, they were able to overrule any dissenting opinions. That included convincing the President of the United States that the plan would work and be untraceable.

The plan itself was to land a number of Cuban exiles back on Cuban shores—after training them to use heavy weaponry—and have them stage a counter-revolution to the revolution Castro had launched just a couple years prior. The leadership in the CIA was convinced that, once the exiled Cubans returned, the average Cuban citizens would rise up in arms and throw off Castro's communist-leaning, dictatorial government.

As it turns out, there were a number of contraindications for the plan spread across the timeframe for the preparation. In fact, a Russian radio station broadcast that the invasion was going to happen just four days before the actual date. Allies and opponents alike knew about the pending conflict—and were vocal about their knowledge. Additionally, CIA operatives in Cuba had interviewed citizens there and found only support for Castro, making it unlikely that the citizens would rebel against their new leader.

Still, Kennedy and, more importantly, the CIA directors in charge of the operation, made no change to the plans. They gave in to their collective ego and ignored the dissenting opinions and information. Leadership's refusal to acknowledge dissenting viewpoints got so bad that some dissenters began to self-censor rather than rock the boat and receive social sanctions in return. In the end, the Bay of Pigs was not only a complete military failure, it was also a political relations failure that many believe led Castro to more fully embrace the Soviet Union and, later, paved the way for the Cuban missile crisis.

Because groupthink results in the team all thinking basically the same way, it's easy for the team members to end up with a false sense of security. When everyone around you agrees that an idea is good, it tends to reassure you in the decision. More importantly, it means there is a huge social pressure to not push back. Solomon Asch[15] studied this phenomenon prior to the Bay of Pigs Invasion, performing his famous study back in the 1950s.

The study found that people have a strong tendency to follow the group consensus rather than be a dissenting opinion. The test was a simple comparison of the length of several lines in which the person was supposed to identify which of three lines matched the length of a fourth. The correct choice was clearly evident, and the answer should have been easy. The hard part of the experiment was that the subject would be the sixth or seventh person to give an answer and all the preceding subjects had been coached to give the same, wrong answer. By the time the subject's turn came around, 75% of them would give the wrong answer—the same wrong

---

[15] A pioneer of social psychology and professor at Rutgers, University of Pennsylvania, Harvard, and MIT

answer that the other people gave—even though the correct answer was obvious. Asch concluded that this social conformity was, at least in part, to avoid the social sanctions of disagreeing with the other members of the group (Asch 1956).

One of the things that makes this more complicated is that group acceptance is the most common form of external feedback that bolsters perceived self-efficacy. In other words, we want the group to like us because it helps us feel better about ourselves. We get the idea that speaking out against the consensus decision just makes people annoyed with us. Unfortunately, if everyone is thinking the same way, and the idea they've collectively decided on is actually a bad idea, that external feedback becomes a trap. It becomes like a single person telling himself that he's had a good idea—over and over again. Eventually, the group members will all believe it. That's cognitive dissonance and rationalization at work on a large scale, and it results in groupthink.

Groupthink is why teams should never stay static for long periods of time. When a project is finished, the demographics of the group should change. While this may result in a slight drag on efficiency, it will help keep groups diverse—preventing excessive cohesion and, therefore, preventing groupthink. Deeper than simple team construction, however, are the hiring practices of an organization. While companies would do well to identify required competencies and hire accordingly, they would also do well to make sure they are hiring people of diverse backgrounds. If everyone is a cookie cutter piece, groupthink will only happen that much faster.

Another way to prevent or limit groupthink is to set the expectation that people should play devil's advocate. Having some sort of a deviant voice in the group can help others feel more comfortable speaking up against a decision. In replications of the Asch experiments, researchers have found that adding a single dissenting voice to the lineup ahead of the subject drops conformity rates to around 5-10%. The reason is that it removes the social stigma of being the only person to speak against the decision. It breaks the peer pressure of conformity and lets people be themselves and share their own opinions again. Kennedy did this during the Cuban Missile Crisis following the Bay of Pigs disaster, and the outcome was much more acceptable.

As a Leader at any Level, you can help prevent groupthink by actively seeking opinions outside the scope of normal sources. You may even consider going outside the company to find a handful of trusted mentors. You can bounce ideas off these people in addition to your team. You should also lead by example in playing the role of the devil's advocate at times and bringing up concerns that may not be popular. A leader needs to look out for the wellbeing of his or his colleagues, helping them avoid social stigma is one more way to help.

Social Loafing

Social loafing is another problem leaders have to be on the lookout for. Any time you have a team setting, you will have a group of people with different calibers of intrinsic motivation and ability. Some people on the team are likely to be your self-starters. Your go-getters. These are the people that crave a project they can take and run with. We all wish that all our colleagues were like this but, the reality is, while everyone comes to work in order to work and find success, they all define work differently and have differing levels of ability. Some people are stars, and some people are potential stars; they're all there to work at some level if you structure things right. If you treat people as at least potential stars—meaning with respect— they will respond better.

These potential stars are the people who can get the job done and get it done well, but who aren't as quick to step up and take the lead. They may have less confidence in their ability or they may just be tired that day. In any case, the bulk of your team will be, by definition, average. They're at their maximum depth for responsibility or they're just not interested in taking on more right now. Either way, they're essential to getting the job done, but they're not going to take the lead on the project. And, as much as we love the stars, these potential stars are more likely to be in control of their egos, and they're more likely to work well with others. Stars have more of a tendency to give in to their egos.

Lastly, if you haven't properly set the expectations, or if you've just completed a merger and have a lot of new personnel, you may have that handful of people who have been sucked up into the system and sort of lost in the works. These are usually your low performers. They may have snuck in, or they may have experienced something life changing that turned off their excitement for their work. The easiest and best thing to do is reassign these people somewhere they're more passionate about—if possible. They were most likely performers before and, with the right taste of success, they can be performers again. Otherwise, termination is the next best option. Sometimes, however, they're still getting enough done that you can't just terminate them. In this case, you need to watch for social loafing.

Social loafing is one of the major causes for the loss of productivity groups experience. To visualize social loafing, imagine you have 10 people who can each generate 1 unit of output. Strangely, when you group them all together and have them work on something, they only generate 9 units of output. This could be for any number of group related efficiency issues but one of the more common ones is social loafing.

This has been studied since 1913 when Max Ringelmann did an experiment involving pulling on a rope—similar to a tug-o-war. He found that the force a group generated on the rope was not equal to the force of each individual pulling separately. Later repetitions of the experiment controlled for any lost effort based on the group all pulling the rope in slightly different directions and showed that people exerted less and less effort the larger the group got.

In effect, each person in the group thinks, "I'm doing more than anyone else. That's not fair so I'm going to throttle back a little." Instead of giving it their all, they scale back to avoid what's known as the 'sucker effect.' The sucker effect is the "gotcha" at the end of a candid camera skit. It's what happens when the final product roles out, and a person realizes that he has done far more than his fair share of the work—yet he receives the same credit as the rest of the members of the group. It's named because anyone who puts forth their full effort in a group when other members aren't working hard ends up as a 'sucker.' Sadly, in throttling back, he puts everyone else in a position of being the sucker and, over time, this results in people trying to avoid effort and work so that they aren't pulling any 'extra' load.

Thankfully, as we've already talked about, people don't typically go to work to slack off and be failures. They go to put forth solid effort and earn success. If that wasn't the case, modern society would have fallen apart long before it started. Humans, like wolves, are pack animals. We have an inner, instinctual drive to participate and support the group. We're hardwired for it. This instinct means that you shouldn't have to worry too much about people trying to avoid the sucker effect as long as you deal with the people who are trying to make suckers of everyone else. Group members' efforts may drop some when a new person joins the group but it shouldn't drop much, and it should recover quickly.

The converse of the sucker effect is the free-rider theory and this one is far more dangerous than the previous example. With this form of social loafing, people might think more along the lines of "We've got enough people here to get it all done without me. I'll just sit back and see what happens." This is clearly a cognitive dissonance situation. A person rationalizes his laziness (without admitting it) by telling himself that he'll just get in the way or that there isn't enough work to do or that someone else would do a better job. Or maybe he doesn't rationalize at all and just accepts the fact that he's being lazy. In either case, he doesn't put forth his best effort and ends up as a drag on the group.

Groups will pretty quickly pick up on this kind of behavior and either make the loafer shape up or make him ship out. Slackers who were trying to justify their lack of effort to themselves will usually come back around and start making an effort again. Interestingly, those who are willfully lazy tend to also be those employees who are defiant—losing them is generally a blessing to the organization.

The easiest way to counteract social loafing is to design your groups to be only big enough to accomplish a task. This establishes more transparency and visibility for the members and helps prevent the anonymity that encourages loafing behavior. If you're daring, you could even make your teams just a little too small. This will force everyone to stay on task or risk failing the assignment. You just have to be careful not to make the group so small that they feel understaffed for the task. You don't want to introduce discouragement by accident. That would be far more detrimental than a little bit of social loafing.

Another idea is to administer periodic team assessments. You have each team member anonymously rate each other team member, and then you examine the trends. As we mentioned, groups tend to notice when one or more of their members are avoiding responsibility even if that avoidance isn't consciously called out. By gathering and aggregating the results, you can get a feel for the trends in the group. The key is to look for trends, not individual data points. Look for trends within a given response set and, more particularly, trends over time. Also keep in mind that, if a team on the whole looks at the assessment as a waste of time, it probably means they either aren't having loafing problems, or they're all having loafing problems. If everyone on the team is being ineffective, you should be able to see that in their output.

The thing is, everyone wants to contribute to the goals of the organization and be fairly compensated for their success. They want increasing responsibility, so they can prove their worth and have more success. A lot of people can seem overtaxed when, in reality, they're ready for another task. Another responsibility. Sometimes, when a team feels they need more people, the truth is that they just need the right people. In Chapter 7, we talked about when the purchasing manager came to me and asked for another employee. In that instance, we made the negative a positive by letting go a low performer and giving the star performer more responsibility—and a significant increase in pay. As it turned out, there were some issues with motivation and ability in that department, and, once we rebalanced everything to eliminate the social loafing, we were able to dramatically improve the situation on the team.

As a Leader at any Level, you have to be especially careful of adding headcount when you're in a high-growth business. The growth and the rapidly inflating numbers can mask the inefficiencies and social loafing. Growth spawns an honest need for increasing headcount, but it's extremely easy to let the headcount outpace the growth. Be cautious when you're working through your financials. If productivity ratios start to drop, you need to figure out why. It could be due to the introduction of inefficiencies like social loafing.

Entitlement

The third issue leaders need to watch for is entitlement. In Matthew 20, of the New Testament in the Bible, there is a parable about a manager hiring new staff—specifically a bunch of temp workers. In the King James Version, it reads:

> *[1]For the kingdom of heaven is like unto a man that is an householder, which went out early in the morning to hire labourers into his vineyard.*
>
> *[2]And when he had agreed with the labourers for a penny a day, he sent them into his vineyard.*
>
> *[3]And he went out about the third hour, and saw others standing idle in the marketplace,*
>
> *[4]And said unto them; Go ye also into the vineyard, and whatsoever is right I will give you. And they went their way.*
>
> *[5]Again he went out about the sixth and ninth hour, and did likewise.*
>
> *[6]And about the eleventh hour he went out, and found others standing idle, and saith unto them, Why stand ye here all the day idle?*
>
> *[7]They say unto him, Because no man hath hired us. He saith unto them, Go ye also into the vineyard; and whatsoever is right, that shall ye receive.*
>
> *[8]So when even was come, the lord of the vineyard saith unto his steward, Call the labourers, and give them their hire, beginning from the last unto the first.*
>
> *[9]And when they came that were hired about the eleventh hour, they received every man a penny.*
>
> *[10]But when the first came, they supposed that they should have received more; and they likewise received every man a penny.*
>
> *[11]And when they had received it, they murmured against the goodman of the house,*
>
> *[12]Saying, These last have wrought but one hour, and thou hast made them equal unto us, which have borne the burden and heat of the day.*
>
> *[13]But he answered one of them, and said, Friend, I do thee no wrong: didst not thou agree with me for a penny?*
>
> *[14]Take that thine is, and go thy way: I will give unto this last, even as unto thee.*

The first set of workers had negotiated fair wages for what they were going to do. As the day progressed and more workers were called into the vineyard, they didn't push for more wages; they were just happy to get whatever work they could and make some money. The entitlement rears its head at the end when the householder starts paying out the wages. The first set of workers was paid fairly, but, when they saw that everyone else was getting the same thing, they were offended. They didn't think it was fair that the later workers should get the same amount of money as they did when the later workers worked for less time.

Unfortunately, humans are remarkably comparative creatures. Much of what we say, do, and think is dependent on what's around us. People with controlled egos, solid character, and self-image don't have this problem as badly as those with uncontrolled egos do. When we know exactly where we stand and what we're good for, we don't have to worry about what anyone else is worth. However, everyone's ego gets a little out of hand once in a while.

Entitlement usually stems from jealousy and a perception of unfair treatment. In the parable, the workers though the fair wages they'd negotiated were fair until they saw the other workers getting the same. They didn't think it was fair that they got the same pay for more time working. On the one hand, I think most of us can agree with the sentiment. On the other hand, these guys signed a contract, in effect.

Entitlement becomes so dangerous because it destroys teams (and communities, families, businesses, nations, etc.). Jealousy, the root of entitlement, turns people against each other. It's the idea of keeping up with the Joneses. Only, in today's day and age, it's more like being the Joneses and having everyone else keep up with you. It's an exercise in ego, pure and simple.

People do need to feel appreciated; they do need honest rewards for their honest efforts. However, entitlement goes beyond what is just or fair. Entitlement steps in when people begin to expect more than they deserve and, once entitlement grows up, it's difficult—bordering on impossible—to help those people be satisfied with fair rewards again. Once they feel like they aren't being rewarded fairly, they start to withhold their effort. They start to socially loaf until they reach a level where they feel that the compensation they are getting is sufficient for the work they are doing. This is an act of selfish defiance.

So how does a Leader at any Level help to prevent entitlement? First of all, make compensation fair. Don't try to sneak extra effort out of people. Treat them honorably and reward them for their efforts. The success of the business depends on the success of all the pieces that make up the business, particularly the people. The easiest way to compensate fairly and prevent entitlement is to put people on a commission structure whenever possible.

In some ways, salaried compensation structures can encourage social loafing and, eventually, entitlement. This happens because the person will draw the pay regardless of what gets done. As long as they stay productive enough to avoid getting fired, they will continue to make the same amount. This makes it hard to draw out that extra, discretionary effort with a salary. I mean, if they can do twice as much as their peers but only receive the same pay, why bother?

Salary encourages people to sink to the lowest common denominator. Now, to be sure, there will be people who buck this trend. As we've said, people want to work hard and be successful. In particular, there are the truly noble who want to come to work and bust their chops just because they know they were born to do it and they couldn't care less what you're paying them. Let's be honest though. Those people are precious, few, and far between. Far more common are those who gauge their fair wage by the amount of effort they're putting forward in comparison to the effort they see others putting forward in the same pay bracket.

Additionally, a little understood concept is that, once you're paying someone a salary, you limit their ability to go above and beyond and do something extraordinary. If you're taking a salary and your boss asks you to go take out the trash or clean the toilets in the restroom or whatever else, you have to go do it. You're getting paid for it. You're selling your time, not your talents. You may have certain job-description based responsibilities, but your real job is just to do whatever your boss asks. Including taking out the trash, if that comes up.

With commission, on the other hand, the sky is the limit on what an employee can do to go above and beyond their duties. Once you've established a fair reward for individual deals, the employee is motivated to go out and make deals. If they want more money, they need to make more deals. It's that simple. If they want to scale back and spend more time on other pursuits, that's their choice. You aren't going to be paying them if they aren't getting work done.

Once people get a taste for commission, most of them will crave it. People don't want to be paid for their time. Not the ones with ambition, anyway. The lazy ones want to get paid for their time. Ambitious, successful people want to be paid for their ingenuity and effort. They want to be paid for their success, not for how accurately they punch a clock. They want the chance to find ways to work less but still generate more money for themselves—and, by extension, the business.

Commission gives this opportunity—and it doesn't have to be a straight sales commission because that doesn't work in all instances; it can be project based with certain payouts attached to certain milestones. As a person works through the project, they get paid out according to their results. Piece-work rates are similar but run the risk of lowered quality. Your data entry people can get paid by the line item. The ones who work quickly will make more than the ones who work slowly. And, all things considered, that's pretty fair.

The other thing commission has over salary is a mind for risk-taking. In a salaried position, there is no incentive to change the status quo. Specifically, there is no incentive to improve it. No matter what you get done, you'll get paid the same. Why try something revolutionary? If you cut the time to complete a process in half, it just means you'll have to do it twice that many times in your shift. For particularly onerous tasks, people are likely to try to find ways to improve the system anyway, but it removes the incentive as a general rule.

With commission, on the other hand, there is always an incentive to improve the system. If you can move more product or decrease your downtime between customers or improve the customer management system, you can improve your paycheck. Innovative, inventive, discretionary effort and calculated, intelligent risks are rewarded through access to ever greater numbers of customers and ever greater paychecks. People will see a direct effect between the improvements they make and the rewards they see for their success.

The answer is to set the compensation figures so that a person is satisfied with the reward for a single deal in relation to the work it costs them, and then, as they work more effectively, they make more. This ensures that people hired on later can be paid at the same rate as those hired on in the beginning, and the experienced people won't feel slighted. It also ensures that the people who join your organization early on can negotiate a fair contract and remain happy with it to the end. It doesn't always happen smoothly, but it certainly works better than salary.

Another advantage to you is you don't have to pay people unless they are producing. When we were just starting out, we realized that we needed someone to start selling computers for us. We were both still selling cars at that point and we wanted someone to get out and start moving product in our fledgling business. Problem was, the business wasn't making any money yet, and we'd leveraged ourselves to the hilt to secure our franchises. My daughter's old swim coach, a young man who had just graduated with his MBA, fit the bill.

He actually came to me to express his interest in joining us and selling Apple computers. When we explained that he'd have to work commission, he didn't bat an eyelash. In no time, he was making sales and moving product—and making a decent paycheck for his efforts. Best part was, my partner and I could afford it because the only way the young man got paid was if he was bringing money into the business.

The thing you do need to watch out for in a commission environment is the quality of the deal. When people are paid for output there is a risk that they will sacrifice the quality in order to improve the quantity. The easiest safeguard for this is to withhold payment on a deal until the money is collected from the customer. If the customer doesn't pay, the salesperson doesn't get paid. You also need to watch out for salespeople passing on deals because the commission would be too low. As a Leader at any Level, it's also your job to be an example of integrity and sales technique. You may also want to sample their work and make sure it's meeting the standards imposed. If not, it's your job to train and discipline as necessary.

The other drawback to commission is that people are unlikely to engage in activities that aren't directly compensated. With a person on salary, you can instruct him to go clean the bathroom. With someone on commission, he's likely to tell you what to do with the toilets and where you can put them. You're not paying him to clean the bathroom.

Now, there are some who will argue that money and compensation are simply a hygiene factor, and that they don't really motivate. These people are referring to the Herzberg hygiene factors. This is the idea that, once a person's monetary needs are met or exceeded, money no longer motivates. That may be true but that's the other place where commission excels. Once you clear certain benchmarks, it's not about the money anymore. It's about getting the high score. Commission naturally taps into a person's competitive nature. Salespeople at that level aren't trying to earn another dollar; they're trying to beat their personal record, or that of a colleague. They're trying to see who can earn the most. It's becomes, in some senses, like a game to them. So it's not just about the money, it's about the success. In this instance, the money just happens to be an indicator of that success.

Cutting the Deck

These problems mean that a true leader should trust everyone but cut the deck. People, in general, want to do a good job but, on occasion, they may try to pull a fast one to protect a growing ego problem. More likely, they are falling prey to one of these psychological issues without even realizing it. The group may have grown too comfortable, and, as a result, they aren't thinking creatively anymore. They may be experiencing a loss of efficiency due to social loafing. They may be having entitlement issues.

A Leader at any Level's job is to diagnose these problems, if they exist, and correct them. If a group is suffering from groupthink, consider switching up the composition of the group. Change out the members to infuse some new blood and new ideas. Have them visit with external experts. Alternatively, put them through some creativity exercises. Ask the tough questions and try to jumpstart their minds. Temporarily dissolve the group and send the various members to work in other groups for a period of time. Do something to help them separate their minds from one another and think critically and creatively again.

Be sure to monitor their output trends and peer reviews. Make sure you're watching for social loafing and, if you see it starting, act early. Talk individually with offenders—and do it in private. You don't want to put someone on display if there's a chance that it's a mistake. A public execution was never a pretty thing, but crucifying someone innocent is a double whammy—and it will have severe repercussions for the team in specific and the business in general. These are the sorts of incidents that can quickly alter a company's culture for the worse.

If you see entitlement cropping up, consider working to restructure the compensation plan to reward people for their efforts instead of their time. Try to limit salaries in favor of commissions and avoid bonuses for 'hard work.' Just be sure that you base commissions in hard data and metrics, not anything that could be subjective. Again, you want to reward them for obtaining business results. Verifiable ones. You can't just reward people for 'hard work,' as we've talked about before. It's too easy to muddy the waters with something so vague and, the moment people sense an imbalance, you run the risk that they'll be after you like vultures. That's another way to ruin your corporate culture.

But the key in all this is to cut the deck. You want to trust your friends when you're playing cards with them, but that doesn't stop you from cutting the deck. Cutting the deck just ensures an even playing field for everyone. You do this whether things are going well for you or not; it's a simple precaution. And you're not asking to be in charge of the whole shuffle; just a single cut of the deck.

Do the same thing with your coworkers. There is a paradoxical phrase, "trust but verify," that floats around. Unfortunately, if you feel the need to verify things, you aren't feeling trust. Still, you can trust your colleagues to do a good job and then take a random sample of their work—like sending in mystery shoppers. You don't need to inspect everything, that's too much like beating people over the head. You don't need to hit people between the eyes with the inspection. If you review everything they do, they will feel belittled and unvalued. They will know you don't trust them.

At the same time, however, you don't want your verification to be in secret. First of all, you want the fear of accountability to keep people from ever straying in the first place. You want them to recognize that, if they get off base, they'll get caught. Sooner rather than later. That knowledge will help them keep themselves more honest. Only the truly psychotic would commit a crime right in front of a police officer. Chances are good that the people you work with are mentally stable. If they know there's a mechanism to catch crooked deals, they'll avoid crooked deals. People generally want to be honest, and, even if that fails, they don't want to get caught.

Second of all, if the time ever comes that you do catch someone in a lie, you don't want him to be surprised by it. You want him squirming in his seat the moment he does something dishonest. You want him to know the expectations, and that he's violated the understanding. You want him worried about getting caught so that, when it happens, he isn't surprised.

This will ensure that he's ready for the consequences. After all, he'll have acted knowingly—and that's defiance; people know the punishment for defiance by now. If you are reviewing people's work without telling them, they will feel betrayed and angry when you confront them. Even though you'll be in the right, you won't really have the moral high ground because you were being sneaky too. A Leader at any Level keeps to that moral high ground.

What's more, if you surprise one of your coworkers by catching them in a lie, they'll gossip about you to everyone else before they go. You'll end up in a situation where your own secrecy has now cost you the trust of your good people. They won't know what to think about how you are acting. They won't know if you're checking into them or not. And, even though they aren't doing anything dishonest or wrong, they'll worry about whether you are underhanded enough to trick them or set them up.

Lastly, if you sneak around, it will only cause the dishonest people to dig deeper and work harder to hide their deeds. The trickier you get, the harder they will be to find. If they feel comfortable and know they can trust you—even though you can't trust them—they are more likely to do something obvious and get caught for it. That's the nature of trust. It lowers barriers instead of raising them.

A Leader at any Level doesn't really do anything secret. A true leader doesn't do anything that needs to be done in secret—not a leader of a business, community, or family anyway. You're supposed to be an example to your colleagues. If you don't want them sneaking around and being shady, you shouldn't be either. If you want them to be trustworthy, you need to stay worthy of their trust.

So trust everyone but cut the deck. Do random quality checks, so people have an incentive to stay honest, but remember that everyone is innocent until proven guilty—and that these people are coming to work to do a good job. The added bonus of doing your homework is that it will keep you more up to speed on what's happening on your team and in the business. That will make you a much better leader. Think of it as reconnaissance.

And because you are then knowledgeable about what's happening, the people around you will be able to trust that you know what's going on—which means they'll be able to trust your judgment. It also means you'll be able to lead, instead of following behind. In short, you'll be better equipped to earn the loyalty of your team.

Chapter Summary
- Groupthink improves efficiency at the expense of creativity—and sometimes common sense; it can lead to disaster if left unchecked
- Social loafing will drag down the efficiency of a team; it's often the symptom of laziness
- Entitlement is like organizational cancer; it stems from defiance and will lead to people withholding effort and trying to hold an organization hostage
- Commission-based incentive structures are an excellent way to prevent entitlement
- Sampling people's work is a simple precaution to ensure quality but must be done with transparency—and should be done in good times as well as bad

DON'T MIX BUSINESS AND PLEASURE – DON'T DRINK AND DRIVE

Loyalty is an interesting animal: it's a blessing and a curse. On the one hand, having a loyal team means you can ask them to go out on a limb and do new and different things—and trust that they'll follow through. You also don't have to worry about cutting the deck as often because people don't want to disappoint you. On the other hand, a loyal team will try to take advantage of you in entirely different ways if you're not careful—it's not nefarious; it's human nature. Let's begin by looking at the specific definition of loyalty:

"Faithful adherence to a sovereign, government, leader, cause, etc" (Random House Webster's Unabridged Dictionary 2001).

In other words, when people are loyal, they will listen to a leader's message and do as it directs. They'll follow orders and suggestions. They'll fulfill their responsibilities without trying to find excuses or ways to get out of them. When a leader has a loyal workforce, he or she can leverage that to accomplish more and be more efficient. Sounds great, right?

Loyalty requires a foundation of trust. That means you have to do what you say and say what you do. We talked about that when we talked about Leaders at any Level being examples of integrity. You can't be tricky or underhanded, as we've just discussed in the previous chapter. However, there's another catch to loyalty and this one will surprise a lot of people: it's worthless as a tool. In fact, it's only included in this book to give a warning about how it can and can't be used—and what it really means for a Leader at any Level.

The problem with loyalty lies in the fact that you can't really leverage it. That may seem hard to swallow, but bear with me while I explain.

If people are doing things because they are loyal to you—and only because they are loyal to you—it means they have no personal belief in whatever you're asking them to do. That's a dangerous situation for a number of reasons: it uses up your socio-emotional capital; it requires no real investment from the people helping you; it sidesteps the safeguards in the business decision process; and it replaces a business focus with an egocentric, selfish one.

First of all, if people are doing things because they are loyal to you, it uses up your socio-emotional capital (good will). In effect, you're having people do personal favors for you. This may be entirely necessary at certain times—like trying to get a new, revolutionary program off the ground—but these times need to be exceptionally rare. These are times when what you are asking only makes sense from a higher perspective, and you don't have the time or resources to pass that perspective down the line. There is no other reason to run this risk.

The problem is, when you have someone do a personal favor for your, you burn up a little bit of the social capital you've built with him. Each time you ask for another favor, you use a little more of that good will. It's like taking withdrawals out of a bank account. Now, if you're being a Leader at any Level, and you try to follow the principles in this book, you're likely to end up with a lot of social capital on your hands. That's a good thing. However, if you rely on it with any level of frequency, you'll eventually use it up—and that can happen a lot more quickly than you think it will. The fact is, the more social capital you have with a person, the more slowly it accrues, and, ironically, the more you use, the more slowly it accrues to replace the withdrawal. What's worse, the more often you ask for favors, the more social capital it takes for any given favor. This is because people will start to catch on to the patterns in your behavior and change their perceptions accordingly, adapting to you.

Worse still, when you ask a favor of someone, the general rule is that you owe him a favor in return. This is the law of reciprocity and, even though it's not actually a law, it carries a lot of meaning and weight in society. This is the feeling you get when someone gives you a gift on your birthday, and you realize that you're going to have to get him something on his birthday now. You know that, if you don't, you'll be frowned on. Violation of reciprocity carries heavy social sanctions.

This is also a double whammy because, while being Leader at any Level will earn you plenty of social capital, it may not earn you favors. In fact, if you're honest with yourself, a true leader is unlikely to earn any favors. You should already be doing anything and everything you can to serve and help the people you work with. That's the whole point of real leadership. That means that cashing in a favor can potentially leave you indebted to your coworkers. Hopefully, after our discussion of needing to cut the deck, you can see how being in debt is a dangerous situation.

No matter how good and honest your colleagues are, everyone is looking for a leg up in this world. Aren't you? Once you owe someone a favor, you can bet the time will come that he or she will cash it in. It may not be right away, but it'll come. It's not that anyone is looking for a way to skirt the rules or do anything illegal, but people want a strategic advantage over you—if they can get it—and you can't afford to give it to them. Now, that may seem harsh and even a little far-fetched so allow me to explain in a story.

Consider the scenario in which you desperately need a report in a short period of time. You go to one of your coworkers and ask him to set things aside and do this report for you. He agrees, based on his loyalty toward you, and, setting aside his other responsibilities for a time, performs the task admirably. Now you owe him a favor. Doesn't seem like that big a deal. Yet.

Later, a promotion opportunity becomes available in a neighboring department. It just so happens that you know the manager over there from time in staff meetings and performance review meetings. Turns out that your report-preparing buddy has applied over for this promotion and, knowing of your relationship with the supervisor, cashes in that old favor to have you put in a good word. Still sounds innocuous, right? I mean, it's just a good word.

Wrong. There was another equally qualified member of your staff who also applied for the position. The one who prepared the report for you gets the job, the other one doesn't. It almost sounds fair since one of them did more work—by preparing that report—except that the reality is that they were dead even for the job—neither was better with people; neither was a harder worker. Whether your recommendation even swayed the end decision or not is actually irrelevant. Everything could have come down to a coin toss; it doesn't matter. The problem is in motion. If the person still on your staff ever finds out about your 'good word' on his competition's behalf, he'll be justified in thinking you're playing favorites.

Can you see how quickly your team could fall apart if people think you're picking winners and losers among them? A Leader at any Level can't afford to appear to be anything but unbiased, impartial, and fair. You can't have the appearance of favoritism, or your ability to lead and coach your colleagues vanishes immediately. The risk is that everyone thinks you're playing favorites and the favorite is someone else. They'll use their selective instance and confirmation bias to see all the times you play favorites and, just like that, you'll have lost all your social capital with everyone.

So, what started out as a harmless situation suddenly blew out of proportion. Is this an unlikely example? Ask yourself that question and take a moment to answer honestly. I don't think it's unlikely; things like this happen all the time. Life is a minefield, and, all too often, we're walking through it blindfolded. A key point of this book is to increase awareness. We're trying to take off the blindfold, so you can navigate the minefield of business and life without taking the wrong step—the one that leads to failure.

It's not like the person who prepared the report wanted the favor so he could do anything wrong. He didn't cash it in to get out of a written warning for absenteeism. He wasn't trying to sneak an excuse for doing something wrong or bad. Everything was acceptable and 'above board.' If the other employee had asked for the same recommendation, you probably would have given it to him too. It just also happened that the process of giving and receiving favors had an unforeseen consequence this time. That's why you don't want to leverage your loyalty. You'll end up owing favors and you may not be in a position to choose how those favors get cashed in. That's not a position a Leader at any Level wants to be in; it's not a position you can afford to be in.

The second risk of loyalty is that leveraging it doesn't require any real investment on the part of your colleagues. They will do the task for you, but, if they don't believe in end goal because it isn't tied to their own success, their work could well be subpar. Let's think about it, they want to help you out because they have loyalty toward you. At the same time, though, they have any number of other responsibilities to fulfill. Are you going to transfer some of their other duties to someone else? What about that person's other duties? The point is, your coworker may not have much time to help you, and, even if he does have the time, he probably has competing priorities to deal with.

If the task is simple enough, he will probably get it done and move on—no problems. Then again, if it were that simple, you'd probably just get it done on your own. If, as is more likely, the task requires some level of effort and investment, it may not be worth his while on its own merit. It may not carry the intrinsic value that his other work does. After all, he has quotas to meet, projects to finish, performance reviews to prepare for, etc. And that's just at work. We haven't even considered the scope of his life outside the office. If your assignment is going to take enough time that he has to stay after hours, then you're competing with every other aspect of his being. Anniversaries, children's birthdays, family reunions, church and community functions, softball league, golf, second jobs, etc.

It's not that he doesn't feel a need to support you. He's loyal to you, remember? The problem is that there are so many competing interests for his time; he just can't do it all. No one has time for everything. In this instance, you may actually cause cognitive dissonance for him. He's loyal to you and wants to help you, but he doesn't have time. Somehow, he has to reconcile that inconsistency. Either he'll downplay a different priority, or he'll downplay you. Regardless of whether or not he chooses to downplay you, the required mental gymnastics can have near-permanent effects on how he perceives you—most likely for the worse.

You may end up on the second tier of priority—or lower—and either not get your favor done on time or get it done at a subpar level. Again, it's not that people don't want to help you—they really do care about you and want you to be successful—it's that you've already got them doing a lot of other stuff. They aren't coming in to work and sitting around waiting all day in hopes that you'll hand them something to do; they already have plenty on their plates. It's an ability issue, not a motivational one. Don't get caught by the fundamental attribution error; just recognize that your priorities may or may not be the same as the priorities of other people. Give them the respect they deserve and don't ask for favors that put them in a difficult position, or you'll pay the price regardless of the outcome.

The third reason that leveraging loyalty is dangerous is that cashing in on it removes a safeguard from the process of business administration. If people are doing something because they're loyal to you, they are less likely to question it. If you think back to when we talked about Constructive Resistance, you want your coworkers to challenge your assumptions and help you bulletproof your plans. Not a knockdown, drag-out brawl, but you want them to have minds of their own. You want them to push back and explore the strengths and weaknesses of your ideas, so you can flesh things out and make them stronger. That's why you assembled this team, isn't it? Otherwise you could have hired a robot or a computer—or someone with no real character.

We'll talk more about the value of disagreement later but, for now, just recognize that you are less likely to receive that critical feedback if you are leveraging your loyalty. The reason is quite simple: if someone is doing a favor for you, he is less likely to think through the implications of his actions. He's trying to help you out, not make a strategic plan. It's an entirely different thought process in his head. More than likely, if you're asking a favor, whatever you're asking isn't on the strategic plan in the first place. If it were, you'd already have it assigned out.

This becomes especially dangerous because you can potentially put someone in a situation where he does something counterproductive by accident. When you think about an actual business decision, how long is the planning and verification process? How many people discuss the pros and cons? Hopefully it's not an overly cumbersome process, but, at the same time, it's likely to have some checks and balances built in to prevent social loafing and groupthink. When you ask a favor, however, your request doesn't have to go through that same process.

No matter how thorough you think you've been, there are parts of any decision that are unclear until they get at least a second set of eyes on. That's due to a psychological concept called "the Curse of Knowledge." In essence, this is the reason professors and highly specialized people have difficulty explaining their advanced concepts to others. They forget that other people don't have the same fundamental understanding to build on. Any time you generate an idea or learn a new concept, you become subject to the Curse of Knowledge. It's the reason lawyers use 'legal-speak.'

The idea is that there are experiences, circumstances, disclaimers, evidences, reasons, and ideas that are related to whatever you are asking for. Things you know about—but your colleagues may or may not. In the normal decision making process, those additional details would be explored and, as necessary, deleted or fleshed out and included in full. When you make the assignment as a favor and forego that exploratory process, you potentially lose clarity in the assignment. As a result, you may be missing consideration of a critical point, but, because the idea has only been in your head, you never made the connection.

Now your coworker has whatever incomplete portion of the idea you gave him, and he's trying to put it into play as a favor to you because he's loyal. Thing is, without those layers of review, it's really easy for you to have made a simple mistake or omission that can cause serious problems. Have you ever tried to make sense of a dream after you wake up? Usually, dreams are full of random jumps and twists that made sense while you were dreaming them but, in retrospect, make no sense at all.

And, the worst part of the whole thing: who's going to be blamed for any problems that your favor might cause? You might take some heat for it, but, more than likely, your colleague is going to come under the real fire because he's the one who actually did it. That's not particularly fair to him, is it?

As a Leader at any Level, you can't risk people like that. You can't put them in a position that their loyalty to you and their sense of the business strategy come at odds. You can't ask them to do anything that might make them feel uncomfortable or put them in a position to end up disciplined.

The final point is related to the third point: taking advantage of loyalty potentially distracts from a focus on the business issues. With the ever-spreading exchange of favors, work becomes a game of personal goals instead of looking at what's best for the company. This goes back to ego and thinking that you know what's best, instead of working with others to figure out what really is best. Alternatively, it still goes back to ego but in the sense that what you want and need is somehow more important than what the business wants and needs.

Abusing your leadership position in this way can confuse the proper lines of communication through the organization. It can cause people to completely lose sight of the business's vision and, ultimately, it will cause them to follow your example and put their own personal goals and ambitions ahead of the company. Instead of viewing the company as a family where everyone sacrifices together to make it a success, they start to look at the organization as a casino. They start to worry about the long-term viability of the operations, and that gets them looking for where they can hit a jackpot before cashing out—with no regard for the continued welfare of the organization.

In families and other relationships, this is called putting the self first—aka selfishness. This is also a very quick, effective way to destroy such relationships. Putting your own ego ahead of the wellbeing of the organizations to which you belong is equally, remarkably dangerous. It's dangerous to your ego because it will contribute to inflationary growth and potentially lead you to lose control of your ego. It's also dangerous to the relationship or business because you shift from a building perspective to an exploiting perspective. No matter how big and strong and established the relationship is, it can only give so much before it gives up. If all you do is take, you'll be running things into the ground. It becomes a question of when you fail, not if.

If you really want to ignite people and get them using that Fourth Gear, don't rely on dangerous games like loyalty. On the surface leveraging loyalty seems like a sure way to win and, to be fair, having the loyalty of your colleagues will help you be more successful. However, you can't rely on loyalty. It's too unstable. Too changeable. Besides, it can put you into any number of situations that result in the loss of your job, the termination of your colleague's job, or the downfall of the company itself.

Instead of loyalty, focus on making sure that the business strategy is right and then focus on making sure it is communicated clearly. If you have the right vision, what's best for the company will also be best for the employee. If you have that alignment, your employees will be motivated to work for the business' success because it will bring them success as well. That's a positive reinforcement cycle, and you want that. Under that scenario, a commission-based pay structure will launch success and productivity to new heights because everyone will be doing the hard work necessary for success—and they'll all be working together for the same success.

Don't harness their loyalty toward you personally; harness their loyalty toward the business instead. Make sure you are asking them to help the business succeed and thrive. Don't ask people to help you succeed, ask them to help themselves succeed—and then show them how to do it. Be the example. If you happen to succeed along with them, all the better. If their efforts lead to rewards for themselves, you won't be indebted with a favor. If your requests are always aligned with the strategic vision of the company, you won't have to worry about they could pass through the standard channels, and you won't have to leverage loyalty. You'll be able to keep you people focused on the things that bring growth and success. People go to work to make a little money and experience a lot of success. If you help them gain that, loyalty and respect are just bonuses to the process.

Which brings up another distinction that needs to be made: that of loyalty versus friendship.

The Double-edged Blade of Friendship

While loyalty and friendship often cohabitate, they are not the same. In fact, if loyalty is dangerous for a Leader at any Level, friendship is absolute suicide. A true leader—a good leader—needs to establish and maintain barriers with his or his coworkers, not friendship. This, again, sounds a little harsh but allow me to explain.

If you recall the example about Joe Money from Chapter 3, he had all the right qualifications. He was smart and trained and talented, but he was also complacent. He'd turned lazy. When I asked his boss to fire him, the boss refused. The reason behind that refusal was the man's friendship with Joe.

As you can see, their friendship cost them their jobs. Now, that's not to say that their friendship was the direct cause of their termination, it wasn't. Joe failed and then turned defiant. He needed to be terminated for his actions. His boss hadn't done anything wrong yet but quickly adopted the same defiant attitude and had to be terminated because he had become a liability. Business can sometimes be a heartless place but, the truth is, it was a cognitively dissonant situation.

Pomeroy IT Solutions was not a place that harbored the defiant. We couldn't risk being in that situation again so, rather than simply terminating Joe, we had to also terminate his manager. They had become friends and that prevented the manager from seeing clearly and doing what needed to be done. I can't say I enjoyed terminating either of them. Joe was a high-caliber guy. I had high hopes for him. I'd expended a lot of effort to get him on board. His manager was a good man too.

Unfortunately, friendship has no place in business decisions. Whether or not you like a person can't have any bearing on whether or not you view them as a contributor or a liability. Joe had become a liability because his defiance was adversely impacting the performance of his branch. When his boss couldn't terminate him, I had to step in and take broader steps. Now, that's not to say that friendship can't spring up in the business arena. It can and often does. I have any number of friends today that I made during my years of work. The difference is that, when the time comes to fire your friend, you can't hold back just because he's your friend.

As messy and painful as it was, there came a time when I had to buy my partner out of our fledgling computer business. We talked about this briefly when we discussed exit strategies but allow me to elaborate a little here. My partner was growing more distant from the business, and, from that perspective, it was time to buy him out. It was a hard decision. We had been partners in the truest sense. We'd been bad cop and good cop. We'd been like two halves of a coin. We'd built our business from a shoebox closet and shoestring budget into a multi-million dollar corporate entity. We'd shot up like a rocket, pilot and co-pilot. To buy him out would mean taking on both sides of the business where I'd only ever had to cover one side before. It wasn't an easy choice.

Still, we couldn't lead together anymore. We'd built a small but lucrative retail business. We'd had a great run of it. However, my vision had developed one way, and my partner's had gone another way. I could see us growing to a billion a year in sales, hundreds of sales people, and offering services instead of just products. I was aiming for the stars one realistic step at a time, but he was still focused on successful retailer mode.

Even with our exit strategy on paper, it was a battle. An uncomfortable battle. That's what you get when you have a face-off between two hard-nosed salesmen though. And, worse than a normal leader-employee relationship where you can just fire the person—maybe write them a nice little severance and be done with it—this was my partner. I had to buy him out and he wanted more than I was willing to give him; more than his share of the business was worth. Ultimately, as I said before, I had to offer to let him buy me out instead. In retrospect, I guess that goes back to the principles of true leadership: never ask someone to do something you're not willing to do yourself. In any case, the company had gotten too big for the both of us to run it together.

A week or so went by while my partner tallied his resources in preparation to buy me out. Finally, he came back, put his cards on the table, and accepted that I'd called his bluff. He took my original offer. I bought him out and he moved on. He was a friend and, after the dust settled, we were still friends. He was a good man. In my view, though, he was impeding the business. He had become an obstacle to progress and, as much as I loved him and as close as we were, I had to separate the needs of the business from my own needs. To have kept him on would have been a horrendous exercise of ego on both our parts.

I don't wish that situation on anyone, and the easiest way to avoid it is to not get so close with your colleagues. Now, I suppose I should pause here to define what I consider a friend to be. To me, a friend is someone you can call on the phone and just chat with. You don't have to have a reason to talk, you can just talk. It's someone you look forward to seeing in person for no reason. My belief is that real friends are probably fewer and further between than we care to admit—especially in this social-media age. Real friends take a continuous, dedicated investment of time and effort and attention. It's not always easy to keep a real friend. Thankfully, it's worth the hard work.

Except in the case of making friends with your colleagues. Be polite and amiable at work, but don't hang out after. When I hear about managers going and getting drinks with their staffs, I cringe. I suppose it might be okay once in a long while—a very long while—but you have to remember the risks of loyalty. Friendship takes those risks and multiplies them tenfold. Even if you think you can get away with owing a favor to a loyal coworker, you won't get away with owing a favor to a friend. What's more, one of the purposes of this book has been to teach self-awareness, so you could better control your emotions and, in so doing, better control the situations you face—especially the negative situations.

Friendship is an inherently emotional thing. Introducing friendship—and all its attendant emotions—to the workplace just complicates things unnecessarily. Don't hang out with your coworkers after work. Go home and be with your family or significant other or dog or sit in the corner and watch TV alone for all it matters. A Leader at any Level can't afford for the emotional baggage that inevitably follows friendship to be interfering with work.

You also need to recognize that your staff has nothing to lose in it. In fact, it's in their best interest to be your friend because it makes it harder for you to be a disciplinarian with them. On the flip side, that makes it harder for you to coach them to rise above their current level. Who wants to punish their friends? As draconic and cynical as it may sound, it's true. If you become a friend to your employees, you will be giving them a huge advantage over you—just like Joe Money and his boss. Maybe you're strong enough to handle it; maybe you can control your ego that well. My question is, why bother? Why put yourself in a difficult situation? Enough issues come up all on their own; there's no reason to tempt fate.

This principle counts double when it comes to family. By virtue of being family, people often think they are entitled to something from you—and, to be fair, they are. They're just not entitled to anything from your business because it's a separate entity. Family deserves your love and respect and care, but that doesn't mean your business has to give the same things. You are not your business—to think otherwise is a huge ego trip—and you need to make sure that is clear to everyone. Set the expectation that you won't mix business with pleasure and set that expectation starting now—including the rule that you won't go into business with family.

Of course, none of this is to say you should be mean to the people that work with you. That's not the answer either—far from it, in fact. As a Leader at any Level, it's your job to help people find success by mentoring them. The solution is simply to set barriers; set limits on after-work activities. Let the team go and mix and mingle and bond, but don't go with them. Remember that, as a Leader at any Level, you have an example to uphold. You need to be mindful of the fact that your example stretches beyond the walls of the office building.

If you go out and do something untoward with one of your colleagues for instance, you can show up to work the next day with a sexual harassment charge on your desk. Don't do that to yourself. Don't put yourself in that kind of situation. Draw your boundaries and stick to them. People may think you're being unreasonable or impossible or whatever, but just take it as a compliment. A Leader at any Level needs to have a tough but fair kind of attitude in order to make the decisions necessary to keep the business running in the right direction.

The Best Motivator

So, if you shouldn't use loyalty and you can't use friendship, some of you may be asking what you should use to lead people. The answer is frighteningly simple: fear. Now, as Machiavellian as it might seem, fear is still and has always been the best motivator. Bear with me here. The catch is, you aren't trying to make a culture where people are looking over their shoulder all the time, waiting for a knife in the dark. Far from it.

You're not trying to make people cower at your name; you want to be their hero—the one who leads them in the paths of safety and helps them avoid fear. You want to be the example of success—the person who meets all the expectations and lives fear-free.

First of all, make sure you set up goals and rewards in such a way that no one can 'steal' from anyone else. If there is going to be competition, you want it to be "co-opetition[16]" not coworker vs. coworker. You don't want an attitude of fear or anger throughout the office; you only want fear as a very subtle motivator. This will come from setting the proper expectations, not any action you take directly. The idea isn't to use fear directly; rather, to use it indirectly.

Once the expectations are clear, people will understand both the requirements and the cost of failure. They will also know that you have backups to backups to replace them with, if necessary, and that you are cutting the deck. Essentially, you're building a rock behind them so they have nowhere to go but forward into the hard place—into success—right where you're going to lead them. You don't make them fear you or the company; you want them to fear failure—to be failure averse. The best fear, if you can manage it, is the fear of disappointing themselves or their family. Imagine going home to tell your spouse or friends that you failed and got fired. That becomes an intensely powerful, intrinsic motivator to ignite that Fourth Gear and push on for success.

So it's not about whips and threats; it's about coaching and training. It's about making the consequences of failure very, painfully clear—and then teaching people everything they need to know to succeed to such a

---

[16] The idea that they are all competing to be at the top, but that they can't sabotage anyone else's efforts

degree that they stay well clear of failure. It's not about being a dictator; it's about being right there in the front lines, leading the way. Every leader wants to be a hero and that's okay. It may be stroking the ego a little—and it may be the wrong kind of ego in some cases—but we all love it anyway. We all want to know that we've been helpful to someone else. It's part of the instinctual programming that drives us for success.

So be a humble hero. That's really what a Leader at any Level is: a hero figure. Teach people failure aversion and then help them avoid failure. They'll love you for the success they have, and you'll be rewarded with success of your own.

Chapter Summary
- Loyalty is a mixed bag: it's helpful to have, but you can't rely on it
- Don't cultivate loyalty to you personally, cultivate loyalty to the business
- Friendship is too dangerous for the workplace; be polite and thoughtful to your coworkers but don't hang out with them outside of work
- Fear of failure—failure aversion—is the best motivator; it will engage the Fourth Gear better than anything else
- Set clear expectations to establish failure aversion; then model the example and offer help to make sure no one fails

NOTHING IS IMPOSSIBLE – THE EXPRESS LANE

Emerson tells us that "Whatever course you decide upon, there is always someone to tell you that you are wrong. There are always difficulties arising which will tempt you to believe that your critics are right. To map out a course of action and follow it to an end requires courage." After forty years of business experience across three industries and in a broad range of very different positions, I fully agree: sometimes, following the roadmap is hard.

As we talked about in Chapter 1, if something in life is worth getting, it's worth working hard for. That's what having a tough but not impossible attitude is all about: hard work. It's not about shooting for the stars like an uncontrolled ego would. It's about setting realistic but difficult goals and then igniting the Fourth Gear to meet them. It's about not giving up at the first sign of trouble—or even the tenth sign—it's about pushing yourself further and harder today than you did yesterday. As the Navy SEAL motto says, "The only easy day was yesterday." Success is about doing more than the minimum and more than what's expected.

When I was financing cars, we had the seemingly impossible goal to become the number one dealership in terms of sales. We were 95th of 105 dealerships in our zone at that point and little place to go but up. Still, that's a steep hill—to climb 94 positions. We knew that we were setting an extremely difficult task in front of ourselves. To tell ourselves it would happen quickly would have been to make the goal impossible. Still, it was something we felt we could do in spite of the odds.

Now, there are any number of factors a dealership could be rated on, but we wanted the factor that indicated success. When you're in car sales, what better indicator is there than that of selling cars? Besides, the district office kept track of all the dealerships in a ranking already so we wouldn't have to fabricate a way to keep track of where we stood; it was already distributed regularly. So we got to work.

The first thing we did was work to better integrate the F&I (financing and insurance) team with the salespeople. Previously, the two departments had been somewhat siloed—operating independently for no reason. Over time, this had led to a certain amount of hording and protective behavior. The salespeople didn't want to hand things over to the F&I people for fear they might lose a customer. I suppose that a hard-driving F&I guy might push too much to upsell a customer on some after-market accessory and, as a result, potentially drive the customer off, but the risk of that was low. We wanted the sales too. In any case, the status quo had the two teams working separately.

We didn't want the status quo though. We've all heard the saying that the definition of insanity is "doing the same thing over and over and expecting a different result." While it's debatable whether or not that actually qualifies as insanity, the saying makes a great point anyway. Perhaps the better way to put it is "if you always do what you've always done, you'll always get what you've always gotten." This isn't entirely true either because, eventually, someone will figure out how to do what you've always done better than you do it, and they'll put you out of business. But I digress. Having a tough but not impossible attitude means looking at the way things have always been done and having the courage to try something new, different, or revolutionary. That's what we wanted.

We wanted to double-team every customer. No one goes to a car dealership unless they're at least somewhat interested in buying a car. What's more, a car is, in today's day and age—and back in the late '70s—not really a luxury. Unless you live in New York or some other big city with a well-developed mass transit system, a car is a need, not a want. You may want a car that's way outside your means, but people understand that they probably won't get a new Ferrari as their first vehicle. With that in mind, you still need some sort of transportation and the best place to start is the dealership. The answer for us was finding the right buttons—finding those hot topics that would move a customer from 'interest' to 'intent to buy.' That's why we wanted to double-team. We wanted to bring all our weapons to bear.

The salesmen knew the products. They knew how to match people to a vehicle and its features. They knew how to sell cars but they had one major problem: they couldn't make people afford the cars they were being sold. No matter how hard you might sell a Camaro to a kid just out of college, he probably couldn't afford it. That's where the F&I team came in. It was our job to look at the credit of the situation and make sure we were playing in the right league. If we had a young married couple on the lot, we were probably looking at something more entry-level. If we had a wealthy business tycoon, we had a few more options. We could also look at trades differently and adjust the sales process to account for them. By combining the strengths of the sales force with the strengths of the F&I team, we could get so much more done; we could start moving more cars.

The next thing we did was to focus on inventory control. In car sales, inventory is life. Sales are success but, if you don't have the vehicle in stock, you can't sell it. No matter how good our double teaming was, we couldn't sell it if there wasn't the right vehicle to sell. For instance, we could've sold Monte Carlos and Camaros all day long from open to close and made more money than would have been healthy, but we didn't have that many. As a small, slow dealership, we were small-fries to the factory reps. We'd beg for the cars we wanted, and they'd ignore us; we didn't have a big enough splash. We needed to start moving more volume if we wanted to earn their attention. Thankfully, moving more cars was already part of the plan.

So we got creative. We started ordering in cars that nobody wanted— cars the reps had to allocate somewhere but couldn't. We used the vehicles as courtesy vehicles for the service department or body shop rentals. By doing that, we earned favors from the reps. That meant better allocation. When we got young customers in, we sold them on the car they really wanted, then double-teamed and educated them on the hard reality of credit and how they would need to get this other, entry-level car for a couple years to build credit—thereby selling them what we needed to move. Then a couple years later, we'd see them back to get them into what they originally wanted. That meant moving inventory which equaled better allocation.

Some cars were doing so poorly in the market that we sold them just to move them—maybe $50 over invoice or, in some instances, maybe not a penny of profit. We just gave them away just to get our numbers up. We even had an advertising blitz about how low our prices were just to get people into the dealership and shop; then we 'sold' them a car at our cost. We were just trying to turn the low-end inventory so we could keep the truly profitable cars coming in. It was tough to put in the time and effort to move a car and get nothing for it but, overall, it was paying off. We were able to increase our sales volume and customer base, and that meant better allocations. Slowly, we were accelerating our success and getting in more inventory. That meant we needed more customers.

So we started offering a nominal referral bonus for customers. It was only $25 but that was late 1970s money. It meant a bit more then than it does today. A gallon of gas was only around $0.60 or $0.70. If anyone needed a car, we wanted a chance to be the ones to sell it to them. Why let them go elsewhere? Now we had the inventory to meet their needs. By pioneering a referral bonus, we were able to get a lot more customers coming into the dealership, which meant that many more sales, which meant that much better allocation.

We also stayed lean, keeping fixed costs down. Where other dealerships had fancy, new buildings and acres of paved lots, we had an ancient office in a run-down part of town and a big dirt lot. It wasn't pretty, but it meant our biggest cost was the cost of the cars from the factory. This little fish was growing up into a fit and trim shark.

Keeping costs down helped us keep prices down too—a fact we advertised heavily. Having prices down helped us bring in still more customers and move still more cars, which meant more volume of sales, which meant we could get more of the vehicles we wanted, which meant we could sell more vehicles that earned us more money. Customers may not have been impressed by the appearance of the dealership, but they appreciated the deals we would cut them, and that kept them coming back. Everything looped back into getting more cars sold, getting better allocation, and maintaining better margins. That was our goal, and we were getting to be the best at it.

Moving from 95th to 1st takes time, effort, creativity, and desire. In fact, it took more than three years to get there. It might be possible to grunt-work your way up that whole ladder but being tough also means knowing how and when to work to get the best results. We were trying things that, today, might seem hokey—or even stupid—but they were revolutionary at the time. We were doing what made sense for our target market, not what made sense to the other dealerships. We didn't want to be like everyone else (ordinary); we wanted to be different (extraordinary). For five, straight years, we advertised a $359.95 AM/FM radio and cassette unit for $69.95. We set our prices low enough that we had everyone believing they couldn't get a better deal anywhere else, taking us from about 30 cars a month to over 500.

Having a tough attitude shouldn't overrule common sense. That would just be giving in to your ego. Having an intelligent, tough attitude means you need to be even more careful about your ego. You have to really watch yourself to make sure you are staying on track and staying reasonable. When you get down to the brass tacks, you need to be sure you're still playing the right game. Anyone can set a tough goal and start moving toward it. A Leader at any Level sets a tough goal and then monitors it, adjusting the expectation as necessary as they get closer to the end and get a better picture of what's required.

Taking things one step at a time allowed us to succeed. When the number one dealership suddenly found themselves as number two, they were shocked. No one had anticipated our tough but not impossible rise to the top spot. Then the tough but not impossible goal was to stay at number one—and, trust me, getting there was easier than staying there. Our rise woke everyone else up and gave us some real competition. As things heated up, it became even more important to stay level-headed and maintain a laser focus on our strategy and goals. To let our ego in just because we'd succeeded would have guaranteed that someone else bumped us back down just as quickly as we'd made that final jump.

The problem is, if you let your ego get away from you, you'll end up locked in a fight that you either can't win, or that you shouldn't win. Remember back to our discussion on ego in the first chapter when we talked about uncontrolled egos setting impossible, shoot-for-the-stars type goals and then falling short? Even if you managed to sacrifice enough to reach a goal like that, you still have to count the cost. Did you spend two dollars to earn one?

I had this happen at Pomeroy IT. After I retired, I stayed on with the company as a member of the Board. I was usually involved in the management process but it wasn't 'my' company anymore because it had been public for years and I was retired. Following some tough times in late 2005, the rest of the Board out-voted me and brought in the wrong kind of CEO. We started to spend a lot of money to 'fix' things, but it didn't work. The new focus was on systems, rather than our previously successful strategy of growth through acquisitions. After spending a lot of money, the Board declared its efforts a success; the issue being that they were talking about operating margins—which had already been positive—completely ignoring the millions they'd spent on 'system improvements' to make the 'profits' happen. They were dipping into the cash and credit reserves to fabricate success that just wasn't there.

They call that a pyrrhic victory, which is really just a fancy way of saying you lost even though you beat the other side. That's what happens when you get more concerned with victory than success. When you let your ego get in the way, it's easy to stray over the line. Issues with the Board at Pomeroy IT prompted me to, ultimately, take the company private again.

I had another experience that was heading for pyrrhic victory at best or defeat at worst following our divorce from Computerland—when we decided to take Pomeroy IT in its own direction—but this time it was of my making.

Computerland just couldn't keep up with us anymore. We had grown too fast, and they couldn't keep up with our growth. We would order inventory, and they would be backordered and out of stock. As an aside, their inability to get the right inventory and keep sufficient quantities in stock later contributed to them going out of business entirely. But, to make things worse, when they did get us product, they would sometimes ship us the wrong things or miss critical deadlines and delivery dates. At first, that was just to be expected in such a new industry. As a more recent example, Apple couldn't keep the first iPad on the shelves either. Demand just outstripped the supply. Really revolutionary products and industries are like that.

After a while though, it was killing us. Now, to be fair, I want to make sure I emphasize the fact that the whole industry was growing so fast that it was a mess everywhere. Still, we had relationships directly with the manufacturers, why did we need some middleman distributor? It didn't make sense for us to source everything through Computerland when that just added one more step in which things could go wrong. We needed to cut them out of the supply chain and eliminate that risk point for product damage or mix-up.

To be clear, because of my frustration with Computerland, and my eagerness to tap into faster-moving business, we did things a little wrong. I can say that in hindsight. At the time, however, Computerland was telling us that we weren't allowed to go public. They were quickly turning into an anchor that threatened to drag us down. Our franchise agreements were just about over anyway, so we broke off and went our own way. We didn't cancel any orders or anything, but we certainly didn't place any new ones. We went straight to the source instead. That ended up as something of a mistake.

The issue, from my point of view, was that they owed us 1.7 million dollars in rebates and miscellaneous receivables. We weren't about to let that go. We couldn't really afford to let it go either. The real kicker, though, was that we didn't believe in quitting, and accepting that debt as a write-off[17] felt too much like quitting financially. We were going to be tough instead. We had a clear case, and theirs was murky, at best.

On the other side of the table, Computerland felt like we'd robbed them of their right to royalties—$3.3 million in royalties, by the time all was said and done. As a franchise, we were supposed to pay a percentage on everything we sold, but we weren't about to pay them until they paid us. Ultimately, they decided to bring a lawsuit against us for failure to pay. The suits and countersuits went on for years—like a thorn in the lion's paw. Still, we weren't about to accept that charge-off and that meant we had to stand tough; we had to hold our ground. Well, we got to trial and pretty soon it was clear that things weren't going our way. The California jury was leaning toward the Silicon Valley company, not the one from Ohio.

I was actually pacing the floor at my hotel room in California during the trial when I realized what had happened: rather than just being tough but not impossible, we had strayed over the line. I had let my ego get involved, and it had pushed us too far.

Consult With an Expert

Over the years, a litmus test I've developed is to call an expert. It doesn't matter whether they're in your company or not; if you're facing a

---

[17] Erasing the debt from the books by taking an equivalent write-down against equity and calling the debt a lost cause

situation that they're an expert in, give them a call. They'll know whether you have legs to stand on, and they'll see right through your ego in about half a second. I only wish that, in this case, I had thought to call an expert sooner.

I ended up calling a man I'd known from Computerland; though neither of us was part of that organization now. He'd worked closely with the CEO during his time there and knew both of us. In talking with him, it became clear that neither side was going to back down quietly. We'd each let our egos get too involved. We were doomed to a drawn-out, bloody battle with at least one of us as a guaranteed loser unless we could get creative. We just had too much ego in the game.

Thankfully, my old contact gave me a suggestion: instead of trying to settle the suits in court, I could simply start doing business with Computerland again. At this point, they desperately needed the sales, and we had a segment of our business that we could move over to them without too much headache. We agreed to pay a little extra on the cost margin, and we made the deal. In just a few minutes, the Computerland CEO and I had unraveled years of lawsuits and arbitration that had gotten us nowhere. Calling an expert had helped me check my ego, which, in turn, helped the CEO of Computerland check his ego, so we could each see clearly again.

And that's the risk you run if your ego gets involved. A Leader at any Level has to be tough. You have to be tough because, if you aren't, the business world will eat you alive. It's cutthroat, make no mistake, and the weak and the small will be trampled unless they stand firm—sometimes even if they do stand firm. The catch is, sticking to your guns puts you in serious risk of letting your ego get away from you, so, in standing firm and being tough, you have to keep extra careful tabs on yourself.

Unfortunately, as we've discussed, once your ego engages, you won't be seeing clearly anymore. The ego has a nasty habit of shielding its own influence to make you think you're still seeing clearly. That's why, normally, I encourage you to steer well clear of situations that might cause you to lose control of your ego. Since avoiding the edge isn't an option in this case, I'm going to recommend a different strategy to keep a check on yourself. It's what I did in my hotel room during that trial: call an expert. The fact of the matter is, the only person your ego can really fool is you. Everyone else will see through your bravado in surprisingly little time.

As best as you can, keep a panel of advisors and mentors—people you can trust to give you their expert opinions on a range of things. Once you have that panel, you can go to them when you've been holding tough and nothing seems to be happening. The idea behind being tough is that you should see movement. You should see progress. It may be painfully slow, but you should still be getting somewhere. Otherwise, what's the point? Once things seem to be stalling or sliding backward, it's time to start checking that you haven't strayed off course and into the realm of your ego.

I've talked about my experience with trying to collect rebates from a huge manufacturer already and I'll talk about it again in the next chapter, but it validates this important point. Rather than focusing on my interactions with the people at the manufacturer, however, I want to take a step back and focus on what was going on behind the scenes for me.

You see, backing me up at Pomeroy IT was the accounts receivable team. In this case, they were my experts. I had learned to master the different financial reports, like the P&L, but that didn't mean that I was creating those reports. I still had experts on the team to crunch the hard numbers of the business. My previous life with Beneficial Financial had taught me the ins and outs of collections, but it had been decades since I'd been in the industry.

So, one day, I was meeting with the amazing people in the accounts receivable department to talk about this massive debt we were owed. We knew we couldn't take a write-off for it. We couldn't afford that; it would have sunk the business. The stock would have dropped through the basement, and we would have lost our jobs and the company. Still, I had learned a lesson in years of bloody conflict with Computerland: you can't threaten people because then you have to follow through. I had fought that losing battle before, and I didn't want to put myself in a position that I would be fighting like that again.

I was willing to be tough and to be an example of indomitable willpower. I was willing to put in all the hard work it took to drag success out of the claws of defeat, but, at the same time, I had to make sure I wasn't straying into the realm of ego. I was ready to be David and stand up to Goliath, but I had to make sure that my determination hadn't blinded me to reality. I didn't want to put in all that time and effort and hard work if it wasn't going to matter anyway. I had to check with the experts and reset my bearings before things went further.

We all sat down in a big meeting and, carefully, I laid out the facts to them. They helped to supply some of the details that I didn't know and, eventually, we all felt like we had a pretty good picture of the overall situation. Then we sat back and looked at each other. It was a huge, difficult task we had set out for ourselves, and I could tell that some of them were wondering how it could possibly be worth it. I may have wondered just a little myself.

Then I looked over at Robin. She had a lot of experience in receivables and I valued her honesty in particular. So I asked her, "Looking at all this, do we have a chance? Is it even worth moving forward or should we just drop the whole thing? Can we do this?"

She looked back at me and said, "Yes. They owe us the money."

And that was that. I was ready to do what it took to protect the company. They were ready to do what it took to protect their company. We buckled down and worked at it. It took a couple years but we made it happen. The situation was tough, but not impossible. As a Leader at any Level, I had to set that example. You can too—by recruiting experts from inside and outside your organization to help you know where the limits of sanity are.

One of the things that amazed me about that whole experience was that none of those people—not one of them—asked for anything in exchange for their extra effort. They knew that hard work was expected, and they were ready and willing to do whatever needed to be done. One of the best experiences was being able to walk down there and give each and every one of them a little cut of that impossible debt after we'd recovered it. Not a bonus for their hard work, a bonus for doing what so many had thought was impossible. A small commission off that huge, impossible debt we had recovered. They had followed my example and stood tough, but, equally importantly, they had supported me and counseled me.

The experience reinforced to me that people don't go to work to sit around. It reinforced to me that people are intelligent and driven, and, if you can give them an appropriate challenge and treat them with the appropriate respect, they'll rise to the challenge. It reinforced to me that people crave success and that their attitude is the driving force behind fulfilling that craving. As a Leader at any Level, you have the privilege of setting the tone for that attitude, and it's your job to make sure that you set it tough.

Nothing is truly impossible in business. It might seem like something can't be done but it's only your ego that makes things impossible. When your ego slips in and takes over, it can make things impossible. It can close doors to you. Like my experience with the rep from the major grocery store chain. When my ego stepped in, that door was quickly slammed in my face. Years and years later, however, my son was actually able to get a foot in that door and bring them on as a client. It would have been impossible for me because my ego had ruined things years before.

The same is true of the 'divorce' from Computerland. Resolving things amicably was obviously not impossible because, in the end, that's what we did. The problem was that I let my ego in early on. I let myself believe that I was right and someone else was wrong, and I stopped considering any other explanations or ideas. When I finally woke up and escaped from the clutches of my ego, the CEO of Computerland and I were able to fix things in half an hour. Tops. After years of failed litigation and far more stress than either of us deserved.

Nothing Is Impossible in Business

That's the real key of having a tough but not impossible attitude. You want to be tough but you don't want to make things impossible by injecting your ego to the mix. Being tough also means you have to be self-aware, observant, and careful. If you'll be those things, nothing will be impossible to you. If you believe otherwise, you should probably get out of business as quickly as you can because the market will eat you alive. If you still don't believe that nothing is impossible, let me give you a few examples that you probably take for granted now.

People once said that cars would never reach a mass market. Turns out, it wasn't impossible. People once said man would never fly. Turns out, it wasn't impossible. People once said there would be a global market for five or six computers and that the average man would have no need or interest. Turns out, it wasn't impossible. People once said we'd never touch space or put a man on the moon. Turns out, it wasn't impossible. People once said no human could break the four-minute mile time. Turns out, it wasn't impossible.

The thing about 'impossible' is that it turns off the imagination. Instantly. The moment something is termed 'impossible,' the implication is that every permutation and combination of every possible idea has been tried. What if Edison had stopped after 500 failures in his quest to find a better filament for the electric light bulb? Thankfully, he didn't, and the company he built, General Electric, later improved on his work to give us the electric lights we have today, nearly a hundred years later.

The great thing about humans is that they are ingenious and driven to make something greater than themselves. I know I've said that before but it bears repeating: people want to be successful. To someone who truly wants success, nothing is impossible. However, the word itself will shut down creativity.

Henry Ford is reported to have said, "Whether you think you can or you can't, either way, you are right."

Certainly, the adaptation of the assembly line to the automobile industry was revolutionary. It had never been dreamed of, and it did wonders to commoditize the car and put it into the hands of the average American and, ultimately, the world. Cars already existed. Assembly lines were already used in limited applications. No one had put the two together, and it was thought impossible that the car would ever become a widespread machine.

Ironically, Henry Ford started versions of the Ford Motor Company and failed twice. The first attempt went bankrupt and the second attempt actually became Cadillac when he left the company and took his name with him. It was only his third attempt—which also almost failed—that finally gave us the global company that still bears his name today.

We've talked about failure aversion and how leaders don't let themselves fail, so it might be helpful to clarify just what 'failure' in that sense means: the only real failure is giving up. Quitting. When something doesn't work, or something doesn't go your way, that's not a failure; it's an opportunity to learn—and it happens all the time. However, if something doesn't go your way and you quit trying? That's failure. When you surrender, you fail.

To have an idea not work, in some respects, is inevitable; it's a side effect of calculated risk-taking. As a Leader at any Level, you need to have the courage and the attitude to be willing to keep throwing things at the wall until something sticks. Just like with the discomfort of cognitive dissonance, don't be afraid of taking a risk and having it turn into a mistake. That kind of failure is just a side effect of learning. It is widely accepted that you learn more from failure than from success. This doesn't have to be true but it often is anyway. The reason is that, when an idea doesn't work, the inventor tends to introspect. He stops and thinks about what he did and how he could do it better the next time around. When you succeed, there's not a lot of drive to stop and think about how to do it better in the future; you got the job done already.

The other main aspect of having a tough but not impossible attitude relates to discipline. Discipline, believe it or not, does not mean punishment. It has come to be synonymous with punishment over the years, but the root of the word is shared with disciple. In other words, follower. Discipline is really the act of helping someone get in line. It's helping them apply themselves in the proper direction. Discipline should take the form of coaching and training, not punishment. It's the act of helping someone become a disciple. The most important part of discipline is the example you set as a Leader at any Level.

Threats Are Less Effective Than People Realize

In relation to this, you should never have to threaten a colleague. This may seem to be at odds with what we talked about in the last chapter regarding fear, but bear with me. When we spoke about fear, we pointed out that it should be neither fear of you nor fear of the company; it should be fear of not being part of the company anymore. Fear of being cast off. Fear of failure.

The critical piece to this is establishing the right expectations and making sure that those expectations are fully understood. Once people can clearly see the dividing line between success and failure, they will know where they need to be. If they aren't there, then you need to take corrective action by determining whether the failure is due to ignorance or defiance. If the problem is ignorance, the person needs discipline; they need training and coaching. If the problem is defiance, the person needs to be terminated. Plain and simple.

Issuing a threat, then, is a useless gesture. All it does is instill the wrong kind of fear in the ignorant and give the defiant more time to prepare against you. The wrong kind of fear will be counterproductive for the person you're trying to train. Instead of learning to trust and follow you, he'll want to avoid you and the discomfort your presence causes. For the defiant coworker, he wants you to threaten him. It tells him he's succeeded in making you angry; it also tells him that he's successfully bought himself more time in the organization. What's more, it gives him a clear warning that the end is coming soon and allows him time to leave a legacy. Typically, it's not a legacy you want left behind.

Instead, be decisive. If you've properly established the expectations—like you will after reading this book—people will know when they've fallen short. Hopefully, they've come to you before it's too late and sought guidance, support, and training. Even if they haven't, it's your job to determine if their failure is related to ignorance or defiance. Don't waste time on threats. Just do what needs to be done. Make it happen.

The problem with a threat is that is has to be acted upon eventually anyway. You can either fire that defiant employee or you can tell him you're going to fire him. If you threaten him and he doesn't shape up, what's next? Are you going to threaten him again? It didn't work last time. Are you finally going to fire him?

It's your choice, but I believe that having to deal with his defiance and the lost productivity it causes is too high a price. And, if you can't ever bring yourself to fire him, you have an ever-growing problem on your hands. Eventually, that defiance will spread. When people see their coworkers acting out and nothing happening in retribution, they'll act out too. People come to work to work, but, if you leave them in a situation where they have to drag a failing teammate along, it's going to impact their productivity too. Remember our discussion about social loafing and cutting the deck?

And what about the ignorant employee? If you threaten him, he is more likely to turn defiant. The natural response to hostility is to return fire with more of the same. If you let your anger out, people are likely to respond with anger of their own. If you start hammering on that employee, and he doesn't feel like he's been trained to do what you're asking, he's going to go away thinking what an ineffective manager you are. He'll spread that around and, ultimately, he'll want off your team in whatever way he can—often by becoming so burdensome and damaging that you have to fire him.

Threats will entirely change the culture of your organization. Punishment is unpleasant but, if the expectation was clear, punishment is understandable and acceptable. Threats, on the other hand, are just psychological warfare. The person has committed the error but not been punished—yet he's still left with the burden of some future, as yet indeterminate punishment to come. It just puts an unnecessary stress on the mind of someone who got up to come to work that morning to have success and contribute to something bigger than himself. All that does is stir resentment which, if left unchecked, leads to defiance.

The fact is, threatening someone is really just stroking your own ego. I mean, ask yourself the last time you were threatened. Did it motivate you to do a better job, or did it motivate you to freshen up your résumé? The appropriate fear is fear of failure—fear of being less than your best. No other fear is appropriate. You want people to have the same tough but not impossible attitude that you do. You want them to stare into the face of difficulty and challenge—and then laugh at it. You don't want them to see you coming up the hall and have them feel the need to go and hide. Threatening someone is just gratifying your own illusions of power by trying to make someone grovel in front of you. A Leader at any Level doesn't need that kind of gratification.

That said, there are situations were intimidation is appropriate—but that still doesn't mean threats. Instead—and more powerful—is a simple reminder of an expectation a person is at risk of failing. Express your disappointment or ask if they are just craving attention. Let them dream up their own punishment. Chances are, their failure aversion will inspire them more than any threat you could make. This is particularly useful in situations like the ones we talked about in turning negatives to positives when we discussed changing the agenda. When people come to complain to you, turn the conversation back around and help them focus on the areas they should be working on. This reminds them of the expectation and, if they aren't meeting it, motivates them with the appropriate fear of failure. They already know the expectation—and associated punishment—they don't need you to remind them while you stroke your ego.

Divide and Conquer

And, while we're on the subject of potential confrontations, let me give you another warning: when people are defiant or failing expectations but are unwilling to accept the consequences, they will often seek safety in numbers. There is real danger for you in this because, once you're outnumbered, it's easier for them to trigger your ego and emotion. The reason is because it triggers your fight-or-flight response and makes you less likely to think clearly. You're outnumbered and that's dangerous.

The best thing you can do in a situation like this is to divide and conquer. Stand firm, be tough and face them separately. If two or more employees come up to you to lodge a complaint or argue with you, tell them you'll meet with them one at a time. Tell them it's so you can make sure you hear their individual sides of the story. Let them know you're interested in the details. As a Leader at any Level, you are interested in the details, right? You want to know everything about the situation, so you can help prevent it from happening with anyone else in the future.

I made the mistake of letting the two young men gang up on me when they came to demand part-ownership in the company. It ended badly. No matter how skilled you are, two heads are better than one. If they outnumber you, they'll likely outsmart you. There is strength in numbers, and you don't want to be on the wrong side of that equation.

That's why I acted so quickly to isolate Jack when he asked the benefits question in the annual sales meeting. I had to be tough with him and put him on the spot not because I wanted to offend him but because I couldn't afford to have so many people ganging up on me at once. No one is brilliant enough to argue with a whole room. That's why politicians always end up looking so dumb when you get them in front of a few dozen reporters. They're outnumbered. Thinking you can beat those odds is just an exercise in ego—and a recipe for failure.

So, again, it comes back to controlling your ego. Having a tough but not impossible attitude means setting clear expectations and being strong enough to hold people accountable for their actions. Don't back down, but don't rise up either. There's no need to threaten anyone, just do what needs to be done without the announcement. If the expectation has been violated, the appropriate punishment has been earned. There's no reason to delay it in order to stroke your own sense of power.

A Leader at any Level has to be tough enough to survive the rigors of business. You can do that. A Leader at any Level has to be tough enough to set hard goals and then work to make them happen. You can do that. A Leader at any Level has to be tough enough to hold people accountable for their actions and mis-actions. You can do that too. In business, nothing's impossible.

Chapter Summary
- Choose your course wisely and then use everything you have to follow that course
- If you start to feel like you've strayed off track, consult an expert to get your head clear and get back in the game in the right direction
- Where there's a will, there's a way; nothing is impossible in business
- Threats are counterproductive; if a person has violated an expectation, they have earned the punishment—no threat required
- When you have a group confront you, divide and conquer or they are likely to engage your ego and make you lose control of the situation

Communication – the Home Stretch

We've talked around the topic of communication again and again in this book—particularly when we covered setting the right expectations in Chapter 5. Obviously, in order to set those expectations, you need to be able to communicate effectively. Now it's time to get into the meat of things—and the dessert of this book—and figure out what it really means to be an effective communicator.

Lou Holtz[18] gave a speech in which he identified three main elements for true communication:

- Are you committed?
- Can I trust you?
- Do you care about me?

It struck me, back when I heard it, how comprehensive that was—and it stuck with me through the years since. As I look back, I still feel it holds true. At the same time, I want to dig a little deeper and see if we can really discover the power of those three elements.

First is commitment. According to the dictionary, commitment is "engagement; involvement" (Random House Webster's Unabridged Dictionary 2001). I like to look at it as presence. Not presence as in the aura a person carries with them, I mean presence as in 'present and accounted for.' Basically, when you are with someone, trying to communicate with them, you need to make sure you're really there. You need to be there not just in body but in mind. Consider the implications of being in a conversation and not really paying attention. To help drive the point home,

---

[18] The head football coach for a number of prestigious universities, sports commentator, author, motivational speaker, and member of the College Football Hall of Fame

let's use an analogy.

Let's say you're in Driver's Ed. Like most teens, you already know everything so there is very little reason to be engaged. You know that the gas pedal makes the car go forward and the brake makes the car stop. You also know the steering wheel changes your direction. Since you already know everything and you've got way more important stuff to think about, you decide to tune out the instructor.

Well, now it's time for the driving component. You go out to the car and suddenly realize you'll be driving a manual transmission. Some of you are probably clamming up right now. Others are thinking, 'I can drive manual.' There's another issue too though: you'll be driving a British car (so you'll drive from the American passenger side) and you'll be driving through an obstacle course. By the way, all the instructions for how to equip your safety gear properly were covered in class—the instructions for how to navigate the course properly too. How are you feeling now?

The sad thing is, we do this to ourselves all the time. Sometimes, it feels almost painful to stay engaged, but, unless you do, there's a good chance you'll miss something important. It's like being introduced to someone before you're really ready, and, halfway through the conversation, he drops your name, and you realize you don't remember his.

In order to display your commitment to another person's success, you must have the determination to stay engaged with the conversation. What's more, you have to have the determination to stay in the present tense of the conversation and stay on board with the program. Commitment to the people around you manifests in the use of true listening skills.

Listening is a complicated skill set to develop because it's more than simply sitting quietly. True listening is a concerted effort to hear what a person is saying, what they mean to be saying, and, most importantly, what they aren't saying—all at the same time. Sound difficult? It takes practice.

Listening For Content

First, the easy part. Listening to what a person is saying. There is a popular saying that "we have two ears and only one mouth, meaning we should listen twice as much as we talk." For some people, this comes easier than for other people. Some people are naturally quiet. They are natural-born listeners in this regard. However, listening and simply hearing are two very different animals.

Hearing is the act of remaining silent while someone else speaks. It's the physical process of sound waves entering your ears and being processed to the brain. It's simple, reflexive and thoughtless. You hear things all the time without even realizing it. Close your eyes for a moment and open your ears. What do you hear? Cars driving by on the road outside? The hum of the a/c or heat blowing? Your coworker tapping on his desk in the next cube? Someone talking just up the hall? Maybe just the brush of your hand across the page of this book. More than likely, you hear something.

The brain receives thousands of stimuli every moment, and, being the amazing organ it is, the brain processes and files all that away. Think about when you hear a car alarm go off. It gets your attention for a moment, doesn't it? You think—even if only briefly—is that my car? But you don't perk up the same way when someone starts talking in the next booth over at a restaurant. That's because most of what you hear each day is just white noise. It's unimportant. Trying to actively process it all would be overwhelming and totally pointless. The problem is, that filtering process can sometimes predispose us to tuning out other people when we ought to be tuning in. For all the multi-tasking our brains do, they can't effectively multi-task conscious thoughts or points of focus. Want some proof? Try reciting your ABCs in your head at the same time that you count from one to twenty in your head. And no cheating by using your fingers to count. Harder than it sounds, isn't it?

This inability to multitask poses a problem for conversation and listening because we can only either process what a person is saying or generate a response at any given time. Listening is an active process that requires focus and concentration—so is the act of planning out what you want to say. It's mentally impossible to do both simultaneously.

Thankfully, it doesn't generally take much time or effort to come up with a response so delaying that action doesn't generally put a conversation off track. At worst, it means you seem like you're hesitating—I prefer to call it 'gathering my thoughts'—before speaking. However, failure to process what a person is saying can lead to all kinds of misunderstandings and train wrecks. Just like our Driver's Ed example a little bit ago. It's like trying to solve a word problem after only reading half of it.

Because speech patterns don't allow us to frontload all the important information, ignoring part of what someone says while you think of a response to what he started with will rob you of precious details that came in the latter portion of his message. Ironically, if we could frontload all the important information, we'd just drop the extraneous stuff and you'd still have to listen the whole way through what a person was saying to understand his full meaning.

So why do we want to jump the gun on responding rather than waiting our turn? It's an ego thing, mostly—and not the good kind of ego. A lot of times, we feel that the rest of what the person is saying will be unimportant. After all, he'll put the really important stuff first, won't he? Why save the best for last? It's like reading a news story. We expect to get all the details in the first two paragraphs so we can move on. However, since space runs a premium for newspapers, why would they waste space by printing extraneous information? People are the same. How often do you add a bunch of irrelevant details into something you're trying to say? Why would anyone else be guilty of it any more often than you?

Another possible explanation is that we feel that what we have to say is too important to wait. Sometimes, someone will say something that you feel like you just have to respond to right then and there. You can't wait and risk losing the thought—not to mention that the speaker might inadvertently change the subject before he's done and you'll lose your chance.

Well, hold the thought anyway. If he is going to change the subject before he really gets through his first thought, the first half of it was more likely to be introductory and only tangentially related to his real area of concern. People typically finish on the note they want you to take away from their comment. It's why everything ends with a conclusion. We're wired to do that from the time we enter school. Ironically, that's why small talk is sometimes so hard. There are no conclusions in true small talk and that makes many of us uncomfortable.

A third reason we want to respond before the person is done speaking is that we may simply feel like we already know what the other person is going to say. Especially when we deal with people we know well, we tend to assume we already understand their thought processes and what they're going to say before they say it. We think we've shared enough experience with a person to read their mind. It's awesome and effective when it works but, unfortunately, more often than not, we're wrong. People aren't robots, and they're a lot harder to predict, in specific, than we give them credit. As a species and in groups, behavior follows some fairly regular patterns. As individuals, however, we're just that: individual. No two people are alike, which means no one can always predict what another person is thinking or feeling. So don't try.

The point is, for whatever reason, we sometimes think we don't need to wait until a person is done talking before we can tune out and tune into our own thoughts: resist the temptation. As a Leader at any Level, you want other people to pay close attention to your instructions. That being the case, you need to be an example of that same level of attention for when others are talking to you.

The idea behind truly listening to someone is that you should be able to rephrase and repeat what he tells you. You should be able to summarize the highlights of what he told you. Try it sometime. Don't parrot it back word for word; instead, internalize what he said and paraphrase it. You'll find that, in doing so, you often elicit more information as the other person tries to clarify what you understood. Sometimes, you'll find out that what he said was actually nothing even remotely close to what he meant. Paraphrasing his words will help him realize this and give him a chance to have a second try.

Whether he tries to clarify or not, he'll know you were listening to what he was saying; he'll know you are committed to him and his success. That earns you respect and trust—and it earns you time to think through your response and clarify as necessary to make sure you are delivering the message you think you are. If you're giving him your full attention, more than likely, he'll reciprocate. Commitment breeds commitment, and, if you will show others you need success for them, they'll need it for you in return.

Trust is the second key of communication. It comes in two major forms. First, people need to be able to trust that you will give them the time of day. They need to know you'll actually listen. This goes back to commitment and listening. People want to know they'll be taken seriously. If you don't pay attention to them, you'll violate that expectation and lose their trust and their respect.

Second, they need to trust that you won't throw them under the bus for what they're saying. They need to know that what they tell you will stay between you and them. As a Leader at any Level, you will often be privy to information that others don't receive. It's one of your responsibilities to keep secrets. When one of your coworkers makes a mistake, don't put him on display to everyone. Don't make him an example. Save that for the people who come out in defiance. For people who honestly make a simple mistake, give them the benefit of the doubt. They're coming to work to do a good job.

When my grandchildren do something wrong around me, I don't go to their mother. I handle it myself and consider the matter finished. Once I've taken care of it, there's no reason to get anyone else involved—and risk a second round of punishment for the child. In the same way, when one of your coworkers comes to you with a mistake, do what needs to be done and have done with it. There's no reason to parade anyone's "dirty laundry" around for everyone else to see. That will only guarantee that they never come to you again.

You want people to know they can come to you for help in fixing their mistakes. This has some pretty big benefits for you as a Leader at any Level. If people willingly come to you with their mistakes, it ensures that you'll hear about those issues in a timely manner and also means that you'll have more chances to coach and train. When we talked about ego, and then again with turning negatives into positives, we mentioned that you want to turn around your mistakes as quickly as possible instead of trying to hide them. The same holds true for the people working around you. If they trust you, they're less likely to exercise their ego and try to hide problems. This gives you a lot of power.

However, the moment you begin using secrets against people—either by blackmailing them or by ratting them out—you will lose all respect and trust. All the power you may have had will evaporate. In other words, don't let the trust go to your head; don't let your ego get control of you. Giving in to your ego will cost you more than the trust and loyalty of those close to you; it will have much further reaching effects as well. It will instantly craft a very dangerous reputation for you. So make sure that, when something is told to you in confidence, that you keep it that way.

In conjunction with your ability to keep confidence, people need to know that you won't take advantage of them for what they're saying. As opposed to blackmail, this is more like mockery and teasing. It's the idea that they'll say something in the wrong way, and you never let them live it down. That destroys trust and confidence too, and makes a person less likely to engage in conversation with you in the future.

Listening For Meaning

In order be effective at maintaining this aspect of trust, you need the second skill of listening: the ability to listen to what a person is meaning, not just what they're saying. This can get very complicated very quickly. The English language—or any language, really—is full of double meanings, references, quotations, citations, puns, irony, sarcasm, etc. The list of things that confuse normal communication goes on and on and on.

In fact, in American English, nearly anything can mean nearly anything else in the right context and delivery. It's almost like words hold no real meaning of their own and everything is conveyed by the other characteristics of the speaker and delivery. Is it any wonder that miscommunications abound? So the second key of listening is not to simply hear the words a person is saying and pay attention to process everything; the second key is to dig below the surface.

For this skill, you have to listen to not only what is said but how it is said. Look for signals in the speaker's body language. Look for environmental cues. Listen carefully to the patterns of intonation and word choice. Look for signs of the person's emotional state and what baggage they might be bringing to the table. Listen for negatives that can be turned to positives. Listen for Constructive Resistance and defiance. Remember that, when people are in cognitively dissonant situations, they often choose words that help to relieve themselves of the weight of the dissonance. Words that help them rationalize things. Consider the following two statements:

"We lost another customer today."

"We successfully divested a troublesome account today."

I'll grant that the information is ever so slightly different. In the first version, there is no indication that the account was difficult. However, there's no guarantee that the second statement was entirely accurate in that regard either. Think back to our discussion on cognitive dissonance. The mind has a very powerful ability to rationalize things away. The fox couldn't know that the grapes were sour, but he convinced himself they were because it was easier than accepting the idea that he'd failed. We run the risk of doing the same thing when we face a failure situation. No one wants to be a failure, and no one wants to admit that he gave up—which is true failure. No matter how strategic it might have been to quit, no one wants to be a quitter.

Getting back to the example, the account might not have ever had any trouble in the past, but, at this meeting, the customer had some requests that the second salesman didn't think could be met. Maybe the requests truly were outlandish. Maybe they were just outside what the salesperson was willing to do. Maybe it just would have taken discretionary, unrewarded, extra effort for the salesman to fulfill the request and he's in the middle of a tight month.

In any case, the salesperson may have decided that the request was only the first in a never ending list of demands and, therefore, decided that the customer was now a difficult one. Again, the specific reasons behind this example are less important than simply realizing that multiple explanations exist, thereby remaining self-aware and helping us avoid the fundamental attribution error. We ultimately want to know if this salesperson is undertrained or just lazy. Is he ignorant or defiant? We won't know without further research, and we'll never learn if we've already made up our minds.

Going back to the report itself, though. You can see how both phrases, in essence, say the same thing. At the core, both mean 'we have one fewer customer.' The key is in the pitch. The spin. Don't believe me? Go listen to the politicians on both sides of a sensitive debate. Each side will spin the other side's message to paint it in a worse light and spin their own message to make their view sound more appealing.

Which news would you rather receive? That you just lost a customer or that you divested a troublesome account? Hopefully you said 'neither.'

So you can listen closely to your colleague and understand what he said in literal terms but then you have to look at the deeper meaning. You have to peel away the layers of reference and loaded language to understand the true meaning. Then you can load it back up again and understand another meaning based on the way the information spins. The person in the first phrase was sad to lose the customer. He regretted it, or he at least recognized that it was probably a bad thing. You get more of a feeling that he fought to preserve the relationship but lost the customer anyway.

With the second phrase, you get the distinct—and disturbing—impression that the salesperson is excited to see the account go. The salesman labeled it 'troublesome.' He likely didn't use all his skills and effort in an attempt to keep the account. From the look of things, he was more than willing to let a customer walk out the door than he was to try to save the relationship, nurture it, and make it fruitful again—he was unwilling to put in the hard work to make the negative a positive.

Based on these deeper looks, we may also be able to infer something about the ego of these two people. The first salesman was more humble about the experience. He was pained by the loss of a customer. He values his customers and worries about what their loss will mean for the business. He may be inept, but he's certainly not defiant. If this was an avoidable situation, this salesperson just needs more training. Maybe you could do more joint calls and model best practices and behaviors.

The second salesperson, on the other hand, thinks he already has the answers. He thinks he's got enough experience to know best. He views customers as expendable. He may also be unwilling to accept failure. Losing a customer is an unfortunate reality; it happens occasionally. Sometimes it really is a good thing—or can be turned around into a good thing, as with the multi-national client in Chapter 7. Regardless of whether this loss was favorable or not, it implies a lack of skill on the salesperson's part. He wasn't reporting a mission accomplished or he'd have named the customer to allay any fears in the supervisor. Instead, to avoid the cognitive dissonance this failure might cause, the salesman spun it to make a failure sound like a success. This is a prime example of rationalization—self-brainwashing.

Would you rather have a salesperson who is honest with you or one that only brings you good news? You answer to that question might say something about your ego…

I remember hearing about a young man once who was having trouble with putting together his résumé. He had several years of work experience but the only job he'd ever had was on his family farm. Doesn't sound like much, huh? Well, as it turns out, the young man's family owns a huge, multi-million dollar operation. This guy was in charge of a team that did all the work for a specific region of the farm—including responsibility for the million-plus dollar budget for purchasing and maintenance. He had a team of a dozen or so people that he had to manage. How many twenty year-olds do you know who have managed a million-dollar operation and more than a dozen, full-time employees? They're out there, to be sure, but they're few and far between. What the young man didn't realize was how the spin of what he'd done mattered if he wanted people to understand what he'd really done.

In addition to watching for word choice and speech patterns, another part of this second listening key is the idea of watching the nonverbal cues. When people take a protective stance, for instance, it probably means they're worried by what they're going to say and are getting ready to defend themselves. If they take an aggressive stance, it might mean they are presenting something controversial and are daring you to challenge them. It might also mean they are very confident in their assessment. While polygraphs have been pretty well debunked by science, people often still wear their emotions on their sleeves—if you know how to look. Ironically, it's usually because they haven't trained themselves how to be self-aware and in control of their emotions.

The location where someone chooses to engage in communication with you also means something. If your supervisor calls you to his office, he probably has something serious to discuss. It might be either good or bad but he's probably not calling you in to chat about the weather. If a colleague bumps into you in the hall and starts a conversation, on the other hand, they're either in a serious hurry to get the message across or topic probably isn't particularly important. If your significant other invites you out to a fancy restaurant, he or she is probably either looking to escalate things or terminate them. The seriousness of the setting will most likely reflect the seriousness of the message.

This reality is based on cognitive dissonance. You don't go to a busy fast food place to do something serious because serious things don't happen in fast food restaurants, they happen in serious, up-scale restaurants. You don't talk to your supervisor about a pay raise or new promotion in the hall because those discussions don't happen there, they happen in private places. You don't go to the conference room and fire up the projector to talk about the movie you saw the night before, you stay at your desk or somewhere out of the way. The point is, people will usually seek a setting that seems to fit the overall importance and mood of the message they want to deliver.

Of course, this is not foolproof, and you need to be careful because the delivery and setting of a message shouldn't outweigh the message itself. Still, being able to put things into context can help add layers of meaning or clarify vague components. As a major caution, though, don't trick yourself into believing that this second key of listening will work in absence of effective use of the first key. If you can't bring yourself to listen to the message, no amount of context clues will help you clarify its meaning.

Listening For Omissions

Listening deeper into a message will help to establish trust and show commitment. The other thing it will do is begin to show that you care about the speaker—the third component of effective communication. In order to show that you really care, you need to employ the two listening skills we've discussed and one more. The third skill is the ability to dig even deeper below the surface to find out what's not being said. This shows your concern and care because it shows that you are really trying to look out for the person's best interests.

Oftentimes, when we don't say something, it's because it's embarrass-sing to us. Other times it's because we feel the information is irrelevant. Or, maybe, we just weren't thinking about it at the time. As a Leader at any Level, you want to be able to really understand all the facets of the conversation and the situation. Sometimes, very serious sources of influence aren't ever mentioned. If you can dig in far enough to understand those factors and take them into consideration, you will be showing people that they are important to you. That you care about them and what's best for them.

Make no mistake, though, this is by far the most difficult skill because the signs tend to be more ambiguous and be more open to interpretation. For this skill, it helps to know the person with whom you are conversing. It helps to know how he approaches conflict and what his ego is like. The better you know him, the more likely you are to be correct.

You can still listen for what's not being said without knowing a person, but it's more difficult. Points to focus on are things that would normally come up in a similar conversation. It's almost like trying to find a light switch in the dark. You know where it should be, in general, but that doesn't mean you'll get your hand on it on the first try. Then again, once you do track it down, you can light up whole rooms of information you couldn't see before.

For example, if you're talking to one of your vendors, and he isn't bringing up a critical point—like delivery date or capacity—you want to be mindful of that. It's possible that he just forgot to bring it up, but it's possible that he's hiding something or about to make a deal that he might not be able to keep. It might not be malicious—or even intentional—but that won't help you when he can't meet your demand and the product arrives late.

Likewise, if you have a customer who doesn't bring up volume discounts or doesn't really seem interested in invoice terms, you might want to explore that more. He could either be so flush that you can score yourself a better deal, or he could have no intention of paying you for any product you ship him. The point is to know the battlefield so you can look for the clues of things people aren't addressing.

I was on vacation once and went to a fairly upscale hotel. I said very little to the people at the check-in counter and went quickly to put my bags in my room. I hadn't been there long when the phone started ringing. It was the concierge. They had noticed my tennis bag and wondered if I would like them to schedule some time on the court for me. Then they continued on to explain their dinner options and ask which I would be most interested in. I had said nothing about tennis or dinner when I checked in, but the personnel were trained to look for cues. I felt like they cared about me individually because of the time they took to read between the lines and guess my needs.

A couple times now, we've brought up an example of when Pomeroy IT was buying enough volume from one of the manufacturers that we had accrued about $20 million in rebates. It was money we needed, and money that the manufacturer wasn't interested in paying us. Over the course of a couple years, five or more meetings with senior people at the company, and any number of phone calls and letters, we were able to resolve things. I remember one meeting in particular, though.

I was meeting with the CFO and we were going through the numbers. In storms the President of the PC division—the guy who owed us the $20 million—and slams his fist on the table before saying something like, "I'm sick and tired of you and your little company and this rebate nonsense. We're not paying your exaggerated numbers, so just stop wasting our time."

I didn't threaten back, and I didn't get emotional. Instead, I replied, "You've got to pay us. You can slam your fist on that table as many times as makes you feel good, but the facts are the facts. Now, I don't know how you treat your thousands of other retailers and I don't really care, but Pomeroy IT Solutions is one reseller you are going to pay."

I could tell he was mad. I could tell he didn't want to pay us the rebates. He'd said as much before, and this wasn't the first time I'd met with him. But that wasn't the whole of it. What wasn't he saying?

Probably that we were just one of thousands of distributors, and, if they paid us, they would have to pay a lot more people. I wasn't going to talk about it to any other companies—that wasn't my style—but things like that tend to get out eventually. In that regard, we were only the tip of the iceberg. We may have been a mighty big tip, but, no matter how you looked at it, we were still only one of thousands of retailers for them. Even if everyone else was only doing a fraction of our business, that was a lot of fractions. Anything times 5,000 starts to add up quickly.

Thankfully, I had learned some lessons. I was able to keep control of my emotions and keep control of the situation. I decided to listen between the lines and took a different approach from my previous meetings:

"So let's say you only owe us $10 thousand of the $20 million. Would you pay us the $10 thousand?"

"Sure, I guess."

"Okay, we'll send you some information." That was the start we needed.

By listening to what wasn't being said, I was able to pick up on a few things. First of all, it was a big chunk of money, even for this industry-dominating manufacturer, and there was some sticker shock over swallowing the whole thing. Second of all, there were a lot more sharks out there who might come calling if they smelled blood in the water, and just rolling over and letting us take the whole pound of flesh would have left a lot of blood in the water. Lastly, and perhaps most importantly, they weren't interested in getting involved in a legal battle over it. Neither was I. I'd tried that in the past during the divorce with Computerland and it hadn't worked, so I made sure not to threaten this time.

Still, by using what we'd learned from what wasn't said, we were able to slowly work through the process, proving things one step at a time. Eventually, after long, painful weeks and months, we were able to recover our money.

That's one of the biggest risks to real conversation and quality communication: ego. I'd had previous experiences that were fairly similar—with Computerland and with the rep from the grocery store—in which I'd let my ego get the better of me. It had caused me to believe that I was right and the other party was wrong and, no matter what, I wasn't going to back down. I learned my lesson from those. This time, I kept my ego in my back pocket where it belonged. I tried to listen and learn—and it paid off.

The problem with ego is that it tricks you into thinking that you know best. Once your ego starts creeping in, you stop using these three listening skills. You stop looking for clues of what people aren't saying because you stop feeling like they know anything important. You stop reading the environmental and verbal cues because you stop thinking there might be multiple interpretations to what a person is saying. Lastly, you stop even really listening to what they say because you are too busy thinking you already know what they're going to say, and you're too busy thinking about what you're going to say back. In that environment, communication is dead.

And, once your ego starts to show, you can say goodbye to any feelings of commitment, trust, or caring in the conversation. If you let your ego out, the only person you'll be caring about is yourself. If you let your ego out, people will know they can't trust you. If you let your ego out, people will see that you put yourself above everything else—that you are where your commitment lies.

As a Leader at any Level, you need people to be willing to approach you for anything and everything. In order to encourage that kind of behavior, you have to make it safe to talk to you. You have to show them that you're committed to them, that you are trustworthy, and that you care about them individually. The best way to do that is to master the listening skills we've discussed—and then go out of your way to use these skills.

Sadly, truly good listeners are something of a novelty—these are skills that ordinary people just don't spend the effort to develop. The good news is that you can be extraordinary; you can develop all these skills. It's up to you; do you want to be ordinary, or extraordinary? Even small steps in the direction of effectively listening will make the people around you notice. They may not consciously stop and think that you're becoming a great listener, but they'll know it anyway when they feel your care and commitment. They'll know it, and they'll show their trust by coming to you more often to seek your advice and help.

Chapter Summary
- True communication requires commitment, trust, and genuine care
- Listening is more than just hearing; it's synthesis, thought, and attention
- People often say one thing yet mean another; a good listener will pick up on the meaning, not just the actual words
- Emotional, sensitive subjects often cause people to leave out critical information; by listening for what's omitted, you can show people that you are fighting for their best interests and concerns
- True listening skills are not only rare, they are the hallmark of a great leader

---

Success – You Have Reached Your Destination

I had the good fortune, early in my career at Pomeroy IT to ask an older gentleman about what it takes to be successful in business and how you know when you're 'there.' He told me that it takes five years. Five years to build a strong customer base and a strong capital base. I have always valued his wisdom. In many ways, he was a very short-term mentor for me.

Success is an interesting animal in that regard. He told me it takes five years grinding away at it. At the time, I'd only been in business two years. I don't put stock in his five-year deadline anymore, but it was exactly what I needed to hear to keep me hanging tough in the early, dark days.

I have a friend now to whom I gave the same advice. This friend was starting an insurance company, and he wondered how long it would be to see success. I told him five years. After five years, he was unconvinced—so, laughingly, I told him to go another five years. It's been more than ten now, and he has, indeed, found success. The point isn't the five years, it's the long-term horizon. Success is a marathon; it takes time and requires patience.

Success doesn't come by the wave of some magic wand. Success comes by dedication and perseverance to a goal; it comes by igniting that Fourth Gear into relentless determination to avoid failure. Unfortunately, success only rarely comes quickly. For most of us, we work at it our whole lives and only see it when we look back. In fact, just reading this book is a success in its own right.

So what does all this mean? We've talked about a lot of things in our time together. I hope they've enriched you and helped you to clarify your vision and determination. As I think back over all the lessons the 'school of hard knocks' has taught me over the years, I wonder if there's any way to ever really do those lessons justice. I think this book does.

At the beginning, I posed the question "Why do people fail when they think they know what it takes to succeed?" I hope you realize some of the answers now. People fail because they don't plan ahead far enough; they don't set up their backups and their exit strategies. They fail because they don't study to understand people and human behavior. They fail because they don't treat people with respect; they don't recognize that their employees are intelligent and driven by challenge and success. They fail because they forget to separate business and pleasure, and they cross lines that shouldn't be crossed. They fail because they don't take time to understand the language of business and the financial health reports that show the inner workings of the company. They fail because they decide they can lead from some corner office instead of leading by example.

But, when it all comes down to it, the Ego is the biggest reason people fail. It's a lack of self-awareness which becomes, in effect, the root of all business evil. Proverbs 16:18 in the Old Testament of the Bible tells us that "Pride goeth before destruction, and an haughty spirit before a fall."

From Enron to the Ma & Pa stores that go under; Ego is the real culprit for failure. Mostly because it's so easy to have a little success in business. Having a lot of success is exponentially more difficult because the external pressures grow exponentially; still, anyone can have a little success, and that can very quickly go to the head. Unfortunately, the moment it does, we set ourselves up for failure. Success and ego cannot coexist for long.

There was a man I worked with, once upon a time. He'd started a computer retailer, same as me, and, over the years, we'd gotten to know one another. He was a nice guy. Likeable. Driven. Smart. Well, over time, his business started to struggle. He was having a more and more difficult time staying afloat. Things weren't looking good. So I did something I don't normally do: I threw him a lifeline and hired him, merging his business into mine.

In exchange, I set out some clear expectations about how he was going to run the business with me. I knew his ego was going to be a problem, but I also knew how brilliant he was—and we needed that kind of intelligence. We needed his help mastering a just-in-time inventory, reducing shrinkage to zero, eliminating product losses, etc. He was very smart when it came to distribution, and Pomeroy IT needed that. He and I worked closely with one another, and, for five years, he did some pretty amazing things for the company. He helped bring in acquisitions and overhauled our distribution system and saw a lot of success. Unfortunately, I could see tiny instances where his ego was threatening to creep in: customer complaints about not listening, employee complaints about ego, instances where he tried to take more credit than he was due, a tendency to always blow his own horn, etc. The issues started small at first but, over time, things got worse.

Then one day, he came to me and asked to be president of the company. He was running a huge chunk of things already so, in some respects, it was the next logical step. Still, I told him it wasn't the right time because I could see his ego threatening on the horizon. He asked why, and I decided to give him a chance to prove my point. I laid out a list of things that I expected him to do over and above the things he'd already done. These were things related to keeping his ego in check, not just business goals. He stormed out.

Sadly, he had only reinvented himself to a point. He'd failed in his own business, gotten his second chance, and, by his intelligence and hard work, gotten some success. In the face of that, his old habits started to resurface. He started to indulge his ego again. For those first five years, he'd kept his ego under control and done amazing things. When he started to let it out, he started to have problems again.

People started to see through his ego. He started to make mistakes. He started to think more of himself than the business and the people in it. He started to feel entitled to run the company, not because he wanted to improve it, but because he wanted the status of being the CEO. Unfortunately for him, I couldn't let that happen, so he resigned. I had to remember to keep the company first.

We've covered a lot of topics in these pages. It's been an interesting exercise for me to try to boil down my experience into a manageable form. This book has actually been a decade in the preparing and writing, but if you have learned just one thing from these pages, then it has all been worth it. My goal isn't to set myself up as the wizard behind the curtain. I'm here in front of you, mistakes and all. I know well enough to know that you'd see through my ego if I tried to fill these pages with it. You're too intelligent for that.

But that intelligence is the very reason that I know you can succeed. You can be a Leader at any Level. You can ignite your Fourth Gear and be an example of the principles taught in this book. Are they guaranteed to uncover all of life's mysteries and solve all your problems? No. Are they guaranteed to help? Now we're talking.

You see, humans, at our core, are social beings. Since the cavemen, we've been communal creatures. We live together, we hunt together, we fight together, we bleed together, and we die together. That's what it means to be human. It means we take care of one another. It's not about ripping off someone else, so you can take an imaginary step forward. We're not a race of parasites all trying to suck the life out of everything else. That's not what makes humanity great.

What makes us great is our ability to conquer our fears and walk into the field of battle trusting that our colleagues are behind us—never looking back. What makes us great is our uniqueness, our differences, and our ability to learn to understand one another in spite of those dissimilarities.

What makes us great is our ability to confront an uncomfortable situation and, instead of shrinking and begging for someone else to take over, rise up and make it our time to shine. What makes us great is our ability to plan ahead and stage contingencies, allowing us to turn bad situations on their heads and bring home victory. What makes us great is our ability to understand complex problems and principles and, through perseverance and communication, work our way through them in the pursuit of success. What makes us great is our ability to master the most difficult enemy out there: our selves.

The truth is, what really makes us great is our ability to go even further and step outside ourselves and contribute to something greater and grander than what any one person could ever be on their own. It's that Fourth Gear.

It is my hope that this book will, at least in some small way, help you do just that. Best of luck on your personal, communal road to success.

BIBLIOGRAPHY AND ADDITIONAL READING

Aguinis, Herman, Ryan K. Gottfredson, and Harry Joo. "Delivering Effective Performance Feedback: The Strengths-based Approach." *Business Horizons* 55, no. 2 (March-April 2012): 105-111.

Asch, Solomon E. "Studies of Independence and Conformity: I. A Minority of One Against a Unanimous Majority." *Psychological Monographs: General and Applied* 70, no. 9 (1956): 1-70.

Baum, L. Frank. *The Wonderful Wizard of Oz*. Chicago: G.M. Hill Co., 1900.

Bennis, Warren G. *Managing the Dream: Reflections on Leadership and Change*. Cambridge: Perseus Publishing, 2000.

"Chief Executive Officer." *Investopedia.com*. n.d. http://www.investopedia.com/terms/c/ceo.asp#axzz2K9EAt gKN (accessed December 2012).

Festinger, Leon. *When Prophecy Fails*. Minneapolis: University of Minnesota Press, 1956.

Kotter, John P. "Leading Change: Why Transformation Efforts Fail." *Harvard Business Review*, 2000: 59-67.

Lepper, Mark R., and David Greene. "Turning Play into Work: Effects of Adult Surveillance and Extrinsic Rewards on Children's Intrinsic Motivation." *Journal of Personality and Social Psychology* 31, no. 3 (1975): 479-486.

Ordóñez, Lisa D., Maurice E. Schweitzer, Adam D. Galinsky, and Max H. Bazerman. "Goals Gone Wild: The Systematic Side Effects of Overprescribing Goal Setting." *Academy of Management Perspectives*, 2009: 6-16.

Pascale, Richard. *Managing on the Edge*. New York: Simon and Schuster, 1990.

Random House Webster's Unabridged Dictionary. New York: Random House Reference, 2001.

APPENDIX A: THE BRIDGE BUILDER

By Will Allen Dromgoole

An old man, going a lone highway,
Came at the evening, cold and gray,
To a chasm, vast and deep and wide,
Through which was flowing a sullen tide.
The old man crossed in the twilight dim;
The sullen stream had no fears for him;
But he turned when safe on the other side
And built a bridge to span the tide.
"Old man," said a fellow pilgrim near,
"You are wasting strength with building here;
Your journey will end with the ending day;
You never again must pass this way;
You have crossed the chasm, deep and wide—
Why build you the bridge at the eventide?"
The builder lifted his old gray head:
"Good friend, in the path I have come," he said,
"There followeth after me today
A youth whose feet must pass this way.
This chasm that has been naught to me
To that fair-haired youth may a pitfall be.
He, too, must cross in the twilight dim;
Good friend, I am building the bridge for him.

Assets

Tangible Assets – These are any part of a business you can walk in and touch. For instance, inventory is a tangible asset. So are land, buildings, furniture and equipment. You can think of these as hard assets, things that could be repossessed or foreclosed on. Typically, these are the assets most easily used as collateral for financing. Cash would also be a tangible asset. Typically, all the tangible assets with show up on a company's balance sheet—one of the three main financial reports.

Something to note about these assets is that banks will adjust their lending based on the age of the asset. In the case of buildings and land, that adjustment is less noticeable. With inventory, however, age risks obsolescence and, taking that into account, banks are willing to lend less—especially in the technology industry. Think in terms of a grocery store. How much are you willing to lend a grocery store so they can buy a pallet of tomatoes? Depends on how old the tomatoes are, right?

This is also noticeable in the case of accounts receivables. Are you collecting from your customers within 30 days, or are many of your receivables reaching the 90-120 day mark? That makes a difference for you and for banks. Underlying the overall number in your receivables account is another potential danger: the makeup of who you're lending to. Are your receivables for Fortune 500 companies that are sure to pay you back or are you lending to consumers? If you're lending to consumers or small businesses, you should consider contracting with a finance company to underwrite those receivables. Otherwise you're adversely impacting the quality of your receivables and, therefore, impacting the way the banks will treat that asset for lending purposes. Just remember, accounts receivables tracks money you've lent to other people. Are you comfortable with the people you've lent money to?

Intangible Assets – This is anything that provides value to the business that you *can't* walk in and put your hand on. For instance, things like patents, employee intelligence and experience, brand loyalty, and Goodwill. Because these things can't be repossessed or foreclosed on in general, banks tend to be more hesitant to use them as collateral.

To further complicate intangible assets, many of them don't necessarily show up on a company's financials. At least, not directly. You often have to read between the lines. For instance, if you total up all the assets on Coca-Cola's balance sheet, you'll see that they are worth about $80 billion. Now, that's a lot of money but their market capitalization (the value of all their stock at market prices plus all their outstanding debt) is over $165 billion (as of this writing, 4ᵗʰ quarter 2012).

In theory, with $80 billion you could build everything Coke owns from the ground up. So what is the difference in that value? Why should the real Coke be valued at more than double the worth of its hard assets? Intangibles. The company is valued at a much greater level than what the raw assets would imply because it has more than 100 years of brand development—plus personnel expertise, distribution channels and agreements, client relationships, etc.

Goodwill – Goodwill is a special animal. It is a type of intangible asset that shows up on a lot of company financials but is somewhat misunderstood. Goodwill is a measure of brand loyalty, on a certain level. It's also, indirectly, one of the reasons you have to read between the lines when looking at a company's financials. The reason for this is that a company only records goodwill on its books during a merger or acquisition. Going back to Coke, their brand is one of the most recognizable in the world. That has more value than most people would believe. However, the only way to capture that value on paper is for someone to buy Coke. Anyone got a couple hundred billion dollars on hand?

The way it works is that, when buying a company, the accountants will go in and determine the value of all the hard (tangible) assets (called the fair market value, or FMV). They'll go in and value the intangibles too but that requires a bit more faith, practice and guessing. Ultimately, they'll come back with a number. When the company is purchased, all those numbers are transferred to their respective places on the balance sheet. However, the company was probably purchased for a premium, meaning the buyer paid more than the company was 'worth' on paper. This is to cover the intangibles that aren't listed on the balance sheet—things like trained employees and brand recognition. Whatever that premium was is now recorded on the acquiring company's balance sheet as Goodwill. It seems a little confusing but it has to be done that way to make sure that Assets continue to equal the sum of Liabilities and Equity.

Capital Expenditures – Companies are expensive to run. For Pomeroy IT, we were spending 97% or so of everything we brought in. This went to cover new buildings, utilities, salaries and commissions, inventory, business trips and functions, shipping and freight, etc. When an expense is made to cover something that will be used up in a year or less, it is recorded as an Expense, doesn't touch the balance sheet and generally counts as a tax deduction. However, if that expense is for something that will provide value over the course of more than one year—like furniture and buildings—it is considered a capital expense instead. Instead of being treated as an instant expense and becoming a tax deduction, items like this are 'capitalized' and treated as assets. This is because they are expected to provide continuing, future benefit for the organization.

To illustrate this, let's use an example. You need to take the kids to soccer practice. You and some of the other parents in your neighborhood decide to form a carpool. Since you've got the minivan, you get elected as the driver. Each week, you pick up all the kids and take them to soccer practice then bring them home again. The other parents decide to pitch in to help you cover the cost since you're doing all the driving. How much do you charge them? What's their fair share? The minivan cost you $25,000. Over the course of the summer, you spent about $100 in gasoline to haul the kids back and forth. Do you split the full $25,100 with the other parents? They'll think you're crazy. Instead, you'll split the cost of the gas and maybe charge them a slight premium for your time and the stains that will never come out of your van's seats.

Now, obviously this example is extremely oversimplified but the point is that van has much more useful life than simply one summer for soccer practices. That's the idea behind a capitalized expense. Where we stray from our example is that, in business, you would calculate the expected useful life of the van and then factor the cost of however much of that useful life was consumed. Because that's too complicated, however, businesses just break down the cost over a specified time period and allocate the cost in chunks over the course of a certain number of years.

Depreciation and Amortization – Depreciation and Amortization, in general, are the same thing. Depreciation tends to apply to tangible assets while Amortization tends to apply to intangible assets. In either case, it is the portion of a capitalized expense that gets counted in a given year. To continue with our earlier, extremely simple example, if our minivan had an expected life of five years, we would be able to depreciate $5,000 per year ($25,000 purchase price / 5 years). There are a host of other factors that play in when you're talking about capital expenditures and depreciation (like MACRS – Modified Accelerated Cost Recovery System) so go and make friends with your accountants to get a better understanding of how these principles work in real life. Again, you *must* step outside the scope of this painfully limited discussion if you want to succeed. Think of this as an appetizer for the main course your accounting team can give you—the one you need so you can have the strength to succeed.

Liabilities and Equity

Current & Long-term Liabilities – In general, a liability is money the company owes to someone else. It includes things like bank loans, accounts payable, lines of credit, etc. Current Liabilities are usually defined as the subset of liabilities that will come due over the course of the next year. This is as opposed to Long-term Liabilities which are typically considered debts that will come due beyond one year's time. For instance, a mortgage is a long-term liability. You will pay it back over 15 or 30 years (or whatever other term you've chosen) and few people would argue that as being anything but long-term. However, there is a portion of that mortgage that will come due this year. That portion is considered a current liability because it is shorter term in nature.

The distinction has implications in business valuation and strategic planning. A company with high long-term liabilities could be said to be putting off any repayment and, in doing so, setting themselves up for future difficulty. On the other hand, a company with high current liabilities could be considered risky in the present because they will need to pay out cash in order to meet those obligations—or float a new piece of credit and refinance the liabilities. In either case, these are typically debts that a company owes to banks or vendors.

Shareholder's Equity – Whether a company is public or private, it has shareholders. A private company tends to have fewer shareholders (usually just the founders) than a public company but the distinction is irrelevant for our purposes here. The point is that someone owns the company. The Shareholder's Equity on the balance sheet tells you just how much of the company those owners really own. It includes things like common stock and retained earnings. Knowing how much of the business the owners actually own becomes especially important in the world of business finance because banks don't want to control too much of a company.

ABOUT THE AUTHOR

David B. Pomeroy is the founder and former CEO of Pomeroy IT, a NASDAQ traded company. He has 40 years of business experience at all levels of organizational hierarchy, and has employed more than 2,500 people.

David served on an advisory boards for IBM, U.S. Bank, and Xavier University. He has completed 40 mergers and acquisitions and has had three public offerings.

David has earned the following awards:

- Ernst and Young Entrepreneur of the Year Award for his ability to start and grow a small business;
- IBM Reseller of the Year Award;
- Hewlett Packard Reseller of the Year Award;
- Compaq Reseller of the Year Award;
- Microsoft Regional Reseller of the Year Award;
- Oracle Regional Reseller of the Year Award;
- Sun Regional Reseller of the Year Award;
- EMC Regional Reseller of the Year Award;
- Proctor & Gamble Vendor of the Year Award;

David's company received the Top 50 Fastest Growing Companies award for the 1990s.

David's Computerland franchises were in the Top 10 of 450 for several years.

He was the first IBM PC reseller in the U.S.; 1981.

David's company generated annual revenues of approximately 1 billion dollars.

He is currently semi-retired, acting in consultancy and advisory roles to a number of small and large businesses and foundations.

David stays abreast of all of the management and leadership literature, and reads nearly every book that is published on the subject.

As long as we're telling the complete story, David has also gotten 5 hole-in-one shots in golf.

www.ingramcontent.com/pod-product-compliance
Lightning Source LLC
Chambersburg PA
CBHW081442170526
45166CB00008B/2291